WORDS 2003
FOR TODAY

Notes for d

GW00993160

**International
Bible Reading
Association**

Cover image – Revd Peter Kettle

Editor – Nicola Slee

Published by:
The International Bible Reading Association
1020 Bristol Road
Selly Oak
Birmingham
B29 6LB

Charity Number 211542

ISBN 1-904024-03-3
ISSN 0140-8275

Typeset by Christian Education Publications
Printed and bound in Great Britain by
Biddles, Guildford

CONTENTS

EDITORIAL

The cover of this year's *Words for Today* shows a group of Indian women and girls bathing and relaxing under the refreshing waters of a glittering waterfall. It is a wonderful image of joy, life and community, full of colour, movement and sound: we can almost hear the roar and splash of the water as it cascades down on the women's bodies. The image speaks to us of the sustenance, cleansing, refreshment and teeming abundance with which we associate the waters of creation and the waters of redemption into which we, as believers, are invited to plunge. Yet, as Alan and Clare Amos remind us in their notes on 'Waters of Life', the water which is a source of life and nourishment and refreshment can also be experienced as a destructive power in our world. Flood waters, rivers breaking their banks and the surging depths of the ocean can be a fearful, terrifying force, sweeping away all life in their path and wreaking havoc and chaos. Water, too, is a political commodity, used as a means of control over groups and nations in many parts of the world. Indeed, it is reckoned by some world commentators that water and its control may well become the source of major wars in years to come.

What is true of the natural phenomenon of water – that it is an ambivalent force, capable of being used for both good and evil, creation and destruction, liberation and oppression – is true, too, of religious faith. We do not need to look far to see how religious faith can be employed as a weapon of warfare, mastery and oppression by some, even as we can identify contrasting examples of religion as a source of empowerment, refreshment and genuine life-giving health for many. The scriptures, too, can be used as a defence against others who are different and as a weapon to attack them. Words and texts can become like a water hose trained on a crowd with the intent to control and subjugate – a force which bruises and crushes – or, by contrast, like a canal or a water sprinkler which irrigates and nourishes the land and enables new life to flourish and grow where previously there had been nothing.

What makes the difference between a religious faith which is life-enhancing, welcoming and open to the other, and one which is death-dealing, suspicious of difference and exclusive? That is a question too large for this editorial. Yet *Words for Today* seeks to play its own small part in nurturing the kind of faith which is a force for life, rather than a force for death and destruction. It does so by encouraging its readers to come to daily reading of the Bible with a self-critical, questioning and questing spirit, an openness to truth, wherever it may come from, and a willingness to be challenged and converted again and again.

I am grateful, as always, to the writers who have contributed their experience, expertise and distinctive perspectives from around the world. There is, as ever, much diversity in the pages that follow. But what all the writers share is a common commitment to truth, inclusivity, justice and the larger life of the gospel which is always beyond our possession and control.

May we each find ourselves refreshed and washed anew in the waters of life as we read these pages, and may our own faith be a force for life and renewal of others, and never a tool of destruction.

N. Slee

Nicola Slee – Editor

Acknowledgements and abbreviations

GNB Good News Bible (The Bible Societies/Collins Publishers) – Old Testament © American Bible Society 1976; New Testament © American Bible Society 1966, 1971, 1976.

NIV Scripture quotations taken from The Holy Bible, New International Version © 1973, 1978, 1984 by International Bible Society. Used by permission of Hodder & Stoughton Limited. All rights reserved. 'NIV' is a registered trademark of International Bible Society. UK trademark number 1448790.

NJB Taken from the New Jerusalem Bible, published and copyright 1985 by Darton, Longman and Todd Ltd and Doubleday & Co. Inc, and used by permission of the publishers.

NRSV New Revised Standard Version © 1989, Division of Christian Education of the National Council of Churches of Christ in the United States of America.

REB Revised English Bible © Oxford University and Cambridge University Presses 1989.

RSV The Holy Bible, Revised Standard Version © 1973, Division of Christian Education of the National Council of Churches of Christ in the United States of America.

BCE Before the Common Era. BCE and CE are used by some writers instead of BC and AD.

Readings from the Revised Common Lectionary

How to use a 'quiet time'

Have a visual focus — a cross, a plant, interesting stones... Create a prayer table on which to display them with other symbols. Place on it pictures or articles from the daily news.

Use silence Relax and empty your mind of all that's going on around you. Know that God's loving presence encircles you, your family, your community and the world. Learn to enjoy God's presence. If, because of personal problems, you cannot free your mind of the day's concerns, remember that these are your prayers and offer them to God. Know that you are loved and valued, and seek the strength and peace God offers.

Read the Bible passage for the day and then the notes. Read the verses again, allowing the words to fill your mind. Try to discover their message for you and the world around you. Refer back to other readings in the theme, so that you can see how the thoughts link together. If the writer of the week's notes comes from a different culture or background from yours, ask yourself what is new and fresh. What surprising insights have come to you from his or her perspective?

Listen Remember that the most important part of prayer is to hear what God is saying to us. God speaks to us through the words of scripture, the daily news, and often through people around us — our children, our friends, our neighbours, the person who asks for help, the stranger... Frequently the voice of God disturbs our complacency, and calls us to 'Go out' and do something we've never done before!

Include the world Hold the news of each day in your mind. Enter the situation of those you hear or read about and try to pray alongside them — with them. In a wonderful way, prayer transcends the thousands of miles between us. Through prayer we draw strength from the mysterious fellowship that binds us to one another and to God.

Pray without ceasing Remember that prayer is not only the 'quiet time' we set aside. It becomes part of the whole of life, a continuous dialogue between God and ourselves, through all that we do and think and say: a growing awareness of the loving presence of God who travels with us and never leaves us.

MORNING PRAYERS

Protect me, O Lord;
My boat is so small,
And your sea so big.   *Traditional Breton fisherman's prayer*

Lord Jesus Christ,
grant us the humility and the insight
to be able to recognise
when you are speaking to us,
though it be through words or actions
which challenge our assumption
that we already know what we should be doing.
Make us more aware of your presence
in everyday experiences;
and enable us
to recognise your call
when it comes,
whether through newspaper article,
Bible passage,
a stirring call to action
or quiet inner promptings.
Open our eyes to the signs
which declare that your kingdom
is already in our midst
and make us more ready to be led into new ways.

From Reaching for the Infinite
by Edmund Banyard (NCEC, 2000)

Wake us up, God,
with your life-giving water.
Splash our faces
with the cold of your truth
which can make us gasp and catch our breath.
Draw us deeper
into the depths of your ocean
where we may learn to swim more freely in your waters.
Surprise us with creatures and beauties of the deeps
which enlarge our vision
and kindle our adoration.
Fill us full with your rivers of life
so that we may overflow
with life-giving goodness for others.

Nicola Slee

EVENING PRAYERS

As the grey wave
creeps on to the shore
and the sail limps
for port,
so, Lord, do I
throw myself
into your harbour; crawl into the circle
of your welcoming arms.

May I know your forgiveness.
Then may I forgive
as you have forgiven me.

And now the blue comes flooding in,
transforming sea and sky with light;
the white wave tops are bracelets of glory;
the sand
a new page
on which to write my story. *Kate McIlhagga, taken from*
The Word in the World, compiled by Donald Hilton (NCEC, 1997)

In the night of weariness let me give myself up to sleep without
struggle, resting my trust upon thee.
Let me not force my flagging spirit into a poor preparation for thy
. worship.
It is thou who drawest the veil of night upon the tired eyes of the
day to renew its sight in a fresher gladness of awakening.
Rabindranath Tagore

We are needy for your grace and your mercy:
Take the towel, Christ, and serve us!
We are ready for your healing and your cleansing:
Bring the bowl, Christ, and wash us!
We are longing for your presence and your touch:
Set the table, Christ, and sit with us!
We are waiting for the renewal of our lives:
Call the chosen, Christ, and sup with us!
We are hungry for your truth and your word:
Break the bread, Christ, and feed us!
We are thirsty for your life and your love:
Pour the wine, Christ, and satisfy us!
Nicola Slee, from the Queens Eucharistic Prayer

FAR OFF AND NEAR
1. Broken barriers

Notes based on the New Revised Standard Version by
Lesley G Anderson

Lesley G Anderson is a Methodist minister from the Republic of Panama. He is the President of the Panama/Costa Rica District Conference of the Methodist Church in the Caribbean and the Americas (MCCA); Chair of the Praesidium of the Caribbean Conference of Churches (CCC); Vice-Chair of the Board of Governors of the United Theological College of the West Indies (UTCWI), Jamaica; and Chair of the Board of Directors of the Institute of Ecumenism, Society and Development (IESDE), in collaboration with the University of St Mary (USMA), Panama.

Today many persons are overwhelmed by the many barriers they have to face. There are national, linguistic, religious, societal, colour, racial and class barriers to name a few. The world appears to be seething with anger and hatred. There is a need to replace these with the love of God. Christians need to testify to the world that God is love. We need to display love in our lives and share it with others who are not like ourselves. Breaking down barriers is not necessarily an easy task, but we can rely on our Lord, who is faithful, to assist us. We are challenged to reach out in love and service to the voiceless in society, the marginalised, the ostracised, the oppressed, the suffering poor and others like them, whose tears could fill cups. They are in need of deliverance. Christ is calling us to break down barriers of hostility and follow him in his mission of love to the world.

Wednesday January 1   *Ephesians 2:1–10*
Salvation for all through Christ
Salvation had come to the Jews and the Gentiles without distinction. There were to be no barriers between them. They were made to live together, united in this new life. This is the powerful point of this passage. Previously, the Gentiles, living in the pit of sin and evil, had sunk to the lowest denominator of life. In Christ, however, they were saved by grace and transformed into a new people, a new creation, and had found their rightful place among the people of God.

As we begin the new year 2003 we too can experience a similar transformation and walk from the path of sin to the path of life with Christ. 'Walking' refers to the whole body of laws relating to conduct known as the 'Halachah'.

When we walk with Christ we will learn that there is no barrier that is insurmountable or obstacle that is insuperable. With him we can break down the wall of sin and walk into the hall of righteousness. We can break down the wretchedness of hostility and walk in the path of love. We can break down the barrier of hatred and enable unity between persons of different nationalities, languages, religions, colours and races. We can break the hostile power of evil, that good may prevail. Let us therefore think with the mind and spirit of Christ, and determine to live by his code: 'Do not be overcome by evil, but overcome evil with good' (Romans 12:21).

✳ *My Lord and my God, as we begin the new year, enable us to move from death to new life which will endure for ever.*

Thursday January 2   *Ephesians 2:11–20*
Deliverance from sin through Christ
The covenant God made with Abraham involved a promise that he would be the founder of a great nation – Israel. God therefore commanded that all Abraham's male descendants should be circumcised. This was to be the physical sign that they belonged to the people of God. It was a rite of a purely spiritual nature. The flesh for Paul was the stronghold of sin, representing our sinful nature, desires and impulses. Christ, however, delivered us from sin by reconciling us to God in his very flesh.

Circumcision or admission into membership of the people of God, is a matter of what we believe and how we behave. The outward sign on its own is not enough; it has to be matched by love of other people and obedience to God. There are to be no barriers. Therefore Gentiles who became Christians did not need to be physically circumcised, for 'uncircumcision' in Jewish thought was not a sign of natural wickedness or original sin. What was important was the coming into a right relationship with God. It was this which enabled them to become heirs to the promises of God.

Paul therefore explained that under the gospel, in the dramatic act of baptism, the Christian could share in Jesus' death and be raised with him to new life. It meant a complete break with the past, a removal of sin, and the start of a new life lived in the power given by Jesus Christ himself. All this could become a reality through faith in the power of God, who raised Jesus from the dead!

✴ *O Lord, my Saviour, deliver me from the power of sin and clothe me with the new life of righteousness.*

Friday January 3   Romans 3:1–20
God is faithful

The covenant of God with Abraham involved a promise of blessing for Israel. Israel was a favoured nation. They had the benefit of the scriptures. According to Romans 9:4–5, they were also the beneficiaries of divine adoption (sonship), glory, the covenants, the law (divine legislation), worship, the promises, the patriarchs and the Messiah, through natural descent. What, however, is their advantage in possessing the scriptures and all these other blessings, if they are condemned for disobeying them? Paul's answer in 3:1–8 is complex and difficult to comprehend. He struggles to reconcile the impartiality of God with the election of the Jews.

Paul takes the position that the covenant made with Abraham involved a promise of blessing for Israel, which as a nation they broke. They therefore forfeited the blessing. God, however, has remained faithful (2 Timothy 2:13), regardless of whether some of the Jews were disbelievers or unfaithful to their trust. He therefore concludes in 3:9–20 that the universal effect of the law is rebellion against it (1 Corinthians 15:56) and that all Jews and Gentiles are under sin. This being the case, in God's court, all are answerable to him.

✴ *Lord Jesus, you have cleansed me from guilt and sin in the blood of your sacrifice on Calvary's cross. I am thankful!*

Saturday January 4   Romans 3:21–31
God's righteousness

Paul's central theme in this passage is God's righteousness, which is revealed in the gospel 'through faith for faith' (Romans 1:17). God's righteousness is for all who have faith or belief in Jesus Christ. No distinctions are made. There are no barriers to this faith.

We live in a world engulfed by sin. We who are sinful have fallen 'short of the glory of God' (verse 23). The glory of God is the divine likeness and to come short of it is to sin. Can we be set free from sin?

Through Christ, God has set us free from sin by his grace (*charis* in Greek). We can do nothing to earn it. The notion of grace expresses Paul's idea of salvation as God's free gift. We are justified, vindicated, and delivered from the oppression of sin.

For it is Christ who came to give his life as a ransom (*lutron* in Greek) for many (Mark 10:45; Matthew 20:28), understood as the payment of money for the freeing of slaves (emancipation). There can be no mistake about this redemption. God has intervened decisively to set us free from the bondage of sin.

God's justice demanded some kind of punishment for sin in order to break down the barrier between himself and us. He himself made the propitiatory offering of his Son, Jesus Christ, as the sacrifice for our sins (propitiation = to placate or expiate).

✳ *Help us, O God, to keep our faith in you and our focus on Jesus Christ, our Saviour.*

FOR REFLECTION – alone or with a group

● Reflect on your relationship with people of other nationalities, religions, languages, colours and races.
● What is that relationship like?
● Are you prepared to break down barriers of hostility and build bridges of friendship?

FOR ACTION

Discuss with your family and friends ways and means of breaking down community barriers. Decide what you can do to assist with the process.

FAR OFF AND NEAR
2. Christ for all peoples

Notes based on the New Revised Standard Version by
Lesley G Anderson

The gospel is that wonderful news that Jesus Christ came into the world to die for the sins of all peoples. To die for others is the ultimate sacrifice. Through belief, faith and trust in this Jesus – Servant of God, King of kings, Lord of lords, and Saviour of the world – millions of people have received forgiveness of sins, healing of mind and body, and the opportunity of a new life. On Calvary's cross he demonstrated the deep-rooted love of God for all people, regardless of their social prestige, political power, or poverty-stricken situation. Jesus Christ reached out in love to all peoples. Although we are all different, he reminds us we are all God's children. We can all rely on him to be merciful to us and give us a new hope and direction for life.

Sunday January 5   *Isaiah 49:1–12*
The servant of God: call and mission

One of the great privileges in life is to serve others. Unfortunately, some persons serve because they wish to be in the limelight, to be well known, to be popular and to receive awards. Others serve for glory, acclamation, personal gain and advantages. Jesus, the servant of God, teaches that the person who humbles himself or herself and genuinely serves others is 'great' (Matthew 20:26–28). He became the ultimate sacrifice on Calvary's cross. Does this not show how much God loves and values us?

What lessons can we learn from the servant of God, who gave his life as 'a ransom for many' (Matthew 20:28)? First, like him we need to acquire the discipline of listening to God's word so that we can be formed for servanthood. By listening we can respond positively to his call to service – not to privilege, glory or honour. Second, we need to keep our trust and confidence in God's judgement for our lives, not be swayed by the judgements of others. We need to recognise that God is our strength. Third, we need to learn that following the servant of God demands a cross, without which there is no crown of righteousness. We need to be ready to face opposition and suffering if necessary.

In his mission the servant of God reaches out to all. Those bound by the chains of oppression will be set at liberty; those lost in the darkness of sin will see the light of their salvation; the marginalised and voiceless in society will neither hunger nor thirst, for God himself will lead his servant to triumph on their behalf.

✳ *Lord Jesus, teach us how to serve without distinction or discrimination all who are in need.*

Monday January 6　　　　　　　　　　　　　　*Matthew 2:1–12*

Jesus the Messianic King, truly God and truly human

In time and history God saw fit to send his Son into the world. The reaction to the supernatural birth of the new-born king was twofold: hostility from the 'home crowd' contrasted with a warm reception from the 'foreign crowd'.

Matthew, therefore, wisely devotes attention to the visit of the wise persons or Magi. The Greek word *magoi* refers to fortune-tellers, magicians and astrologers. The wise men, having followed a star, were believed to be astrologers. They were known in later tradition as Caspar, Melchior and Balthasar. They came bearing gifts (gold, frankincense and myrrh) in their treasure chest and were the first to worship the new-born King. Their gifts have special symbolic significance. Gold is the gift that befits a king and Jesus was the Messianic king. Frankincense conveys the idea of belonging to the service of God, and Jesus is truly God. Myrrh was used to treat the bodies of the dead to delay decay, and reveals Jesus as truly human, who will die for our salvation.

Herod, who was jealous, insecure and evil, is the opposite to the wise men and displays trickery and cunning. Let us emulate the wise men who worshipped rather than the jealous king who contrived to oppose God's way.

✳ *Most gracious God, thanks for your unspeakable gift, Jesus Christ, the Messianic King.*

Tuesday January 7　　　　　　　　　　　　　　*Matthew 2:13–23*

Jesus the Nazarene, Saviour of the world

God intervened, breaking the silence of eternity to reveal his Son, Jesus, fully and finally to all people. He came into a world tainted and stained with sin. Danger lurked everywhere. His life was not safe. Herod was scheming to get rid of him. Joseph was warned in a dream to take Mary and the child to safety in Egypt.

Herod, in many ways, makes us become aware of the tragic and violent nature of our sinful selves. He helps us to recognise our need of Jesus, the Nazarene, who is truly the Messiah and Saviour of the world.

The name, Nazarene, was used as a term of contempt (see John 1:46). It means a shoot or branch. Nevertheless, it is with pride and great honour that we are followers of the Nazarene. We rejoice that in him we have the gift of life – everlasting life. When we believe in him, his enduring love will remain alive in our lives, flowering in new growth which constantly springs from the tree of life.

✳ *Loving God, we behold the glory of our Lord, who came into the world as a gift for our salvation.*

Wednesday January 8   *Matthew 8:5–13*

Jesus has the power to heal

The centurion knew that Jesus had the power to heal his servant who was a bedridden paralytic. His condition was dreadful. He was 'in terrible distress' (verse 6). The centurion was certain Jesus could heal his servant (in Greek, *doulos* , slave). The word 'heal' (*therapeuso*) means to serve, or give medical attention, as well as to cure or restore to health. The centurion was certain that Jesus, even at a distance, had the power to heal his servant. He was so full of faith that he felt Jesus only had to speak the word (verse 8) and his servant would be restored to health.

The belief in the days of Jesus was that the world was divided into two kingdoms: one belonging to God and the other to Satan, who is called 'the devil', 'the evil one', and 'the prince of demons'. Satan was considered the cause of sin, ill-health and death. To be healed was to become whole or wholesome again, to be freed from the chains of sin and the grip of death. It was to be liberated from the power of Satan. The healings were powerful blows against Satan's kingdom and steps toward the establishment of the Kingdom of God.

In our times of illness we, like Bartimaeus, can cry out to Jesus. He who has the power to heal will reach out his nail-printed hands to embrace us and give us new life and new hope.

✳ *Lord Jesus, divine healer, grant me the faith that can move mountains.*

Thursday January 9   *Mark 2:13–17*

Jesus calls us to a new life

Levi (called Matthew) was a Jew, whose father's name was Alphaeus. He was a tax collector for Herod Antipas, who was a puppet ruler. He was therefore a hated and despised publican. His fellow Jews saw him getting rich at their expense and classified him with sinners.

Jesus saw Levi and challenged him saying, 'Follow me' (verse 14). Levi did not hesitate. His response to the call was positive.

He made the choice to open his heart and mind to Jesus. His decision to follow Jesus was decisive.

At the reception he held for Jesus and his disciples, there were publicans and sinners present, those with whom a strict Jew would not associate or share table. But it was these who had decided to follow Jesus, thus receiving from him forgiveness of their sins and a new life free from sin, rather than the scribes and the Pharisees, who could not see beyond their own offence.

✳ *O Holy Spirit, grant us a new life in Christ that we may sincerely follow him.*

Friday January 10   *Acts 1:1–8*

Witness to the resurrection of Christ

I always wonder why people have a preference for 'seeing' and 'touching' things, in order to substantiate their belief. Does it help their unbelief? For centuries unbelievers have requested 'proofs' of the resurrection of Jesus Christ. It is true that to see and touch may help us to believe. The experience of Thomas, however, is a reminder that there is a greater satisfaction – and that is to have the faith to believe without seeing and touching.

We go through life enjoying the air we breathe. It is an invisible reality we take for granted until something happens to us and we have to receive oxygen medically in order to survive. Like the air we breathe, there are other invisible realities such as love, trust, confidence, friendship and patriotism, upon which our lives are based.

Let us remember that although we cannot see or touch God, God is real. People today, like those of old, want 'convincing proofs' of the resurrection. But God has provided the evidence in the appearances of the Risen Christ to the disciples. He presented himself alive to his eleven disciples in Jerusalem (Mark 16:14 and so on), showed them 'his hands and his side' (John 20:26–29), appeared to seven disciples at the Sea of Tiberias (John 21:1–23) and on the mountain in Galilee (Matthew 28:16–20 and so on), and finally to Paul (1 Corinthians 15:8).

✳ *Lord, help my unbelief. Help me to accept in faith your resurrection and witness to the truth of your living presence in my life.*

Saturday January 11   *Acts 2:1–11*

The baptism of the Holy Spirit

The first Pentecost took place after the death, resurrection, and ascension of Jesus. On that occasion, the disciples were baptised with the Holy Spirit, which came upon them like 'the rush of a violent wind' (verse 2). The emphasis here is on the sound, the roar, not the wind itself, and upon the effect of the Spirit on the assembled company: for the first time they became a church. Empowered by Christ and suddenly gifted by the Holy Spirit, they began to praise God and speak in other languages. The audible sign was followed by the visible sign of each tongue having a fire-like appearance, fire being the symbol of purity, power and the divine presence. It was with boldness and conviction that they powerfully proclaimed the gospel. Peter told his astonished and bewildered listeners on the day of Pentecost that the prophecy of Joel had come true. God had poured out his Spirit on all believers.

When we receive Christ and become Christians, we receive the gift of the Holy Spirit, who lives within us. The Spirit helps us to realise our oneness in Christ. He guides and directs us, and gives us the assurance that we are truly children of God. He helps us build the mind and character of Jesus in our lives. He blesses us with the gifts of love, joy, peace, patience, kindness, goodness, faithfulness, humility and self-control. In addition, he gives us the privilege and power to serve God.

✳ *Holy Spirit, give us your gifts of love, joy and peace, that we might live in unity.*

FOR REFLECTION – alone or with a group
- Think of the many ways you can be of service to your best friend.
- Think of the many ways you can be of service to your worst enemy or the person who does not like you.
- Do you envisage there will be a difference to the quality of service you are prepared to offer to each?

FOR ACTION
Read again Isaiah 49:1–12 and follow the example of the servant of God. Use every opportunity to serve others, praying for a genuine love for God and all peoples.

IBRA INTERNATIONAL APPEAL

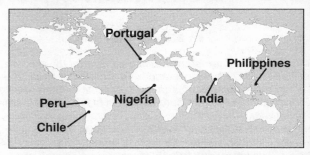

In five continents you will find Christians using IBRA material.

Some will be using books and Bible reading cards translated into their local language, whilst others use English books. Some of the books are printed in the UK, but more and more countries are printing the books and cards themselves. The IBRA International Fund works through churches, Christian groups and Christian publishing houses overseas to make these publications available.

Each year we receive more requests for help from the IBRA International Fund, with greater emphasis on helping our overseas friends to produce their own version of IBRA material.

The only money we have to send is the money you give, so please help us again by giving generously.

Place your gift in the envelope provided and give it to your IBRA representative, or send it direct to:

The IBRA International Appeal
1020 Bristol Road, Selly Oak,
Birmingham B29 6LB, Great Britain
Thank you for your help.

FAR OFF AND NEAR
3. One humanity

Notes based on the New International Version by
Salvador T Martinez

Salvador T Martinez is an ordained minister of the United Church of Christ in the Philippines and an International Associate of the Common Global Ministries Board (Christian Church [Disciples of Christ]) and the United Church of Christ in the USA. He resides in Chiang Mai, Thailand, and is appointed to teach theology and ethics at the McGilvary Faculty of Theology, Payap University in Chiang Mai. He also serves as a volunteer in the HIV-AIDS and prison ministries of the Church of Christ in Thailand.

After 11 September 2001, notwithstanding the efforts of western leaders to form a broad coalition, the world remains divided. Some Muslims believe the war is against them and no doubt some Christians blame Muslims for the acts of terror committed by a few fanatics. More than ever we need to open our minds and hearts to accept that all human beings are created by God. It is not only the biblical revelation that proclaims this. The sacred scripture of Islam also declares: 'You were created as different nations and tribes, not that you should despise one another, but that you should learn from one another.' (*Qur'an, Sura 49*)

Our hope is that the vision of Isaiah (11:6–9) will be fulfilled in our time: 'The wolf will live with the lamb, the leopard will lie down with the goat, the calf and the lion and the yearling together; and a little child will lead them ... They will neither harm nor destroy on all my holy mountain, for the earth will be full of the knowledge of the Lord as the waters cover the sea.' This is our prayer; this is our hope!

Sunday January 12   *Genesis 3:20; 5:1–2*
One Creator

At a seminar workshop held in Chiang Mai, Thailand, in January 2000 on 'Doing Theology with Creation in Asian Cultures', there was one constant in the stories of creation told from different cultures: all human beings come from one source, the Creator. The first woman was created and became the mother of all human beings. In the biblical narrative, the woman is called Eve – the mother of all living. Creation stories from other cultures give her different names, but they all point back to the same creative source. Therefore, together with a tribe in north-east India, we can sing:

> Oh, children of the earth
> Let us celebrate
> Let us sing and dance
> Let all hear the melody of drum
> It is harvest time
> God has answered our prayer.

✳ *O God our creator, out of your overflowing love, you have created and made us into your likeness. But because of our disobedience, we have distorted your image and failed to see your handiwork in other human beings. We sin against you when we see only ourselves and do not recognise all human beings as your children. Forgive us and grant us a deeper understanding of your nature that we may see in every person the glory of your creation.*

Monday January 13   *Genesis 9:18–19; 10:32*

Common ancestry

At the time of writing, the bombing raids in Afghanistan have entered their fourth week. In spite of the claims that the bombs will target only government and military installations at pinpoint accuracy, innocent civilians were tragically killed. Repeatedly, the US President proclaimed that the war is not against Muslims and the military experts are saying that it is going to be a long protracted war. Hopefully, by the time you are reading this in January 2003, peace and reconciliation will have long been achieved.

The biblical revelation is clear that we are all kin. Though we are from different nations, symbolically we are all Noah's children. It is both our privilege and our responsibility to pray for all people and nations, to help those who are in need and to live peaceably with each other.

✳ *Creator God, you brood over the world to bring order to chaos. Come and brood once again over our world and bring order and understanding among the warring nations. Let the seed of peace grow and empower those who lead and those who follow in order that all may establish a world that is built on freedom and love rather than force and hatred; on peace and justice rather than war and prejudice. May your love be the guiding force of all decision-makers, through Christ our peace.*

Similar instinct
The one thing common to every human being and community is their instinctive desire to seek God. Paul outlines the reason for this very neatly: God created all things; God does not live in temples made by human hands; God provides for all human needs and God directs and controls human destiny. In spite of these truths, the Athenians had not directed their worship to the true God and God remained unknown to them, even though they confessed, 'In him we live and move and have our being.' As far as Paul was concerned, there was simply no reason for the true and great God to remain unknown to the Athenians! Is the true and almighty God known to you?

* *O eternal God, from whom we come and to whom we go, and in whom we move and have our being, may we recognise your sovereignty and our kinship with all human beings. Help us to understand that you are in charge of our lives and that we fulfil your will when our lives are shared with others. Help us to learn that what really counts before you is not our elaborate rituals and worship services but our acts of justice and loving mercy towards the powerless and needy. For Christ's sake.*

Gospel for all
Paul argued that since we all came from the living God – 'we are God's offspring' – it would dishonour God if we worshipped God with images made by human hands. To worship God in that way is inexcusable, especially in the light of the resurrection. Some Athenians found Paul's claim ludicrous. Others wanted to hear more before they decided. But some were convinced and believed. One such was Dionysius, who, since he was a member of the Areopagus, was undoubtedly a well-educated Greek aristocrat. The other was Damaris who, judging from the status of women at that time, was most probably from a lower class. What these two conversions signify is that the gospel is for all, regardless of class and status in life.

* *O God, you are without beginning and without end. We thank you that because of the resurrection we know that in suffering there is joy, in death there is life. Show us how to share this joy and this life with others. Help us to dedicate*

our lives in prayer and action toward the realisation of a
world where all (in spite of differences in race, religion and
gender) care for each other as brothers and sisters. In
Christ who prayed that all may become one, we pray.

Thursday January 16   *Psalm 8:1–9*

Unique creation

Why should God notice a man or a woman?
Why should God care for a human being?
God made him/her a little lower than Godself,
And crowned him/her with glory and honour!

Like the psalmist, we cannot help but realise the insignificance of a human being when we see the starry skies on a clear night, and yet, as one poignantly puts it, 'astronomically speaking, man is the astronomer'. This psalm puts the human being in charge of all other creation. He is endowed with power and authority. He is distinguished from the rest of creation in that he is able to communicate with God. God blessed all creation, but God not only blessed human beings, God also spoke to them (see Genesis 1:21–22, 27–29).

Created in God's own image, we are greatly privileged and, therefore, have a great responsibility. Have we been grateful for the privilege and have we been faithful in fulfilling our responsibility?

✳ *'O Lord, our Lord, how majestic is your name in all the*
earth!' You have created all things and you have appointed
us to be stewards of your creation. But either in pride or
selfishness, we have not only abused your gifts to us, we
have even used them for death when they are meant for life.
Forgive us our transgression and grant us grace to live
more worthily in the light of our calling. Renew your
likeness within us and let us be reconciled to you, with all
people and with the rest of your creation. Through Christ
our Lord, we pray.

Friday January 17   *Galatians 3:23–29*

One in Christ

The word 'pedagogue' (from the Greek *paidagogos*, verse 24), used in the modern sense synonymously with 'teacher', originally referred to a person, usually a slave, who accompanied his master's son to school and back. He was also the son's moral guardian, 'in charge' of keeping the son from mischief until he reached the age of maturity.

Paul uses this as an analogy of the role of the law in our lives. The law is in charge until we are justified through our faith in Christ. Those who become united with Christ through baptism become one in Christ – have 'clothed themselves with Christ' – in whom all racial, social and gender discrimination is obliterated.

✳ *O God, who in Jesus Christ came to fulfil the law, we thank you for freeing us from the tyranny of the law. Forgive us our complacency and disobedience. Forgive us for regarding others as less than we are. Fill us with your love and compassion that we may overcome all our hatred and prejudices and be able to share our lives with all human beings regardless of gender, race and social status. In Christ who loves all human beings alike, we offer this prayer in faith and thankfulness.*

Saturday January 18   *Revelation 7:9–17*

One world

This passage is often used in funeral services. It promises the satisfaction of every hunger and thirst after death. It was probably inspired by that passage in Isaiah which proclaims: 'They will neither hunger nor thirst, nor will the desert heat or the sun beat upon them. He who has compassion on them will guide them and lead them beside springs of water' (49:10). Today, we speak of globalisation and information technology that will supposedly revolutionise the world. Yet more than half of the world does not have enough food, does not have access to safe water and cannot read or write. Many still die of hunger and thirst as in the time of Isaiah and the writer of Revelation. Only when we become truly one world, when 'every nation and tribe and people and language' are drawn together before God, will there be real peace and justice. Only then will all hunger or thirst be satisfied. This is our hope.

✳ *O God, creator of all humankind, in humility and hope we confess that we have allowed self and class interest to take over our hearts' desires. Take away from us the spirit of prejudice and may the disputes and differences that have arisen in our own community be fully and speedily settled and justice be established among us. Grant us saner wisdom, better understanding and firmer resolve to follow your will so that unity and peace will prevail among us. This is our fervent prayer for the whole world, for the sake of Christ, our Lord.*

FOR REFLECTION – alone or with a group

● Look back on your life and think of the moment when you became aware that you are a person in a community of people.
● Do you think it is possible to live by yourself?
● What can you do to help foster the fact that we are 'one humanity'?
● What can your church do to contribute toward strengthening unity in your community, in your nation and in the world?

FOR ACTION

Take a look at a world map or a globe. How many of the nations on the map do you recognise? Who are the people that inhabit them? Select one (or two) of the nations you don't know anything about and read about its history, its people and its culture. You can do this easily via the internet or a good library. Pray for the people in the country of your choice. Better yet, try to find someone from the country you selected via the internet and send him or her a greeting by e-mail or letter.

FAR OFF AND NEAR
4. One people of God

Notes based on the New Revised Standard Version by
Andrew Williams

Andrew Williams, a minister of the Uniting Church in Australia, now works as the Secretary, Personnel and Training, in the Council for World Mission (formerly the London Missionary Society). He has worked in several parts of Australia, most recently Sydney, where he was the Secretary for World Mission in the New South Wales Synod of the Uniting Church. He has a MTh (Hons) in Missiology with a thesis on the concept of partnership in mission. He is enrolled in the ThD programme of the University of Birmingham researching patterns of missionary sharing.

'All one in Christ' – can it ever be a reality, or is it just a vision of romantic idealists, an empty slogan, good for church gatherings but not really grounded in the real world? In the global body of Christ today there is so much diversity. Different cultures and contexts are points of celebration as people discover that we all come with cultural insights to the gospel story. But our differences can also create misunderstandings. The reality of thousands of different denominations in the world today is evidence of Christians fracturing the body of Christ because they believe that their way is the correct way. Finding ways to let the gospel break through and break down the barriers we erect is the subject of our readings this week.

Sunday January 19   *Acts 10:1–16*
In the wrong place at the right time

The story of Peter and Cornelius is crucial to Luke's account of the early church – so much so that he devotes one and a half chapters in Acts to telling and re-telling the story. There are some interesting features in the story from the start. Peter is staying with Simon, 'a tanner, whose house is by the seaside'. Anyone who handled the skins of animals was technically unclean, and this may be the reason that his house was by the sea, to avoid contaminating orthodox Jews. Already then Peter is in a risky situation. Cornelius, as a 'man who feared God', was probably someone drawn to the Jewish faith, but short of being a 'proselyte', which involved circumcision. His almsgiving would have been to Jews. We have then two people who are already in unexpected places: a Jew putting himself where there is ritual 'unclean-ness' and a Gentile spending time at the synagogue! More than this, we have the very un-Jewish (and un-Protestant!) assertion that God has heard Cornelius because 'your prayers and your alms have ascended as a memorial before God'. Un-Jewish because God is not meant to be paying much attention to the Gentiles, and un-Protestant because God is not meant to pay attention to good works like almsgiving! Peter's vision is also interesting, having echoes of Peter's earlier encounters, when he had fallen asleep while praying and when the lesson had to be repeated three times so that he could understand.

Sometimes when we put ourselves in unexpected places God can speak to us in new ways. Sometimes God needs to speak slowly, clearly and repeatedly until the lesson sinks in, particularly when God wants to challenge our most deeply held and cherished beliefs and practices.

✳ *Lord, wherever you place me today, may it turn out to be the right place for me. Meet me in unexpected ways today and give me the grace to recognise you.*

Monday January 20   *Acts 10:17–33*
Why send for me? I'm only mortal!
Peter is still puzzling about the meaning of the vision (verses 11–16) when the servants of Cornelius arrive to bring Peter to their master. In this part of the story several elements are repeated and there are several new themes. First is the theme of how the Spirit speaks to those who are open to hearing God's voice. Cornelius and Peter both act, not on their own initiative, but at the Spirit's direction. We have the image of two people, anxious to draw closer to God, who are willing to obey the Spirit's leading 'without hesitation' (verse 20). When Peter finally arrives at Cornelius' house, Cornelius falls at his feet and worships him (verse 25). Peter raises him to his feet, saying, 'I am only a mortal'.

Here is an amazing encounter. Did the two men look each other in the eye? Was Peter feeling awkward at being in the house of this Gentile? Was it at this point (after four days, and when face to face with a stranger) that the lesson of the previous vision began to sink in? The vision had been about eating unclean food but here, face to face with Cornelius, Peter was able to grasp the meaning and express it as 'I should not call *anyone* profane or unclean' (verse 28). Bigger revelations were in store for Peter in the next part of the story, but this must be considered quite a breakthrough. Also understand that Luke was writing after the devastation of the Jewish War when the political hopes of the Zealots were crushed. Here is Peter in the house of one of the occupying forces, making the dramatic discovery that the peace which comes with Jesus is not won through weapons, but through love, forgiveness, and acceptance of one's enemies into the covenant community.

✳ *Lord, it's easy to be defeated and say, 'What can one person do?' Help me discover what I can do. Send me today.*

Tuesday January 21   Acts 10:34–48
God shows no partiality

The first ever sermon to a Gentile audience begins with Peter's amazing claim, 'I truly understand that God shows no partiality, but in every nation anyone who fears him and does what is right is acceptable to him' (verses 34–35). I wonder if the church of today would proclaim that as boldly? Peter's powerful preaching covers all the basic Christological themes, but one also gets a sense that Peter, the first to proclaim Jesus' messiahship, and perhaps his most intimate disciple, is himself gaining a new insight into the universality of the gospel message. As if to cement that idea, while he is in mid-sermon the Holy Spirit is poured out on those who are listening, and because of this Peter orders their baptism. In the New Testament the order of such events (saved, filled with the Spirit, baptised) often varies. The New Testament seems less concerned with the *sequence* than with the life-transforming *content* of such events.

It is hard to put ourselves in this context though – God is doing a new thing, unparalleled. Those who were presumed to be outside God's grace are now found to be bearers and recipients of God's grace.

✳ *Lord, if I have been guilty of dividing the world too neatly into those who are 'in' and those who are 'out' then work with me and show me anew how inclusive your love is. 'Amazing grace, how sweet the sound, that saved a wretch like me!'*

Wednesday January 22   Acts 11:1–18
Peter defends his actions

Peter returns to Jerusalem, perhaps because he has been summoned back to give an account of his actions. He may have expected criticism because he takes six supporters (verse 12) to help corroborate his story. And what is the complaint that the Jewish Christians (the circumcised believers, verse 2) have? 'Why did you go to uncircumcised men and eat with them?' The complaint is not that he has baptised Gentiles but that he has associated with them and sat at their table; he has broken the Law. (Gentiles ate unclean food, were uncircumcised and were outside the covenant relationship with God.)

Peter summarises all the events of the previous chapter with new vividness. The reality is that Peter, by his actions, has changed them from strangers into companions in the most literal sense, for the word companion comes from two Latin words: *cum* – with, and *panis* – bread. A companion is someone with whom we share bread. When the believers hear the story they are silenced. God really has done a new thing and has opened the way for Gentiles for a 'repentance that leads to life' (verse 18).

When God does a new thing, though, it sometimes takes humans a while to catch on. Much of the remainder of the book of Acts deals with the early church's struggle in including both Jews and Gentiles in the saving plan of God.

✳ *Lord, if today I must give an account of myself, help me do so with grace, courage and humility.*

Thursday January 23   *Acts 13:44 – 14:1*
Speaking boldly
This story is from Paul's first missionary journey and takes place in Antioch where we hear that 'almost the whole city gathered to hear the word of the Lord'. This could be something of an exaggeration and may have meant that the crowd was too large to fit into the synagogue. Anyway, the Jews were jealous of the apostle's ability to draw a crowd. This should be a sobering lesson for those who like to count the size of their congregations! From the earliest days people have been looking over their shoulder to see what was happening 'over there'. Many churches today feel they had better brighten up their life so that they can compete with the church down the road which is attracting more members and attention.

Surely the lesson from this passage is that we need to ensure that the message we proclaim is sound and leave the rest to God. Let God decide who is in and who is out and, for our part, proclaim the word boldly (verse 46) for there will always be those who criticise and complain. Speak boldly!

✳ *Loving God, remove from me any jealousy that I harbour. Remove the anxiety that leads me to look at others and*

compare myself with them. Let me know today how much
you love me.

Friday January 24   *Colossians 3:5–15*
To 'put off' and 'put on'
In verses 5–11 Paul contrasts the qualities that those who follow
Christ must 'put off' – and the list is extensive (fornication,
impurity, passion, evil desire, greed, anger, wrath, malice,
slander and lying) – with the qualities that a Christian must 'put
on' (read verses 12–17 again). For our theme, though, we must
dwell on verse 11 which has echoes of Galatians 3:28. It is not
only the old sinful habits and attitudes that are done away with in
the new creation which Christ brings. All the barriers which
divided human beings from one another are done away with as
well: racial barriers, like that between Jews and Gentiles (which
was also a religious barrier, as the reference to circumcised and
uncircumcised indicates); cultural barriers, which divided Greeks
and barbarians, or those outside the pale of Graeco-Roman
civilisation, like the Scythians, from those within; and social
barriers, such as that between slaves and free persons. Within
the community of the new creation – 'in Christ' – such barriers are
irrelevant; indeed, they have no existence.

   Our world continues to be racked by barriers of one kind or
another. In Christ, these barriers must come down – colour bars,
class distinctions, national and cultural divisions, political and
sectarian partisanship. In the unity of the body of Christ there is
no room for these old categories: Christ is all and in all.

✳ *Loving God, help me put off all aspects of the old life which*
   hold me back from following you. Help me put on Christ and
   break down all the barriers that divide me from others.

Saturday January 25   *Matthew 28:16–20*
The Great Commission
The 'Great Commission' has been the most important single text
informing the modern missionary movement. This new
understanding dates from its use by William Carey in 1792. Many
people down the years can testify that their involvement in
mission is a direct result of obedience to these words of Christ.
Indeed many preachers used the text as a last line of defence as
if to say, 'How can you oppose mission to the heathen if Christ
himself commanded it?' Eventually the theme of obedience to the

Great Commission tended to drown out all other motifs. At the beginning of the Student Volunteer Movement, William Ashmore is reported as concluding his address to the students with the challenge, 'Show if you can, why you should not obey the last command of Jesus Christ!'

There are several ways that the Great Commission is now being approached with more care. It has become questionable to use it as an attack on those who do not see mission 'our' way. It needs to be rescued from any simplistic, biblical literalism and proof-texting. It must never shift the church's involvement in mission from the realm of *gospel* to *law*. Lastly, the use of the term *nations* is being re-examined. Previously this was interpreted as requiring the missionary to convert, baptise and teach individuals from the nations. Now, at a time when religious fundamentalism, sectarian violence and terrorism are rising and fragmenting life both locally and globally, the term nation takes on the special meaning of an inclusive entity that comprises communities, cultures and even religions. The church is called upon to disciple the *nations* that they might fulfil the life which God intends for them.

✳ *Lord, show me where to go and who to disciple. In your invitation there is life. Teach all nations the way that leads to peace.*

FOR REFLECTION – alone or with a group

● What is the difference between diversity and disunity in the body of Christ? How can we affirm the former and overcome the latter?

● What can one person do to make a difference? On their own? With others? With God?

● If the Acts 10 story were translated into your own context, who would be the 'insiders' and who would be the 'outsiders'?

● How do you understand the Great Commission in your own local context, taking into account its social, religious and ethnic diversity and needs?

FOR ACTION

Organise a local ecumenical study group to explore together how you can co-operate in your area in mission and ministry. Plan some practical project that will be a witness to the love of God to your local community.

FAR OFF AND NEAR
5. The stranger among us

Notes based on the New Revised Standard Version by
Kate McIlhagga

Kate McIlhagga is a minister of the United Reformed Church in north Northumberland, a writer and a grandmother. She is involved in retreat work and is a volunteer at the local hospice. Kate is a member of the Iona Community.

As I write in the autumn of the year when the world went to war against terrorism and not knowing what the next few weeks or months will hold, the words 'the stranger among us' have taken on a dark meaning. Both the Old and New Testaments, however, call on us to welcome the stranger, to love our neighbours both far off and near.

Perhaps if the world had acted justly towards the alien and the orphan the conditions for terrorism would not have been so favourable. Perhaps in welcoming the asylum-seeker we might have found we welcome angels unaware or even the Christ himself.

There is a thought with which to struggle prayerfully!

Sunday January 26   *Mark 12:28–34*
The rest is commentary

'What you hate for yourself, do not do to your neighbour. This is the whole law; the rest is commentary.' That was the reply given by Hillel, a Jewish teacher, to the often-asked question as to which of the 613 precepts of Old Testament Law was the greatest.

Faced with the same poser, Jesus goes to the root of the question and answers with reference to Deuteronomy 6:4–5 and Leviticus 19:18. Clearly the questioner wants the answer to help him live a good life. He is not just trying to catch Jesus out. He receives Christ's answer and his approval.

The first part of the answer is the first of three texts recited twice each day by pious Jews: 'Hear, O Israel: the Lord our God, the Lord is one'. Flowing from that oneness comes the command to love God with everything that is in us – with all our heart and soul and mind.

Consequent on that is the second commandment: to love our neighbour as we love ourselves. Modern advertising has spotted a niche – buy this 'because you're worth it'! Many of us, who fall into the trap of forgetting that if we are made in God's image we are loveable and ought to love ourselves, put more into loving our neighbour than ourselves. In modern jargon, Jesus is saying that we need to love ourselves to be able fully to love another.

The two commandments that Jesus quotes are connected by the word 'love'. That had not been done before. That was a Jesus 'thing': a gift to the world; a gift to us. To deny self does not mean to hate self.

✳ *Loving Christ,*
in love you were made and made us.
Help us to accept our loveliness
and as we reach out to our neighbour
help us to know that we too are precious.

Monday January 27   *Leviticus 19:17–18, 33–34*

Reproving your neighbour

All the neighbourly love we looked at yesterday does not preclude justice. If your neighbour, for example an international conglomerate, has increased the debt owed by one country to another, or employs slave labour, then that needs to be challenged out of charity and with an eye to righteous living for both yourself and the erring neighbour.

Love the alien as yourself.

In a world where the movement of peoples is common for all sorts of reasons, we are called to welcome the stranger. Whether it be Jew or Arab, Protestant or Catholic, black or white, male or female, those who may seem different, come from another culture or have a history apart from ours are worthy not only of our respect but also of our love.

Many countries throughout the world have the story of the Christ coming in the stranger's guise. You'll find it in Russia and in Africa as well as in Europe. A man or a woman dreams that Christ is coming to visit them. They make ready themselves and their home. A child runs in with a scratch on their knee or without shoes and is dealt with lovingly. A neighbour calls to borrow some flour or some sugar. A traveller asks for shelter or directions. By nightfall the one who had eagerly awaited Christ's visit goes to bed disappointed. 'Why did you not come?' they cry. 'Oh, but I did' replies Christ.

We saw a stranger yesterday.
We put food in the eating place,
drink in the drinking place,
music in the listening place.
And with the sacred name of the triune God

he blessed us and our house,
our cattle and our dear ones.
As the lark says in her song
'Often, often, often.
goes Christ in the stranger's guise'.

(Celtic Rune)

Today is Holocaust Memorial Day. Let us pray for those who are victims of ethnic cleansing, racism and prejudice. And let us pray for those who are their persecutors:

✳ *Loving Christ,*
your arms were stretched out on a cross to embrace the world.
Cast a halo of your presence around all who suffer today.
Forgive those who perpetuate cruelty
and lead us all to respect and love our neighbours.

Tuesday January 28   *Luke 10:25–37*

When 'Who is my neighbour?' is the wrong question

Here is the 'good neighbour' story which has embedded itself in our culture. The lawyer wants Christ to define who his neighbour is. Implicit in that question is the assumption that there may be some to whom we need not be neighbourly. Christ turns the question upside down and tells the story of the Good Samaritan. Fear of defilement prevents the priest and the Levite from helping the man struck down by robbers while the Samaritan responds with merciful compassion.

In a 1960s rock and roll passion play performed in a housing estate in Bristol, the singer cries, 'Who is my neighbour? Please tell me, do. I love my mum – will that do, chum? What more do you want?' Like the lawyer she's asking the wrong question. It's not about who 'belongs' and to whom therefore I must be neighbourly. It is about how we should behave as members of God's family. Christ tells the lawyer and tells us to be like the Samaritan and to act mercifully.

That puts a different slant on how we listen across the garden fence or across the divides of faith, race or culture.

✳ *Loving God,*
may we seek
not so much to compartmentalise people,
but to respond to them with your compassion and love.

Walls and water

Walls are built to keep some in and others out. They divide. St Gildas, the sixth century saint, whose day it is today, was born within the shadow of Hadrian's Wall. The wall stretches across the northern part of England from the Tyne to the Solway and was built to keep out the marauding Scots. Today it is a mecca for tourists.

In Christ's time also, as in modern times, there were divisions in his country, not least between Jews and Samaritans. Here is a neighbour on the doorstep, who is usually ignored. Christ not only speaks to her, but asks her for a drink! The woman enters into theological discussion with him until the disciples return and she leaves her water-pot and hurries to tell her neighbours what she has seen and heard.

She becomes the first woman missionary. It appears that Christ was left thirsty. He never got that drink. But another division between neighbours had been broken down. Jesus is even greater than the patriarch Jacob. He is the Saviour of the world.

As St Gildas was to preach, the simple charity of asking for and receiving a cup of water is more important than any fast – a timely reminder as we approach the Lenten season.

✳ *O Christ our neighbour,*
you asked the Samaritan woman for a drink;
quench our thirst
as we ask you for living water.
Satisfy our desire
for right living and loving.

On Gentile soil

Mark is anxious to explain to the non-Jewish followers of Christ how it came about that the gospel was inclusive and not exclusive. Again we have a dialogue between Christ and a woman – a Gentile woman this time. A woman whose daughter was sick. The thrust of the story is not the healing of the child, but the acceptance of a Gentile within the community of God's purpose. The Gentiles are no longer strangers but pilgrims together with the Jewish Christians on the way to salvation.

✳ *Trinity of compassion,*
pour your grace
without stint

on those in distress.
Reveal in us your glory,
stir in us your power,
that we may come
from north and south,
from east and west,
to sit at table
in your kingdom of love.

Friday January 31   *Deuteronomy 24:14–22*

Remember

These humanitarian and cultic laws are rooted deep in Jewish tradition. Wages must not be withheld or the death sentence given to anyone other than those who had committed the crime. Above all, the resident alien in company with the orphan must not be deprived of justice. Here is a social security system which allows gleaning rights to those on the margins of society – the alien, the orphan and the widow. These laws were not born merely out of kindness or even a desire for justice. They were a reminder that the Jews too had been slaves in the land of Egypt.

In every country and every culture there will be aliens, strangers, refugees, asylum-seekers. We all need to remember that we too have been 'slaves in Egypt' as we learn to live alongside them.

Far and near,
near or far,
my neighbour
is my duty and my joy.
Her eyes are the eyes of Christ;
his hands are Christ's hands
reaching out to me,
as I reach out to them.

✳ *O God, help us all to be good neighbours.*

Saturday February 1   *Luke 7:1–10*

St Brigid's day

Today is the day in the Celtic calendar when St Brigid is remembered. Her festival falls on the day of Inbolc, which marks the coming of the light after the dark days of winter.

The historical Brigid, Abbess of Kildare in Ireland in the sixth century, is also remembered in folklore as midwife and wet-nurse and is often associated with Maia of the Byzantine tradition, perhaps the daughter of the innkeeper who assisted Mary at Jesus' birth. After Brigid's death a fire was tended by her nuns outside the wall of her abbey. It was said to have been kept alight for nearly a thousand years.

This light symbolises the light of Christ which reaches out across the world, breaking down barriers between Jews and Gentiles, men and women. In the episode in the gospel concerning the valued slave of a Gentile centurion, a God-fearer, Luke emphasises how 'unclean' Gentiles are open to receive Jesus' message.

The ones who are worthy to receive the healing love of Christ are those with faith, like the centurion who is worthy not because of his good deeds but because he believes that God in Jesus conquers death.

✳ *Green-hearted winter snowdrop,*
symbol of God's renewing love,
turn your face to the sun
as the days lengthen.
White candies of hope,
remind us of the light
we share with neighbours
near and far.

FOR REFLECTION – alone or with a group

● Take a blank piece of paper. Then draw intersecting circles flowing from the centre. Reflect at which point in your life you intersect with a 'neighbour'. Mark where Christ meets you in your circles and community.

FOR ACTION

Give support to a community project in your neighbourhood which welcomes the stranger. It may be your time, your money, your prayer or your presence that is needed. Where will you meet Christ at work today?

FAR OFF AND NEAR
6. Coming together – forgiveness and reconciliation

Notes based on the New Revised Standard Version by
Nicholas Alan Worssam

Brother Nicholas Alan SSF is a member of the Anglican religious community, the Society of Saint Francis. After time spent in Korea with the Church Mission Society he joined the Franciscans in 1995. He is now living with another brother at a hermitage in Yorkshire in the United Kingdom.

Forgiveness and reconciliation are central to the gospel. They involve a transformation of the heart, requiring nothing less than the all-embracing love of God.

In the early centuries of the Christian church, men and women felt called by God to go out of the towns and villages into the deserts of Egypt, Palestine and Syria. It was a call to flee from the world, and yet also to embrace the suffering world with tears of penitence and prayer.

Each day's comments end with a phrase to be repeated 25, 50 or 100 times in the traditional way of meditative prayer in the Orthodox Church. (For further reading on the desert monastics, see *Wisdom of the Desert* by Thomas Merton, published by New Directions, and others.)

Sunday February 2   *2 Corinthians 5:14–21*
Arsenius

One of the earliest of the monastics of the desert was Abba Arsenius. He was a Roman of senatorial rank, and a tutor to the Emperor's sons. One day while praying in the palace he asked God to show him the way of salvation and heard a voice saying, 'Arsenius, flee from the crowds and you will be saved.' So he left everything, boarded a ship for Egypt, and joined a community of monks in the desert. Again he asked for direction from God and a voice replied, 'Arsenius, flee, be silent, pray continually, for this is the path to sinlessness.'

Silence, solitude and prayer: this became his way of life. On Saturday evenings, to prepare for the celebration of the resurrection of Christ, he would turn his back to the setting sun and lift his hands in prayer to heaven. Not until the sun again shone on his face would he sit down.

How could such a life be one of reconciliation? Only by bringing all people in one's heart to God. Evagrius, a monk already in the Egyptian desert when Arsenius fled from Rome, once said, 'A monk is one who is separated from all, and so united with all.' One died for all, therefore all have died. One weeps with the tears of Christ, and all are washed clean and made new.

✳ *O God, make speed to save us,*
O Lord, make haste to help us.

Monday February 3   *Luke 15:11–32*
Anthony
Anthony of Egypt became probably the most famous of the desert monks. One day in church he heard the text, 'If you wish to be perfect, go, sell your possessions … then come, follow me' (Matthew 19:21). This he did, going first to an old monk in a neighbouring village to learn the art of prayer, then retiring to greater solitude in an abandoned tomb. There he wrestled with demons who appeared to him in the form of wild beasts. Villagers passing heard the roars and howls of wild animals and found Anthony lying exhausted and beaten in the morning. Moving on to the inner desert, Anthony spent 20 years in solitary prayer, finally emerging not as a man deranged, but as one completely sane, restored to the natural unity of humanity with God, radiant in health and compassion for all. People came to him for healing and discernment and returned reconciled to God.

Whatever form the demons take as they battle against our soul, whether as greed, lust, hatred or despair, the love of God is stronger than them all. Just as the prodigal son strayed far away before returning to his father's embrace, so we have only to say 'Father, I have sinned' to know the rejoicing of God and all his household.

✳ *Father, I have sinned against heaven and before you.*

Tuesday February 4   *Matthew 5:21–26*
Agathon
Once a group of monks came to test Abba Agathon. Trying to make him lose his temper, one of them said, 'Aren't you the proud and lustful Agathon we have heard people talk about?' 'Yes, that is true,' Agathon replied. They continued, 'Aren't you that Agathon who talks no sense when he speaks?' 'Indeed, I am.' Realising that the conversation was not going as planned, the monks tried again. 'Aren't you Agathon who denies the truth about God?' 'That I do not,' replied the old man. So they asked

him, 'Why did you accept the first two insults but not the last?' He replied, 'The first two I accept as good for my soul, but the last I deny for it would separate me from God.'

Those who insult us, say the desert monastics, are not our enemies, but our friends, who teach us humility and patience. Is anger of no use then? Yes, its energy is powerful in the struggle with the demons, whether seen as spiritual beings or as latent tendencies of the mind. Amma Syncletica, one of the spiritual mothers of the desert, once said: 'Why hate the one who has hurt you? It is not they who have done wrong but the devil. Hate sickness but not the sick person.' All that separates us from God should be resisted in the powerful name of Jesus, with all the strength that he gives us.

✳ *Jesus!*

Wednesday February 5   *Matthew 5:38–48*
Robbers
There were some robbers making their way through the desert when they came to one of the remote monasteries there. Going into one of the cells, they said to the monk weaving baskets as he prayed, 'Watch out, old man, give us everything you've got!' 'Take whatever you want, my sons,' the monk replied. So they took his few belongings and left. Soon after they had gone, the monk noticed a small bag hidden in a corner that they had missed. He picked it up and ran after them, calling out, 'My sons, take this bag which you left behind!' Amazed at his patience, the robbers brought back everything they had taken and asked for forgiveness, saying, 'Truly, here is a man of God!'

'Those conflicts and disputes among you, where do they come from? Do they not come from your cravings that are at war within you?' (James 4:1). The radical poverty of the desert disarms conflicts by addressing the war within. By letting go of possessive attachments, there is nothing that can be stolen, and so there is no robber or victim. Just as in the gospel reading, this is not a passive resignation, but an active empowerment. Love your enemies, and you will meet only friends.

✳ *May all be filled with the fullness of God.*

Thursday February 6   *Matthew 6:7–15*
Moses
Abba Moses was once a robber in the Egyptian desert of Nitria. He was a black African, tall and powerful. Late in life he became a monk renowned for his hospitality.

Once, at the nearby monastic settlement, a brother had committed some wrong. Abba Moses was invited to join the disciplinary meeting, but declined. Someone was sent to call him, saying, 'Join us, we are all waiting for you.' So Moses got up, picked up a basket and filled it with sand, and took it with him to the meeting. The other monks saw him coming with the basket over his shoulder and asked him what he was doing. Moses said to them, 'My sins flow out behind me without me even knowing, and here I am to judge the failings of another.' Hearing this they no longer accused the brother, but let him go in peace.

Not judging our neighbour was a constant theme of the desert monastics. Yet if there is judgement, it begins with ourselves. 'Forgive us our debts, as we also have forgiven our debtors,' says today's passage. Have we as individuals and as nations even begun to release the world from its burden of debt? Forgiveness must be given even as it is constantly received from God.

✳ *Abba, Father, may your name be holy.*

Friday February 7   Matthew 18:21–35
Brothers
Two monks had been living together as hermits for many years, without ever quarrelling with each other. One said to the other, 'Let's have a quarrel like other people. I will put a brick down here and say that it is mine, then you say that it is yours, and so we will begin a fight.' So they put a brick between them and the first one said, 'This brick is mine!' and the other replied, 'No it isn't, it's mine!' Then the first said, 'Well, if it is yours, then take it!' And so they gave up trying to have an argument and continued to live in peace.

The vast disproportion of the two debts in Jesus' parable shows how ridiculous it is for the slaves to be quarrelling. The generosity of the king is far greater than that required of the servants. Yet still they fail.

We are so slow to learn generosity, so quick to seek security at others' expense. Yet God is patient, forgiving us from the heart, coaxing us to the mercy that is all-embracing.

✳ *Lord Jesus Christ, Son of God, have mercy.*

Saturday February 8   Acts 9:1–19
Isaac
Isaac of Syria was a great hermit, unwillingly made Bishop of Nineveh. He didn't last long. Shortly after his ordination two men

came to him arguing violently, demanding that he settle a disputed inheritance. 'What am I doing here?' he cried to the Lord, 'I can do nothing for the people in this place!' So he fled back to his cave in the desert.

Isaac tells of an elder who was asked, 'What is a compassionate heart?' The old man replied, 'It is a heart on fire with love for the whole of creation, for all people, animals, birds, even the demons, for all that exists.'

Saul was a great enemy to the Christian church before his conversion. Ananias is astounded that God asks him to go and pray for him. He is taking his life in his hands. But he goes, and Saul becomes a 'chosen instrument' filled with the Holy Spirit.

We wrestle with our demons, but God reconciles all things. All that is in the shadow is brought into the light. There is ultimately no separation, no reason for fear, nothing that is not encompassed by the love of God in Christ Jesus our Lord.

✳ *Come, Spirit of God, in the fire of your love.*

FOR REFLECTION – alone or with a group
● Which demons do you spend most time wrestling with?
● What in you needs forgiveness and reconciliation with God?
● In what ways are you estranged from your neighbour?

FOR ACTION
Think of one person you find it difficult to love. Find some way of letting God's love speak or act through you to them.

FAR OFF AND NEAR
7. Living together with the differences

Notes on the New International Version by
Johanna Jones

Johanna Jones has worked for Christian Aid in East Anglia for thirteen years, seeking to encourage church groups and the general public to understand and act on causes of poverty in the world's poorest communities. In this time she has travelled widely, meeting Christian Aid's partner organisations in Africa, Asia and the Middle East. Her love of her own two children fundamentally informs her passion that all should have access, as children of God, to a chance for a decent life.

Differences can destroy relations between individuals, as well as between groups in communities and across national boundaries. We all know how destructive differences can be within a family – and in the world. Paul keeps reminding the Christians of his day of their position as the dearly loved children of God and their calling to live a life of love. Holding on to these two convictions we are able to work our way through our differences. Each day remind yourself you are a dearly loved child of God. From that everything else comes.

Sunday February 9   *Ephesians 4:25 – 5:2*
Living a life of love

My daughter asked me, 'How is it, if everyone is Christian, they vote for different political parties?' In this passage Paul instructs the Ephesians on the reality of living together with our differences. He goes from the practical detail to the grand ideal – from not gossiping about others to being imitators of Christ.

Paul says we have to live a life of love which works out in our day-to-day living. Leading a life of love is hard work. It can feel like we are the only ones out there giving up our space, time and energies to respond to the needs of others. In a world where credit goes to those with top jobs and a good lifestyle, those who work with the poorest can often feel they are struggling on their own.

What difference does it make to our efforts to live a life of love when we know that we are 'dearly loved children'? And that Christ loved us first and gave his life for us?

✴ **John Wesley said, *'I have so much to do that I must spend several hours in prayer before I am able to do it.'* Think of the differences that exist in your local community, in your nation, in the relations between your nation and others. Pray for a new start in living a life of love, a life whose ripples will be felt spreading out into the world.**

Monday February 10   *Romans 1:8–17*
Meeting with others
Paul is desperate to get to Rome to meet the new Christian community there. Until he can get to see them he constantly prays for them. What difference do these prayers make to Paul? To the Romans?

The gospel is for all and Paul is anxious not to be seen as preaching to just one select group. Are there ways we keep our gospel to just one group? When he gets to Rome he expects to learn from the Romans just as they will from him. Are there ways we can learn from our brothers and sisters in Christ in other parts of the world?

✴ **Pray and keep praying for a Christian community in another part of the world, perhaps a part of the world that is in the news. Pray that we and they will know themselves part of the one body of Christ, united with so many others throughout the world.**

Tuesday February 11   *Romans 14:1–13*
Live to the Lord
At University I was asked to sign a statement of faith before joining my fellow Christians in their Bible study group. I did not sign so I was not able to belong to the group and learn from them or they from me. Paul says that we are not to judge each other 'on disputable matters'. Instead, the different ways that we live must each be lived 'to the Lord', what we do must be to the Lord. At what point then are the differences between us such that we must declare our disagreement?

The Christians in Rome had a choice whether to be vegetarian or eat meat – so it became a matter for debate what should be allowed. In our own time, many people round the world have had all choice taken from them. Their land is used for cash crops to pay off their country's debts; they eat the basic foods that are left because they have no value on the world market. What perspective does this put on our debates on what 'proper' Christians should or should not be doing?

✳ *Dear God, I come before you to give an account of myself. I place my life before you and let your searching light shine into the hidden places. Forgive me for when I have judged others, both my near neighbours and those far from me, seeing their lives only from my perspective and not from yours. Help me to kneel with them before you.*

Wednesday February 12   1 Corinthians 6:1–8

True judgement

A straightforward way to settle differences is to go to court. The Corinthians were doing this and so incurred Paul's wrath. They were so busy squabbling and fighting for their own rights that they forgot their higher calling: to judge and discriminate about ultimate matters. Similarly, if we are wronged we want the injustice to be known and put right. Why do we find it so hard to be wronged and have such a strong need for our own rights?

Because of the nature of human beings, things will go wrong within local Christian communities, and within the wider church. How do we put them right? There has to be a means for sorting them out ourselves because if we cannot do so before God how can we do so in a secular court? Our witness, as Paul says, is then defeated. Perhaps, rather than being so concerned for our own unsettled rights, we should be asking whether we are doing anything that hurts our Christian brothers and sisters and which demands to be put right.

✳ *Dear God, it can be very difficult to live as a community. When others hurt us or take what is ours, help us to remember that you are all-seeing and all-knowing and it is your love that is our end. Thank you for the times we have been forgiven by others for the hurt we have done them, for what we have taken that is theirs.*

Christians and non-Christians living together

There are several women in my church who come to worship each Sunday on their own and have to leave straight after the end of the service to get their family's Sunday lunch. They are not able to meet with the rest of the congregation because their husbands are unhappy if they are late home. Being married to a non-Christian can be a great source of anxiety and practical difficulty for the Christian. But Paul, who is not known for mincing his words, says a Christian is not to leave their unbelieving partner. The initiative for divorce lies with the unbeliever. The community of Christians is to mix at this most fundamental level with non-Christians.

If Christian and non-Christian can live together in the most intimate setting of marriage, what does this suggest for how we should work in our communities with non-Christians? So often as Christians we feel we have the right or even the duty to act without being compromised by what we may see as the less acceptable beliefs and actions of others. This passage may put a different perspective on such an attitude. Who has the right to keep separate?

✳ *God has called us to live in peace. Pray for situations where Christians and non-Christians live and work closely together.*

Listen to the lowest

When I visited the highlands of Peru, communities gathered together and then the leader of each village community gave a speech to welcome our party. It was often the least well-dressed, the one with the most work-worn face, or the woman with the most hesitancy, who would stand to speak. I was told that the villages change their leader each year and so all have a turn.

Who is listened to in this world? In a local situation it is easy to be swayed by dress and appearance and treat the well-dressed, self-confident person as the one with more to offer. How much more is this the case in the international scene, where generally only those with power and influence are heard. In an attempt to give other voices a place at the table, Christian Aid, the development agency, paid for two banana farmers from the Windward Islands to go to the Hague where European community leaders were discussing the quotas of banana imports. Meeting these farmers made a huge impact on the men in their offices. How can we give the poor as loud a voice in this world as those with the fine clothes and website access?

✳ *Pray for those who have no voice in the important meetings of this world. Inette Durandis, Development Worker for the Methodist church in Haiti, said: 'As Haitians our voices have no influence. But yours do. Use them.' Pray for ourselves that we may find ways to let the voices of the poorest, those without status, be heard.*

Saturday February 15   Philippians 2:1–15
Shine like stars in the universe

One of my colleagues is very good at getting others to become involved with Christian Aid's work – to preach, talk to groups or campaign. The key to his ability to get others doing this work of the kingdom is simple. He tells everyone that they can do the job better than he can! So they are given confidence and start to do things they had not dreamt they could. He is not after getting people to think how great *he* is.

So often it is when things go drastically wrong – a friend is seriously ill, or a community is hit by disaster – that people drop their disputes and rally together. Conversely, our disputes arise when we lose the vision of our common calling and become preoccupied by our own little situations.

Looking at the Milky Way in the night skies of rural Bolivia, I realised how many stars there are and how brightly they shine. In Cambridge you only have a clear sky one night in six. How can we, together, build a community of the world in which each person can shine their light, whoever they are, for the wellbeing of all and the glory of God?

✳ *Jesus, you made yourself our servant. Help us to kneel and wash the feet of others, to build them up so they can shine your love into our world. Help us to reflect the warmth and assurance of your love to others all around us, that our communities can become like the stars in the Milky Way – too many to be counted and radiant with your love.*

FOR REFLECTION – alone or with a group

● Where do differences bring conflict and where do they bring the joy of diversity?

47

- How do we prevent differences from dividing us?
- When do our beliefs become more important to us than sharing God's love in the world?
- How often are our prayers of intercession really 'God, they are different, change them to be like me/us'?

FOR ACTION

Read the foreign pages of a newspaper and before each name that is mentioned add in 'my sister X' or 'my brother X'. It will produce some scary results! Do the same as you put on your clothes or eat your food – made or grown for me by 'my brother/sister from X [name of country]'. See if your response to calls for action from agencies working for change is any different as a result of this exercise.

1 AND 2 TIMOTHY
1. Trustworthy sayings

Notes on the Revised English Bible by
Jan Sutch Pickard

Jan Sutch Pickard is Warden of the Abbey on Iona and a member of the Iona Community, an ecumenical movement committed to seeking new ways of living the gospel in today's world. A Methodist laywoman, she has also worked as a teacher, freelance writer and editor of periodicals and prayer handbooks, linking the local congregation with the world church. She is called to the Ministry of the Word, and enjoys life as a pilgrimage, in the company of other people – all different, all God's children.

Imagine a young man with a letter (a scroll) in his hand, reading it where the Mediterranean sun streams through a window: a young man who has been given a major responsibility – for guiding and giving some discipline to a lively young church. A church whose members are searching for a meaning in life, enjoy controversy and have a tendency to go off at tangents – what we might now call 'new age'. Imagine that you are that young man, Timothy, and listen to what Paul is saying in his letter: 'Let no one underrate you because you are young', 'keep yourself above reproach', 'keep safe what has been entrusted to you.' How much of this advice relates to the Christian community to which you belong now?

Sunday February 16   1 Timothy 1:1–11
A wilderness of words

Do you enjoy meetings? Or avoid them? And what kind of meetings? Like many adults in the church, I'm very familiar with the kind of meetings which are set up to transact particular business, with an agenda and usually a written record in the form of minutes. Good things can happen in such gatherings, if they bring together committed people and are well chaired. People need to explore the principles underlying decisions, listen to each other and come to a common mind. We all learn – and often grow in respect and love – through such meetings.

But as a student I enjoyed meeting week after week with other young Christians to argue about everything under the sun. How outrageous could we be? We were exploring ideas, provoking each other, playing with words. That was an important stage in my faith journey, but somehow the folk of Ephesus were stuck at that stage. The whirling words went round and round!

In that young church, the teaching of Jesus – and the down-to-earth way he embodied the love of God – was being lost in a fog of theory and superstition. We can hear Paul's impatience.

> ✳ *Dear God, give us patience*
> *to listen to and learn from our fellow Christians.*
> *But bless us with impatience*
> *when wordiness takes over,*
> *deafening us to your word of love.*

Monday February 17   1 Timothy 1:12–20
Worthy of trust

Does it feel good to be trusted? It can be a great honour – and a great burden. Most of us have at some point taken on a responsibility – and then wondered whether we can do all that needs to be done. 'There is this feeling', said a very gifted and able leader, 'that at any moment they're going to find you out.'

Having handed a major responsibility to the young Timothy, Paul encourages him with his own experience. After all, it was a very shaky record that Saul/Paul brought to leadership in the church – at the time of his conversion he was in the midst of persecuting Christians. He must have felt that no one could or would trust him. But God did. God knew how he could be used for good. Paul became a living example of what he preached – that sinners can be saved and the unworthy can find their true worth.

> ✳ **For your prayer, use the following breathing meditation,**
> **focusing on these two words: *'trust* and *'worth'*. Breathe out**
> **on the first word, emptying yourself, and breathe in on the**
> **second, accepting that God fills you with goodness.**

Tuesday February 18   1 Timothy 2:1–7
A quiet life?

Between the beginning and the ending of writing these notes, the world that we know has changed, following the terrorist attacks on the United States in September 2001. By the time you read this you will have read of, and maybe experienced more directly, war far away and action for peace closer to home. In the days after the first attack, Christians – and people of other faiths – offered up many prayers. Some of their concerns can be summed up in verses 1 and 2: 'for all in high office so that we may lead a tranquil and quiet life, free to practise our religion with dignity.'

Those in authority need our prayers more than they need our unquestioning obedience. They carry a heavy burden of responsibility – and they are human beings who do not always get things right. In a democracy we do at least have a vote. But we cannot hold a ballot of every major decision that needs to be made by our elected leaders. We can, however, campaign, demonstrate peacefully and enter into dialogue with them – and we can pray. Commitment to such engagement is not a recipe for 'a quiet life', if by that we mean hiding our heads until it is all over. But surely this is part of the practice of our faith, with dignity and dedication, to which we have a right – and which we would not want to deny to anyone.

✳ *O God, give peace to this broken world:*
Bless those in power with wisdom and compassion;
Empower us all to work together for peace, with justice.

Wednesday February 19   1 Timothy 2:8–15

A woman's place

How do you feel on reading this passage? It made me (as a woman, a single head of household, a Christian moved to prayer, a preacher, a person carrying responsibility within the church) feel uncomfortable. What is Paul saying about my ministry – indeed about my value as a child of God? Does it help me to respond, 'At this point he writes as a man of his time, with limited perspectives'? Does this mean that I am not taking scripture seriously?

Read Romans 16, and the greetings and commendations which include women who seem to be key members of the church. Is Paul being inconsistent between these two letters? Or was he addressing a particular problem, when he wrote to Timothy? It is hard for us to know. It is hard for us to be confronted by what seems like narrow-mindedness. It is just as important that we do not let our prejudice get in the way of Paul's larger message: the good news of God's love for all people and the equal value God as a good parent puts on every child.

✳ *Pray that Christians, wherever they gather, may accept –*
and so be blessed by – the gifts and ministry of both women
and men.

51

A model of leadership

Just as Christians in different cultures and in different times have had very different views about the ministry of women, so our picture of church leaders may change. To those who see clergy as essentially celibate, the idea of a bishop with wife and children will not be easy. Yet this letter is assuming that they will have households like other human beings.

Paul's main concern here is that a person's behaviour should be appropriate to their responsibility. Look at verses 4 and 5. There is a great deal of common sense here, and compassion as well as judgement. Those who care for whole congregations can neglect the needs – or even take out their frustrations – on the immediate family. How can we, as 'the whole people of God' help those who become our leaders?

✳ *God, our loving Parent,*
  Christ, Head of the church,
  Holy Spirit, Encourager of community:
  we know that those who carry responsibility
  within the family of the church are only human.
  Help them to act with humanity and integrity:
  realistic about how much they can do,
  and caring for those close to them.

God's household

Here again, Paul is writing out of the experience of the early church – which may have surprised later generations of Christians. For instance, he assumes that deacons may be men or women.

As with bishops, these folk who take on extra responsibility within the church need to behave consistently. We're probably all aware of the dangers. You can imagine how a fragile gathering of new converts could be damaged by drunkenness, or over-emphasis on money, or gossip. But, on the positive side, think how such a fellowship could be strengthened by those who 'combine a clear conscience with a firm hold on the mystery of the faith' (verse 9).

Think of someone you know who fits these words. And think of the church at its best, made up of such people and described in Paul's homely but powerful image – as 'God's household'.

✳ *God, you are the way, the truth and the life,*
  You are the head of our household of faith.

May we live together in your love;
may we speak together of your truth;
may we share together as your family;
may we follow together in your Way.

Hope in a living God

'Keep in training,' writes Paul to Timothy, and through him to the young church. This letter of encouragement doesn't say, 'You've arrived. Now you know it all. Everything is cut and dried, the church has all the answers'.

Reading this letter is like overhearing a series of arguments: for instance the one about food in verses 1–5. This is still a live issue at family meal-tables and in student halls of residence in our own time. It is worth stopping to think about the ethics of the food we eat: whether its production has involved cruelty, the wrong use of resources, exploitation of people or other parts of God's creation. But whether we choose to be vegetarians or vegans, or to eat only free-range meat, it's important to be reminded that 'everything that God has created is good' (verse 4). We shouldn't see it as a problem that the questions keep re-emerging, but as a sign of a living faith. As each generation enters into the arguments afresh, people become aware of why we live in particular ways, and the choices we can make as Christians. This is one aspect of 'keeping in training': not being smug, not taking things for granted.

'Old wives' tales' could be Paul's way of dismissing superstitions which undermine the gospel (incidentally, it is not only 'wives' or women who tell such tales!). There are also those traditions within churches which have taken on the status of 'this is the way we've always done it', but may be more about short memory or narrowness of thinking, whether it is taking communion from little glasses rather than a common cup, or limiting or rejecting the ministry of women or young people.

As Paul writes to Timothy, he is himself wrestling with these issues – and we may not, through our practice or from our perspectives agree with him. But we sense that these letters were being written within a church on the move, trying to find its way, God's way. It still had a long way to go. And that is true for us too – and should be an encouragement for us. We too need to keep in training, keep struggling to find the right way for our communities of faith, here and now. And we struggle on because 'we have set our hope on the living God' (verse 10).

✳ *Living God, bless and encourage us in our struggles*
to find and follow in your Way.
Help us to remember, day by day,
that you are Creator and you are Saviour of all.

FOR REFLECTION – alone or with a group

● What qualities would you look for in a church leader?
● What are the main issues that challenge the 'household of faith' to which you belong? How can you address them together?
● Take diet as an example, and ask different people to talk about the way they choose the food they eat, and discuss any underlying principles.

FOR ACTION

Reflect on the ministry to which God has called you in your life so far or what you might be called to do, in 'the household of faith' or in the wider world. Find out about how this could be followed through: courses, processes, support and advice from those near to you.

1 AND 2 TIMOTHY
2. Pastoral ministry

Notes based on the New Revised Standard Version by
Julie M Hulme

Julie Hulme is a writer in the field of spirituality and a Methodist, living in Birmingham. She is following a call to live the ministry of word and sacrament as a life of prayer, and spends much of her time in writing, art and pastoral encounters. She has published prayers, meditations and short stories, and gives priority to the support of those in ministry, both lay and ordained. Her husband, David, is also a Methodist minister, and they have two teenage daughters.

Paul writes to Timothy, his 'loyal child in the faith', to offer encouragement and guidance for the work of oversight entrusted to him. Paul is concerned, amongst other matters, for Timothy's wellbeing, and offers a view of pastoral ministry which describes the qualities of a good pastor, as well as good practice within a congregation. Paul's overall aim is to promote 'love that comes from a pure heart, a good conscience, and sincere faith' (1 Timothy 1:5), a godliness which holds promise for both the present life and the life to come.

Sunday February 23   *1 Timothy 4:11–16*
Set an example of love

Paul sees the Christian pastor as a living example of the gospel, as someone whose confidence is rooted in God who is the Saviour of all. Characteristics such as age, gender, race or social status are less important than qualities such as faith and purity of life. When these qualities are recognised and used within the congregation, regardless of social standing, then the people are demonstrating the creativity and freedom of Christian love.

Timothy's main task is to nurture others through studying and living out the scriptures, but Paul also urges him to use the charismatic gift that he has been given. His warnings imply a balance between tradition and renewal which is borne out by the experience of many Christian communities today. Without spiritual renewal, the interpretation of the scriptures can become stale and legalistic; while spiritual gifts must be used in a context of scripture, wise leadership, personal discipline and self-awareness, in order to avoid abuses of power.

Read Psalm 16.

✳ *O God of truth, nourish your pastors in your living word,
that they might live as examples of your gospel, training
your people in godliness and sound teaching, to the glory of
your name, this day and for ever.*

Monday February 24   1 Timothy 5:1–16
Live as a loving family
The pastor can encourage the Christian community to live as a
loving family through the tone of his or her dealings with members
of the congregation so that an atmosphere of mutual respect
develops between pastor and people (compare 4:12 and 5:1).

Indeed, the 'family-like' nature of a congregation should include
a willingness to offer practical help to those members who are left
destitute, but only if they have no blood-relatives able to support
them. The church provides a safety-net, not an excuse for children
who wish to avoid their responsibility toward their parents.

Paul also sees that, in a society which restricts women to the life
of home and family, unmarried women need an outlet for their
energies and their emotions, as well as an income. His advice is
pragmatic: younger widows should remarry rather than fall into
idleness and dissipation. His overall concern is the spiritual health
and security of pastor and congregation alike: he is only too aware
that there are adversaries willing to exploit any vulnerability.

Read Psalm 133.

✳ *O God of grace, fill your people with your own pure love,
that with tender hearts and wise minds we might live
together in harmony and care for each other with
compassion, this day and for ever.*

Tuesday February 25   1 Timothy 5:17–25
Act wisely
Leadership demands wisdom, the ability to stand back from
immediate issues to discern what is owed to both the individual and
the group; to the present moment, and also to the past and the future.

Paul knows that good leadership flourishes in an atmosphere
of creativity and trust, where the leaders are nourished by their
work, and are not subject to hasty or unsubstantiated criticism. If
Timothy is to see clearly how to encourage the elders, he needs
to cultivate an appropriate detachment, so that he too is not

bounced into hasty accusations, into favouring one group over another, into lending his spiritual authority without due reflection or into supporting dubious activity or behaviour.

A wise, reflective detachment from urgent and competing claims also allows a leader to adopt a balanced approach to his or her personal needs. And it tends towards patience, the understanding that some truths – whether for good or ill – only emerge over time.

Read Psalm 111.

✳ *O God of life, nurture your people by your creative Spirit, that in wisdom and trust we might encourage each other to develop the gifts that you have given, and so fulfil our mission as the Body of Christ, this day and for ever.*

Wednesday February 26   1 Timothy 6:1–10

Teach contentment

Paul's teaching on contentment emerged from a life of journeying, marked by sharp and rapid change. Prosperity and success could become hardship and adversity within moments. And yet God had also sustained Paul in his difficulties, and released him from danger through amazing events.

In particular, Paul knew that a congregation could be destroyed from within by dissension and quarrelling, even more effectively than by persecution from outside. His spirituality was formed by his experience of transience and insecurity, and by the need for constant vigilance.

This is why he taught that Christians should seek 'godliness combined with contentment' (verse 6). Hopes of wealth and status were a distraction. The concept of human rights had not yet been developed. In a world where nothing was certain and everything could change in an instant, Paul had found an inner stability. From this spring of peace, he could think, speak and act without fear, even with joy. It is this spiritual freedom that he desires for Timothy and those in his charge.

Read Psalm 131.

✳ *O God of peace, quieten the anxieties which irritate our minds, and calm the fears which cause us to lose patience with one another, so that we might live as a community of love, sharing your peace with our neighbours, this day and for ever.*

Keep the faith

At the lowest point of Jesus' life, when he was called to account before human authority and worldly power, he remained true to himself and to his understanding of what God had asked him to do. He kept faith with God, and that faith then kept him through the long hours of humiliation, agony and desolation which followed.

Paul uses very active, dynamic language to describe Timothy's life of faith. He writes of aiming at the qualities of a man of God; of fighting the good fight; of taking hold of eternal life; of keeping the commandment. This is appropriate because, as he knows only too well, such a life is demanding. It is a struggle.

But it is not a trial of strength. On the contrary, it is only possible to the extent that it is lived in the presence of God who gives life to all things, and of Jesus, who knew what it was to remain faithful when alone, powerless and afraid.

Read Psalm 107.

✵   *O God of endurance, hold us in your love, that we might wrestle with life in order to remain faithful to you; and rest in your peace, knowing that you keep faith with us, this day and for ever.*

Set your hope on God

Where do we set our hope? Where does my heart lie? Or, to use Jesus' imagery, as recorded in Matthew 6:19–21, where is my 'treasure'? Those who are rich, who have money, possessions, skills, education, status or achievements, face the constant temptation to invest too much of their time, energy and hope in the wealth of the world. Such riches may give a sense of security, but all too often this is revealed as an illusion.

On the contrary, Paul teaches the joy of hope which rests on the 'good foundation' of God's generous love. Rejoicing in the rich provision of God, we can give freely of ourselves and all that we have been given. This is a way of life that is more satisfying than relying on material things, because it promotes the 'godliness combined with contentment' which gives us an inner peace. It is also more secure than any form of special knowledge, which, in Paul's experience, leads only to pointless arguments and dissension.

Read Psalm 46.

Saturday March 1   2 Timothy 1:1–7

Rekindle the gift God has given you

In these verses, the bond between Paul and Timothy is shown to be like that between a father and his son – a rational, emotional, spiritual love. It means that the distance between them causes them both deep pain, but they transcend it through prayer, through correspondence, and through a common devotion to Christ.

But Paul wants to offer Timothy a more solid encouragement than his professions of gratitude and goodwill. And so he reminds the younger man that the faith within him has two roots which will continue to nourish him when Paul's fatherly oversight is removed.

The first of these is the tradition of devotion within Timothy's family. He is not alone. He belongs to a community of faith, which has included some of those closest and dearest to him, and that tradition is durable. And secondly, there is Timothy's own experience of God's indwelling strength, which, regardless of our circumstances, always tends towards the power, generosity and self-discipline of love.

Read Psalm 90.

✳ *O God of faith, sustain us in your grace, that each gift might be rekindled by your Spirit and used in the service of your reign of justice and peace, this day and for ever.*

FOR REFLECTION – alone or with a group

● From this week's readings, list the qualities which Paul wishes to encourage in pastors and ministers. How does this list compare with your own experience?

● What qualities need to be developed within a congregation or fellowship if it is to live as a loving family? How can these qualities be expressed and encouraged in daily life?

● How might we learn contentment, as Paul describes it, and encourage it in others?

FOR ACTION

Consider how you might take action to encourage your pastor/s, and show your care for them.

---

1 AND 2 TIMOTHY
3. The work of an evangelist

Notes on the New Revised Standard Version by
Burchel K Taylor

Burchel K Taylor – who has been pastor of Bethel Baptist Church, Kingston, Jamaica, for over 25 years – is internationally recognised as a leading Caribbean biblical scholar and theologian.

Our readings for this week are for the most part very personal and, in some instances, quite intimate. Whatever else is thought about the Pastoral letters as a whole, it seems likely that these readings come from the hands of the apostle Paul, and are addressed to Timothy, a younger Christian leader of whom he obviously expected much.

Paul is very concerned to see that this young man pursues his ministry with great faithfulness and dedication. This is so with special reference to the preaching and teaching of the gospel. He charges him to do the work of an Evangelist. The manner in which the apostle expresses this charge indicates that, whilst there is a special ministry of the Evangelist which is the calling of a few, there is also a more general role of evangelism which all Christians are called to share.

In this sense, then, instructions given to Timothy concerning being a witness and messenger of the Good News of salvation through Christ should be seen as addressed to every believer. It is with this assumption in mind that the readings for this week will be explored.

Sunday March 2   *2 Timothy 1:8–18*
Standing up for the gospel

Meaningful and effective witness will depend on what the gospel means to the believer. Its worth and significance must be experienced and appreciated by the believer before there will be a willingness to express public confidence in it and commitment to it.

There will often be the temptation to be reticent about the gospel in a setting where popular and influential opinion claims that the gospel cannot stand up to any serious scrutiny. We may fear rejection of our testimony as irrelevant to what matters most to people. However, the believer who has experienced and seen at work in others the life-transforming power of the gospel, who knows at first hand the new freedom the gospel inspires and the eternal hope it discloses, will have no need to be ashamed of it (verses 8–10).

We should not understand Paul to be chiding Timothy for actually being ashamed of the gospel. Rather, drawing upon his own experience of the pressure of such a temptation, he is offering wise counsel (Romans 16; 1 Corinthians 1:23). The way forward, he believes, is for implicit trust to be displayed in God who is absolutely trustworthy and in turn to remain bold and faithful with the enabling of the Spirit. There is no need to be ashamed of the gospel.

✳ *'I'm not ashamed to own my Lord or to defend his cause.'*
Lord, help me to be true to your calling.

Monday March 3   *2 Timothy 2:1–14*
Sharing the gospel
As believers have benefited from others sharing the gospel with us, so we should enable others to benefit from our sharing of the gospel. Our love, care and concern for others should commit us to this. There is something about the gospel, the Good News that it is, that should make each one of us want to do this. Timothy is being encouraged along such lines (verses 1 and 2).

At the same time, the apostle is quick to note that the expected and encouraged sharing will require certain personal qualities of mind and spirit. What are these? They are strength of character, endurance in the face of opposition, devotion to duty, self-discipline, sustained effort with the hope of a fruitful outcome and above all Christ-centredness (verses 1, 3–8). Thank God, these are not expected to be self-generated or self-sustained. The sufficient grace of God, along with divinely endowed understanding and faith-union with Christ who vindicates his faithful servants, will facilitate such qualities needed for the ministry of sharing the gospel (verses 1, 7, 11–13).

✳ *Lord, very often our own self-doubts are the greatest*
hindrance to our sharing the gospel. Help us to draw upon
what you have made available to overcome our limitations.

Tuesday March 4   *2 Timothy 2:15–26*
Having the right motive
Nothing can be more self-defeating in our service of the gospel than to be governed by the wrong motive. It is the surest way to having misplaced priorities. We end up by serving wrong interests, playing into the hands of opponents and misusing good opportunities for meaningful presentation of the gospel message.

It is quite fitting, therefore, that Timothy is encouraged to adopt the right motive: that of pleasing God. This should be the definitive and determinative motive of all our efforts. This means being undistracted from the main purpose of presenting the gospel and communicating it faithfully, with the sole intention of bringing others to the saving knowledge of Christ. It is not about scoring points in endless debates which are invariably self-regarding and fruitless. Paul gives examples of those who had lost their way by becoming caught up in such exercises, and who had created much confusion for others (verses 17 and 18). Timothy is expected to avoid their mistake.

God has made proper provision for his word to be shared. Those who embrace this ministry will remain solidly grounded and not readily be carried away into useless religious debates and arguments. Seeking to please God and not ourselves will help to keep us thus grounded.

✳ *Lord, help me to be properly focused and rightfully motivated as I seek to share your word.*

Wednesday March 5   *2 Timothy 3:1–9*
Being on guard
The historical context of these words was one in which Christians believed there would be dramatic moral decline nearing the winding-up of history and the ushering in of the promised new age by God. Paul wants Timothy to be fully aware of the state and condition of the times and context in which he lived, but not to be alarmed by them. In such a situation, it is necessary to be on one's guard against the corrosive and corrupting influence of evil and its ability to affect every area of human life and community.

For the Christian believer operating in such a setting and seeking to share the gospel, it is important that there be no compromising of the integrity of the gospel. It is also important that there be a close watch on one's own spiritual and moral discipline. There is no special immunity granted to the Christian against the subtle and seductive nature of evil, which may well masquerade under forms that enjoy popular acceptance in the society around us. There is therefore no substitute for serious spiritual and moral self-discipline on the part of the Christian. And as well as looking to our own wellbeing, we must be careful of the danger of causing others to stumble, too.

✳ *Lord, make me aware of the danger of sharing the gospel while I myself am disqualified by my lack of moral discipline.*

Maintaining godliness

Following on yesterday's reading, these verses imply that the gospel should be lived. Its ethic, virtues and values are expected to be embodied and exemplified in daily living and relationships. The scriptures are to be seen as a key source in helping believers to such an end. It is vital to cultivate the habit of reading and meditating on the word, both in personal devotion and in fellowship with others.

One of the things this will do is to facilitate a life of godliness which becomes the expression of the lived gospel. Such a life will be in contrast with that of those who live with other interests in mind while claiming they are believers. We may expect to draw unfavourable reactions from some, but the life of godliness must be maintained. It tells its own story of God's grace and goodness and his claim on our lives.

It is in this light that we can understand the encouragement Paul gives to Timothy to follow his own lived example. There is an extraordinary power in the witness of the gospel fully embodied and exemplified in human lives. Our witness cannot be in words alone, but must be anchored in deeds, and in the quality of our lives.

✳ ***Enable me, O God, to live a life worthy of the gospel for Christ's sake.***

Seizing every opportunity

No time must be lost. Every opportunity should be grasped to share the gospel, using whatever method best suits the moment, so long as it is in line with the character of the gospel itself. Witness may be, for example, by proclamation, instruction, exhortation, admonition or discussion, or by various combinations of these. There should be a sense of urgency but this should not lead us to methods of imposition, domination, manipulation and deception.

Let us pray for the wisdom and discipline needed to combine urgency with patience in the process of proclaiming the gospel. Neither opposition to our witness nor the apparent success of those who mislead others should lead to disillusionment or desperation. The task of presenting and sharing the gospel must go on with great determination and commitment, no matter what. This is the burden of the apostle's final charge. It is backed up by his own moving testimony. Despite all the odds, and whatever his own personal end, he knows that he has 'kept the faith' (verse 7).

He looks forward, with hope and expectation, to God's gracious favour bestowed not only on himself, but also upon others who have been faithful in the service of the gospel. The all-sufficient grace of God will accomplish all this.

✳ *Lord, give me a heart, mind and spirit to sense the urgency of sharing the message of your saving love, and make me eager to do so.*

Saturday March 8　　　　　　　　　　　　　　　*2 Timothy 4:9–22*

Affirming community

Sharing the gospel both creates and depends upon community. Isolationism and individualism will sooner or later undermine effective sharing of the gospel. Even the most gifted individual needs the support, friendship and companionship of others in the service of the gospel. Thus, it must always be the cause of serious dismay where there is disunity, disloyalty and betrayal in the ranks of the church. In a real sense it represents a denial of the gospel itself, for the gospel is one of unity and fellowship.

The sentiments of the apostle in this section of the letter express lament at the breakdown of relationships. At the same time, he also requests reading and writing material. No doubt this is for keeping in touch with his fellow Christians and sharing fellowship with them. Thus, both in his admonition of them and in his request for his own needs, he affirms the centrality of community. Surely one of the great and urgent needs at the moment is for effective Christian unity and the manifestation of real community at all levels. We need one another to help make real our common commitment to share the good news of salvation with all the world.

✳ *Lord, give me the wisdom and humility to recognise my need of others and their need of me in our shared commitment to the cause of the gospel.*

FOR REFLECTION – alone or with a group

● How do you understand the call to share the good news in your own life and setting?

● In what ways could you share the good news of salvation with others who need to hear it?

FOR ACTION

Look for and grasp opportunities in the coming week to witness to the love of God, in word and in deed.

LENT – COVENANT
1. Creation and Noah

Notes on the New English Bible by
Martin and Ruth Conway

Ruth and Martin Conway met over 40 years ago in the Student Christian Movement. They have continued to explore the contemporary questions and world-wide friendships which the SCM initially opened up. From a physics base, Ruth has recently concentrated on the values issues in design and technology education; she has written Choices at the Heart of Technology – A Christian Perspective. *Martin served on the staff of both the British and the World Councils of Churches, and then as President to the Selly Oak Colleges in Birmingham. He has written an account of the 1998 WCC Assembly in Harare in* Journeying Together Towards Jubilee.

The Genesis writers tackle key issues for life on earth: how do we relate to the Creator, to others in the human community, and to the rest of the natural world? How do these relationships interact? Creation climaxes in human beings made 'in the image of God' with the potential for loving and responsible relationships. God calls us to fulfil this potential: to trust and love God, our neighbours, and the whole earth community which supports and sustains life. God offers this covenant with a compassion that will in the end lead to the passion of Jesus – and waits for our commitment.

Sunday March 9   *Genesis 1:26 – 2:1*
Praise the Creator!

This story of creation is breath-taking. We are taken into the drama of a growing potential for life, life that is increasingly rich in its diversity and complexity. By the time humanity comes on the scene, the Creator is pronouncing the completed whole, with its finely balanced internal relationships, 'very good'. Moreover, human beings have a key role in maintaining this goodness: although dependent on the rest of the natural world, we are made 'in the image of God' with a responsibility to 'rule over' its life.

We are not left to carry out this mandate according to our own devices. Placing us within the magnificence of creation, God blesses us: God assures us that our lives will be fruitful and fulfilling for we have been brought into being with love and for love. Empowered by this blessing, we are to protect the natural world of which we are a part. We are to act in a way that enables life, with all its interdependent relationships, to flourish.

✳ *Creator God, bless us with a sense of wonder at the beauty of your creation and gratitude for the love that fashioned it. So blessed, may we help protect its life and enable its peoples to live to your praise and glory.*

Monday March 10   *Genesis 3:1–19*
Whose goodness?
In ancient imagery, today's story tells of humanity's 'fall' – though it can equally be seen as a 'growing up' – from the innocence of primeval beginnings into the tough realities of actual history.

Food is to be had only from never-ending toil. Children are born only through intense pain. Snakes are a mortal danger. Why, oh why is life so hard?

Throughout human history, we human beings have acted by self-regarding impulses and our own interpretation of good and evil, be it the child screaming 'That's mine!' or bosses awarding themselves over-large salaries. Thus have we shaped and soured all civilisation. We manage natural resources for our selfish interests, manipulate relationships to suit our own power games – and call 'good' what we have done, disregarding God's intentions, shown anew in Jesus' life for others.

Today's reading warns us to re-examine our lifestyles and what we regard as 'good'. Do we take account of the impact of our 'consumer' decisions on the planet's finely balanced ecosystems? How can we turn our life outward in hospitality and sharing?

✳ *Creator God, give us the humility to repent of selfishness and greed; reveal to us your good in others; show us how to care for the goodness of your creation.*

Tuesday March 11   *Genesis 6:5–22*
There is an alternative
The 21st century, a friend recently agonised, seems determined to face us with all the threats of the 20th – and more! At the start of the Noah story God was as depressed as our friend – and more – by the pernicious corruption and pervasive violence.

Yet then, as now, and in contrast to the notorious TINA doctrine ('there is no alternative'), God's initiatives of love remain strong enough, and the potentialities of God's creation diverse enough, for ways ahead to be found.

Noah and his family are the first biblical example of a remnant: a small group, even a single person, through whom the future health of the whole earth community can be ensured. Noah's faith and constructive action make the renewal of life on earth possible.

So Noah's story challenges us to consider: what is humanity being called to by God at a time when the ecological basis of life is so severely threatened? What particular concern or change or opportunity or need has the Holy Spirit laid before me?

✳ *Creator God, give us minds to discern the root causes of degradation and conflict in your world today, hearts open to new ways of living and acting, and faith to carry these through.*

Wednesday March 12   *Genesis 8:1–5, 15–22*

First priority: worship

And so, in the story, life begins again.

The destructive climatic conditions subside. Noah's family and the assorted living creatures, having learned to live together in cramped conditions, are now free to spread out and colonise the earth again. But before embarking on this new life, Noah's first priority is to build an altar to offer worship to God. He acknowledges his dependence on God and, in response, God confirms that the basic conditions for life will be maintained.

And what of us today? It is not only living creatures that have spread over the earth, but the means of exploiting natural resources, communication networks, trade, financial dealings, and security systems. The result is a grossly inequitable world in which, for many people, the basic conditions for life are in danger.

Have we lost our way by failing to honour the purposes of a just and compassionate Creator? Have we so little gratitude for the marvels of Creation that we plunder it with impunity? Is our love for God so weak that we hardly know how to love our neighbour?

✳ *Creator God, turn us towards you in praise and thankfulness. May our worship inspire in us a care for all the intricate relationships that uphold the life of the planet and support its many peoples.*

Thursday March 13   *Genesis 9:1–17*

Look to the skies!

The terms of the covenant are spelt out. God promises no more all-out destruction if we fulfil our part: respect for other living creatures (even if we are now, unlike Genesis 1:29, allowed to kill and eat some) and for the life of our sisters and brothers across the world.

The light by which the Creator brilliantly pierced the darkness of primeval chaos is now seen as a vibrant spectrum of colours in the midst of the recently destructive rain-clouds. The promise of beauty is wrought by harmonising variety and difference. There is a new beginning born out of judgement and disaster. The Creator has not and will not abandon the creation.

The threatening clouds are with us again, but this time they are predominantly human-induced: climate change brought on by greenhouse gas emissions from the guzzlers of fossil fuels in industry, transport and buildings. We have upset the natural balances on which life depends.

The bow in the sky is a reminder that the covenant needs commitment from our side too. Those who live under the lure of rampant consumerism are called to break the spell and demonstrate abundant life by 'living more simply that others may simply live'.

✳ *Creator God, alert us to the irreparable damage we are causing. Inspire in us ways of living that safeguard life for all.*

Friday March 14   *Isaiah 54:5–10*

Costly love

Sharing the Babylonian exile of Israel, the prophet sings lyrically of God's renewed promises and faithfulness, confident that, as with Noah, a new start of lasting peace is at hand.

Today, when in the affluent West many couples face the agonies of divorce, protestations of new-found faithfulness from a once-straying husband sound dangerously hollow. Yet this passage comes after the vision of the suffering servant, murdered uncomplaining for the faults of others. The message to a captive people is startling: they will be restored to a community where peace and justice are paramount through a love that seeks them out in their humiliation and is alongside them in their despair. Far from abandoning them, God shares their suffering. The followers of Jesus were to see him live this out and the victory of love sealed in his Resurrection.

Everywhere today there are signs of anguish. The earth is despoiled, and many communities oppressed by poverty and injustice. Resorting to violence is no solution. The way of love is to listen, to share, to hope and to trust, knowing that God's costly love has the power to redeem.

✳ *Creating and redeeming God, rekindle in us a trust in your unshakeable love. Take us with you to places of hurt and show us your love at work.*

Creation and covenant fulfilled

Noah and Jesus are here seen together: both living by absolute faith in the Creator/Father, both as remnants opening up a decisive new start. In Jesus' case he did more than 'ride out the storm'. He absorbed the worst that human hate, betrayal and violence can do, and met it with love. He accepted the depth of suffering, even death itself, without breaking his trust in the Father, and so was brought through to resurrection life.

Both dramas come to a climax in God's offer of a covenant relationship. Jesus' new covenant binds his followers into a life of self-giving love for others. This is dramatised for all Christian believers in baptism, as each turns from self-regarding ambition to a life of service in several dimensions:

● in our personal and work relationships a new quality of trust;
● in our ways of reacting and responding to people of other communities, cultures and religions a new quality of love;
● in our handling of the natural world and our caring for the long-term future of the planet a new quality of hope.

✳ ***Creating and reconciling God, renew your people in the joy of Christ's resurrection. Enable us to overcome cynicism, suspicion, and hatred with the hope, trust and love he inspires.***

FOR REFLECTION – alone or with a group

● What prophetic word needs to be spoken to political, industrial, commercial and financial leaders in order to reduce the degradation of earth's life-sustaining eco-systems and to ensure a more equitable sharing of natural resources?

● Does the Creation feature regularly in your church worship? Could your congregation adopt an environmental policy covering management of the premises and land and the purchase of goods? What would need to be done to act on it?

● How can you adapt your lifestyle to ensure a lower impact on the environment? For example: saving energy, conserving water, cutting waste, organic gardening, questioning consumer hype, minimising food miles, making fewer journeys using fossil fuels, investing in environmentally responsible companies.

FOR ACTION

Based on your reflections on the above, what practical steps can you, your family and friends, your congregation, or your work base now take?

LENT – COVENANT
2. Abraham

Notes based on the New Revised Standard Version by
Martin Baddeley

Martin Baddeley is an Anglican priest, recently retired and living in Malvern, about as far from the sea as you can be in the middle of England. He has spent most of his time as an ordained minister working with those training for ordination. He was Principal of the Southwark Ordination Course, which provided a three-year course of training for men and women from the Anglican, Methodist and United Reformed Churches through evening classes and residential periods while they continued with their daily occupations.

Abraham, Sarah and Hagar are the forebears of three faith communities: Judaism, Christianity and Islam. Ishmael and Isaac, two sons of Abraham to whom these three faith traditions look in different ways, eventually united to bury their father Abraham in the family burial place purchased by Abraham (Genesis 25:9–10). In these studies we shall listen to four passages from the book of Genesis in the Old Testament and then passages from two New Testament writers about the great ancestor, Abraham.

Sunday March 16   *Genesis 11:1–9*
Building up for breakdown

The Tower of Babel is the last of the parables of beginnings in Genesis 1–11 before the appearance of Abr(ah)am and the beginning of the story of the adventures of faith in the Bible.

Here is a description of the breakdown of community, of confusion and failure of communication. The story also provides a picture of the possibilities of co-operation for humanity. What are the most important questions to be asked of any human achievement? The tower was to be built 'to make a name for ourselves, otherwise we shall be scattered'. If a name for ourselves and not God is at the centre of our efforts, if God-given boundaries are crossed, if human beings refuse to live in dependence on the Divine Creator, will scattering be a divine judgement?

Shinar is the area around Babylon where Babel meant 'the gate of the gods'. A similar-sounding word in Hebrew means 'confusion'. In the centre of this parable of divine judgement is there a hint of hope held out in verse 6? The co-operative building of this tower is not the way forward but are there other possibilities? Will the next chapter indicate a way?

✳ **Lord, we thank you for the variety of the human race and for all the good things we receive from peoples of other countries and cultures. Give us the gifts of discernment and generosity of heart and mind for Jesus Christ's sake.**

Monday March 17   *Genesis 12:1–5*

The call of Abram

Abram is called to go on a journey for God. He is faced with a series of increasingly harder decisions – 'Leave your country, your kindred and your father's house' – in other words, give up your past in obedience to God. The Hebrew phrase used here for 'go' occurs in the Bible only here and in the story of the binding of Isaac where Abraham is asked to sacrifice his son (22:2) and so give up his future.

Abram is to go to a land that the Lord will show him. Here is the threefold promise which will provide a framework for the following ancestral narratives: the promise of land, of descendants and of being a blessing for all peoples. Will Abram be the right person? Noah found favour in the sight of God (Genesis 6:8–9). But then his descendants attempted to build their tower to make a name for themselves. And so God's gracious covenant dealing with humanity will continue through another, Abram, who will be given a part of the earth where a new community could grow to be a blessing for all humanity.

✳ **Lord, give us a forward-looking faith and use us to build communities which will be blessings for all, for Christ's sake.**

Tuesday March 18   *Genesis 15:1–21*

The covenant of promise

Will that threefold promise of chapter 12 be fulfilled? Time after time in the following stories the promise will be set at risk. Will Abram have any descendants or will his heir be a slave from Damascus? No, the promise is reaffirmed in verse 5 and the next verse indicates that Abram too, like Noah (Genesis 6:8–9), is righteous. But then, what about the promise of land? How is Abram to know that he will possess it?

This passage is the first account of a covenant or binding agreement that God makes with Abram. The meanings of the details are lost in the mists of time and that adds to the mystery. Verse 13 looks ahead to Israel's slavery in Egypt, a land that is not theirs and from which the Lord will rescue them in the Exodus under Moses (Exodus 5:1). Do the fire pot and torch represent the divine? We might have expected the human partner as well to have passed between the sacrificial pieces if the action was to express what Jeremiah 34:18 describes. The emphasis here is on the divine action and the promise of the land is reaffirmed in verses 18–20.

✳ *Lord, help us to grow in trust for Jesus' sake.*

The covenant renewed
Compare this second account of God's covenant with the first in chapter 15. Here from the beginning the emphasis is on God's making of the covenant. Here the promise of descendants is repeated. But will Abram wait for God to fulfil his promise of descendants even though Sarai, his wife, is past the age of child-bearing? Will he learn the lesson of 18:14? Is this a test of his trust in God? In fact it was Sarai, in the previous chapter, who suggested that he had a child by the slave girl, Hagar, and Abram had 'listened to the voice of Sarai' (16:2). Is this phrase used to contrast with obedience to God?

New names with symbolic meanings for a new beginning are given after the birth of Ishmael to Hagar: Abram means 'great father' and Abraham means 'father of a multitude'. Although God promises that twelve princes will descend from Ishmael, as twelve tribes will eventually descend from Jacob, the emphasis in this narrative falls on the child of Sarah. The name Isaac comes from the Hebrew word for laughter (verse 17 and notice also 18:12–15). All the males of Abraham's household are circumcised as a sign of the covenant which will be an everlasting covenant. The promise continues.

✳ *Pray for a growth in understanding and respect among Jews, Muslims and Christians.*

Faith as righteousness
Paul uses the figure of Abraham to show that Gentiles do not have to follow the Jewish path in order to become descendants of Abraham. Abraham is not an example of how to be God's covenant people by observing Torah, the Jewish Law, but as an example of the way

through to God through justification by faith. This is not something earned by Abraham's efforts. For God counted the faith of Abraham as righteousness (Genesis 15:6) before he was circumcised (Genesis 17) and so he is the ancestor of both Gentiles and Jews who follow the example of Abraham's faith. Therefore he is the ancestor of all who believe, even of those outside the Jewish circumcised faith community, as well as those who are circumcised and follow the example of Abraham's faith. Abraham has universal significance for salvation for all peoples and is not the exclusive property of any one faith community. The quotation is from Psalm 32.

✳ *Lord of all power and might, who art the author and giver of all good things: graft in our hearts the love of thy name, increase in us true religion, nourish us with all goodness and of thy great mercy keep us in the same, through Jesus Christ our Lord.*

Book of Common Prayer, *Collect for Trinity 7*

Friday March 21   *Romans 4:13–25*

The promise

Paul concentrates on the connection of the promise with Abraham's faith. The promise is God's gift – look back to the threefold promise in Genesis 12:1–3. And this promise was given by God (Genesis 15) before the Torah or Jewish Law was given to Moses in the book of Exodus. Here are two parts of the promise: the land in verse 13, and descendants in verse 16, all those who have faith. God's promise was the ground of Abraham's faith and hope. Abraham then is the pattern for Christian faith.

Promise and faith rather than achievements *(verses 19–22)* apply to Christians as well as to Abraham. Finally life from death for Christians is based on the resurrection of Jesus Christ, the gift of God. For Abraham the birth of Isaac is considered as life from death (verse 19). All people are under the power of sin and the way out is through faith in Jesus Christ, for from the time of Abraham justification by faith has been the way to God's acceptance.

✳ *Eternal God, increase in us your gift of faith; that, leaving the past and looking out towards your future, we may follow the way of your commandments, through Jesus Christ our Lord.*

Saturday March 22 *Hebrews 6:13–20*

Abraham and Melchizedek point to Jesus as High Priest

The unknown writer speaks of faith ancestors in 1:1 and in this passage summons Abraham as his first example of faith from Israel's story (to whom he returns in 11:8–12). God's promise still applies to Israel, Abraham's descendants through Isaac. The divine promise is based on a divine oath (the writer appears to have Genesis 22:16–18 in mind).

God's promise and oath encourage us, the heirs of the promise, to 'seize the hope set before us' (verse 18). This hope leads us beyond the curtain or veil screening the Holy of Holies, where Jesus has gone as a forerunner on our behalf and as the eternal High Priest. Who was Melchizedek? In Genesis 14 he appears suddenly as King of Jerusalem and priest of God Most High and then as suddenly disappears. He blessed Abram and this shows that an unbroken Jewish priestly line in the earthly temple is not necessary for achieving reconciliation with God. Paul had similarly sought to show that obedience to the Jewish Torah was not essential for Gentiles. What is decisive is faith in Jesus Christ.

✳ *Lord, increase our faith and help us where faith falls short.*

FOR REFLECTION – alone or with a group

● What do you mean by 'faith'?
● Does the variety of stories in Genesis about Abraham make it easier or harder for you to consider him as a model or pattern for faith?

FOR ACTION

Can you find ways of trying to get to know members of other faith communities, particularly Jews and Muslims? Where might you find help and advice through your local church?

74

LENT – COVENANT
3. Sinai

Notes based on the Hebrew Bible by
Jonathan Gorsky

Jonathan Gorsky, an orthodox Jew, is Educational Adviser of the Council of Christians and Jews.

This week's readings, taken from Exodus, look at the Sinai covenant. The commentary looks at different interpretations of the covenantal relationship and its radical development, even within the framework of the Exodus texts. It offers an interpretation of the golden calf incident and an understanding of Moses' veiled countenance, when he descends from Mount Sinai and returns to his people.

Sunday March 23   *Exodus 19:1–8*
Covenantal metaphors

The Jewish theologian David Hartman writes that there are different ways of understanding the relationship of God and Israel. Each way draws upon a particular metaphor, offering insight into what is meant by a 'covenantal' relationship.

The best-known metaphor has God as king and Israel as vassal; the covenant is their document of mutual commitment. In the style of ancient political treaties God describes what he has done for the Israelites. In return they will give him allegiance and he for his part will look after them and protect them. God has the right to this arrangement, because it is due to him that the people have their freedom at all; in the absence of his intervention they would still be slaves in Egypt.

The second version, preferred by Hartman, separates the covenant from the preamble about the Exodus. In this version, Israel is *invited* to participate in the relationship, and there is no element of a divine right, based upon the Exodus, to Israel's allegiance. The community freely accepts the invitation out of love for God. Hartman – following another Rabbinic metaphor – likens this arrangement to a marriage, in which the partners freely respond to each other: individuality is retained, but love inspires a deep sense of mutual responsibility.

Hartman is clearly anxious to avoid the authoritarian element of the first metaphor, and he also favours a third possibility, the rabbinic notion of God as our teacher, encouraging his pupils to freely develop greater spiritual understanding and find their way to holiness.

Look again at the passage, and try and understand which metaphor seems closest to a plain reading.

✳ *Help us, O Lord our God, as we tremble in contemplation of your holy name. Grant us the courage to seek your love, and forgive us our errors and our transgressions.*

Monday March 24   *Exodus 20:1–17*

The Ten Commandments

Yesterday we saw David Hartman somewhat unhappy with God's authority over us; today's famous passage clearly presents Hartman with considerable difficulty!

How do we understand the notion of 'commandment'? Clearly it is a powerful obligation which does not allow for choice, debate or possible amendment. Could God not have chosen an alternative mode of instruction, perhaps commending a certain course of action, or strongly advising us to behave accordingly? The advantage would be that we might then retain our individual freedom, acting out of love and reverence, rather than irresistible compulsion.

But when we come to apply this possibility to the specific commandments, clearly there are problems. Refraining from murder is not merely a piece of good advice; we cannot simply suggest to husbands and wives that they might find it helpful to avoid committing adultery. The consequences of both acts are destructive, either of life, or of the mutuality and trust that is the essence of any relationship, without which it cannot exist at all.

Commandment is the only appropriate way of conveying such obligations, as the alternative would imply a tolerance of actions that are destructive and deeply hurtful. Also, even in many secular disciplines, acts of far lesser import might nevertheless be deemed essential rather than voluntary. A music teacher must insist that her students obey her instructions – otherwise they will not make progress. So it is with the spiritual life, and commandment, after all, might be reconciled with Hartman's other metaphors.

✳ *May we know, O Lord, that your commandments are given to us in your great love to guide us on our journey and bring us safely home. As we observe them, help us to know your presence and find our hope and our consolation.*

Covenant and sacrifice

Today's reading is very difficult indeed, particularly the covenant sacrifice and the physical image of God in verse 10, as well as the apparent irreverence (verse 11) at a moment of great solemnity. Perhaps the sacrifice – and the sprinkling of blood – signified the level of devotion entailed by the covenant; the people recognise that they might be called upon to give up their lives for their faith, and accept the gravity of their undertaking.

One Jewish tradition connects the sapphire stone with the bricks of the Egyptian slavery. According to this tradition, at this most sacred moment people were overwhelmed with guilt-ridden images of their previous degradation at the hands of the Egyptians; the vision indicates to them that God understood the depth of their affliction, and saw only the precious stones of their attainments – not the grim consequences of their intense servitude.

The eating and drinking (verse 11) is sometimes contrasted unfavourably with Moses' 40-day fast (34:28) when he experienced the intimacy of God's presence, but an alternative reading has it that they were celebrating the sanctification of the physical life that was made possible by the grace of divine revelation. Such celebration is fraught with danger, in circumstances which demand the greatest reverence, but God accepted that their motivation was pure and of great holiness.

✳ *Help us, O Lord our God, to see how precious are all of your children, the people of your world. Help us to trust and care for them, to know them as you know them, to see them as you see them, and to love them as you love them at all times and in every place, even in our moments of great anguish and almost unbearable hurt.*

The golden calf

How do we understand the fact that so soon after Israel's most profound experience of God's presence, the people are unfaithful to the covenant and seek to worship an idol? We have already seen (Exodus 20:19) how dependent they were on Moses in their relationship with God, and how his apparent disappearance had a shattering impact upon their faith, leaving them fearful and insecure. The idol is initially seen as a substitute for Moses – a mediating image – rather than a supplanting of God, but within a few verses it has clearly evolved into something far more radical, a god of physical and tangible reassurance who does not utter commandments or instil 'fear or trembling'. There is almost a sense of relief in their excessive rejoicing.

The covenant demands a setting aside of all images; it implies fidelity to a transcendent God in whose presence we must forgo all visual understanding. Even an icon, alluding to God without any idolatrous implication, is strictly prescribed. God is apparently unapproachable – the people are fearful of any close encounter. The setting aside of imagery sharply emphasises that God is eternally other, unknowable and ungraspable. We are to relate intimately and faithfully to One whom we can never really know, or even approach without trepidation, and he discloses himself to us only in his commandments and statutes and ordinances. Without Moses, the people are unable to sustain their covenantal relationship, and yearn for the reassurance of a more amenable and tangible religious life.

✳ *As we wander in great darkness and seek comfort in images and shadows, help us to recall our days of old, and remember your holy presence.*

Thursday March 27   *Exodus 34:1–28*

The covenant renewed

The idolisation of the golden calf was rooted in an inherent flaw in the covenantal relationship as it was perceived by Israel. We saw (Exodus 19:4) the intimacy of the relationship as it was seen by God who carried his people out of slavery as if on the wings of eagles, and, in the Hebrew original, brought them to him (an expression reminiscent of David Hartman's marriage metaphor that we encountered at the beginning of the week). But Israel's experience of God had not disclosed his love for them, and they were fearful and afraid in his presence.

Compare today's reading with the initial revelation on Sinai that we looked at in Exodus 19. The new revelation is private and intimate, rather than publicly awe-inspiring; its focal message is one of divine compassion. God is slow to anger: punishment can be delayed for generations and is, for the rabbis, only meted out if they choose to replicate their ancestors' shortcomings, and it might be averted by penitence. (The rabbis read the punitive verse 7 in the light of Exodus 20:5).

Moses' prayer (verse 9) is a plea for God's intimate presence in the midst of the people. In the first revelation the people had sought the opposite. Frightened by the thunder and lightning, they trembled and asked to stand at a distance from the divine presence. In chapter 20, God answers their request and speaks to them 'from the heavens' (verse 19ff). But in our passage, this is not what Moses prays for, as he seeks a relationship rooted in intimacy and forgiveness.

At the end of this lengthy passage Moses, who had himself hewn the stone tablets at the beginning, is instructed to write the words of the covenant upon them himself. These features did not occur in the first set of tablets, which were given to him by God (compare Exodus 24:12). A rabbinic explanation has it that whereas the first revelation expected us to be heavenly beings, transformed by the experience of God's presence, the second recognises our human fragility, and asks us to gradually inscribe the divine words on the tablets of our own hearts (referring to Proverbs 3:3).

✳ *Help us, O Lord our God, not to be afraid. You who know our failings and our fragility, calm our storms and write your words on the tablet of our hearts.*

Friday March 28   *Exodus 34:29–35*
Moses' radiance
St Jerome, in his fourth century Latin translation of the Bible known as the Vulgate, understood the Hebrew description (verse 29) of Moses' radiance literally, and the rays of light became the 'horns' of Michelangelo's famous statue.

Christian scripture has used the image of the radiant Moses and his veiled countenance in two ways. The most explicit is 2 Corinthians 3. St Paul contrasts the letter (Moses) with the spirit (Christ). If the letter which ends in death is glorious to the degree that people cannot look upon it, then the spirit which gives life must be the more so. Moses' veil means that the Jewish people continue to read their Testament without perceiving its ultimate light, but when they turn to God, the veil will be taken away.

This understanding, presumably spoken in anger, remains difficult and harsh for the Jewish reader. For Jews, the Torah is not a letter devoid of spirit, but a God-given grace that is the beginning of the journey to sanctification. As in Proverbs 6:23, God's precepts are candles that shine with the radiance of the divine, gradually leading us to the light of holiness, which, unlike the Pauline text, we do not expect to be fully disclosed.

The second image – the transfiguration – grants Jesus the radiance that Moses achieved on Sinai, but has him in companionship with Moses and Elijah, rather than as an antithesis. Like the people who draw back from Moses, Jesus' disciples are awe-inspired and afraid. In the Markan version they are afraid of Jesus; in the Matthean and Lukan accounts they are fearful of the voice of God in the cloud, and Jesus has to reassure them. God is hidden by a cloud, as in Exodus, and the disciples are moved to build 'tabernacles' for their holy companions, offering shelter as an expression of their reverence. Covering that which is precious or sacred – an Old Testament word for modesty literally means 'hidden' – is an ancient Jewish response. It is recalled in a famous anecdote of the Desert Father Abba Pambo, of whom it was said: 'God so glorified him that no one could look at his face, because of the glory which his face had.'

✳ *In our times of anger, O Lord, grant us the covenant of your peace and make us worthy of the holiness of all life. Shelter us in the tabernacle of your presence and grant us once again the gift of your eternal love.*

Saturday March 29   *Exodus 15:11–18*
The Song of the Sea
The Song of the Sea celebrates the end of a world where might was right – where the brute force of political power defined the lives of all human beings. It is the song of a people who had been redeemed from slavery to an all-powerful regime which seemed destined to reign for ever. This regime had no care for individual people and few qualms about abusing the powerless and the vulnerable. It was capable of being shaken by irrational fear of strangers in its land, and doing terrible things to maintain their subservience.

A new vision has been born of a God who instils compassion into international affairs, who hears the cry of the suffering peoples and delivers them from their oppressions. God's kingship is celebrated because it heralds the end of the barbarous power of this world. The centre of this kingdom is to be a sanctuary rather than an edifice of military might. God's covenant with a small and vulnerable people of slaves represents a new world order. It means that he is no longer automatically connected with the great power, who assumed that Divine strength was always with them, inspiring victory and justifying depredation. The horse and its rider are no longer invincible, and the Lord shall reign for ever and ever.

✳ *Lord whose presence has transformed all life, hear the cries of those who live in suffering all of their days, and teach the powerful the ways of your peace and your love.*

FOR REFLECTION – alone or with a group
● How do you understand the golden calf story?
● What does the covenant metaphor mean for our relationship with God?
● Are commandments necessary?

FOR ACTION
Alone, or with a group, undertake further study of Jewish understandings of covenant. Consult your local synagogue for help, or the Council of Christians and Jews.

LENT – COVENANT
4. David

Notes on the Hebrew Bible by
Rachel Montagu

Rachel Montagu is the Assistant Education Officer at the Council of Christians and Jews based in London, and teaches biblical Hebrew at Birkbeck College Faculty of Continuing Education and Allen Hall. She has worked as a congregational rabbi and is particularly interested in Jewish feminism.

In David's life we can see reflected the difficulties of being a religious leader in a time of transition. How does David know what God wants him to do? What is his role as king? David is only the second king in Israel and the first, Saul, lost his kingship because he disobeyed God. When the people first wanted a king, the king was to judge them and to lead them in battle. What will be David's and his descendants' religious role? God promises never to forget the covenant with the people even if they sin.

Sunday March 30   *2 Samuel 6:1–23*
How to dance in praise of God
Where should be the appropriate resting-place of the ark containing the stones on which were written the Ten Commandments, seized in battle by the Philistines and then returned to Israel? When David began to bring the ark up towards Jerusalem, the danger of those unauthorised – those not descended from Aaron – touching the ark of God was demonstrated. Uzzah steadied the ark in case it fell, a sensible thing to do, one would think, yet he was killed for it. Only when the presence of the ark brought blessing to Obed-Edom did David dare to bring the ark to Jerusalem, 'the city of David' where his new palace stood. This is when we see the beginning of Jerusalem's centrality in the lives of Jews and Christians, established by David who made it the centre of the monarchy and of religious life.

David danced and spun about in delight as the ark reached Jerusalem safely – and Michal saw him and, instead of rejoicing with him, despised him, thinking his behaviour unkingly. Only one generation of monarchy and already it is so clear to Michal that a king must put dignity before his emotions and passion for God.

David married Michal because she loved him, the only one of his wives who we hear did so (1 Samuel 18:28). We do not know why their relationship went so wrong but we can regret it and her subsequent barrenness.

✳ *The Song of Songs says that love is as strong as death. We pray that our love for those precious to us and theirs for us lasts for ever.*

Monday March 31   *2 Samuel 7:1–17*

Who can build God's house and how grand should it be?

The relationship between king and prophet is an important theme in these historical books of the Bible. Here and in the story of Bathsheba (2 Samuel 11) we see Nathan giving David advice. Nathan first gives his own instinctive response but then has to return, once he has been given a prophetic vision, and report God's message which is different. It is David's as yet unborn son Solomon, and not David himself, who will be deemed worthy to build a house of cedar for God to dwell in.

The mediaeval Jewish commentator Kimchi says that the tent that David pitched for the ark (1 Samuel 6:17) was clearly a temporary home until a better Temple would be built, but it also acted as a reminder of the portable shrine in the wilderness in which it had first been kept.

God promises David that he will not be treated like Saul, the first king of Israel. He will have a great name and the people whom he and God rule over will live in security. His descendants will be punished when they do wrong but their disobedience will not completely rupture their covenant with God as Saul's did. Perhaps God deals with Saul strictly just as parents are often stricter with their first-born than with those who follow.

✳ *'How pleasant are your tents, Jacob, your dwelling-places, Israel'* (Numbers 24:5). *May our homes always be filled with awareness of God's presence.*

Tuesday April 1   *2 Samuel 7:18–29*

God's covenant with the people

David sits in the tent before the ark and this is described as sitting before the Eternal. We can pray to God anywhere but it may be especially easy to have a sense of God's presence in places where God has been manifest, where many others have prayed before or where there are Bibles or prayerbooks. Tova Mirvis, in her novel *The Ladies' Auxiliary*, describes the synagogue secretary just sitting in the synagogue to have a few minutes of peace and sense of the presence of God in the middle of her busy office day.

David speaks now of 'house', meaning not a physical dwelling but the body of his descendants and God's promise of an everlasting covenant. He links the past Exodus from Egypt and the everlasting future which God promises in this new understanding. David had offered to build a house for God and instead he is promised a house and descendants. His thanks to God sound like a psalm of praise. When he says in verse 26 that God's name will be great for ever, he suggests that God's people will offer praises for ever in response to what God does for them.

✳ **Blessed are you, Eternal God of our father Jacob, from everlasting to everlasting. Yours, Eternal, is the greatness and the might and the splendour and the glory and the majesty. Eternal, everything in heaven and earth is yours.**

1 Chronicles 29:10–11

Wednesday April 2   *Psalm 89:1–8*
God's loving-kindness
The first word of the main body of the psalm in Hebrew is *chesed*, loving-kindness. This is the key word of the psalm. Making a covenant with human beings demonstrates God's love and mercy. This is one of those psalms where we see God both as immanent, present in this world and concerned with human beings, and as transcendent, infinite, eternal and mighty. In verse 2, loving-kindness and faithfulness are part of the essential structure of the universe. The verbs used are 'be built' and 'be fixed', solid structural verbs. Later Jewish tradition says that 'the world could not exist if built entirely with justice or entirely with mercy' but loving-kindness transcends these opposites.

Here, as in yesterday's passage, we hear of God making an everlasting covenant with 'David my servant'. David's religious identity is being God's servant, continually in God's presence and obedient (usually!) to his commands. David's sense of wonder at the promise of an everlasting dynasty is obvious here.

✳ **God's loving-kindness endures for ever (Psalm 118).** *Let us praise God for the loving-kindness manifest in our lives and try to bring loving-kindness into the lives of others.*

God's faithfulness to the covenant

A covenant is a permanent agreement between two parties. God promised Abraham that the covenant would be with his descendants for ever and promised the whole people at Sinai that they would be God's treasured possession and a kingdom of priests and a holy nation. Here God promises the people that if they do wrong they will be punished but the covenant itself will remain unaltered. The word used for breaking the covenant is *halal*, meaning 'make unholy'. The covenant is made with loving-kindness and faithfulness and God cannot betray it or go back on such a covenant once it is made.

The analogy of marriage is frequently used for the relationship between God and the Jewish people. There may be moments when husband and wife feel that it is hard to be aware of their partner's feelings or tolerate their behaviour but that does not alter their fundamental commitment to each other.

✷ *I will betroth you to me for ever, I will betroth you to me in righteousness and justice, with loving-kindness and mercy. I will betroth you to me in faithfulness and you will know the Eternal.*   *Hosea 2:19–20*

David's song of joy

This is one – and an unusually long one – of the fifteen psalms of ascents, traditionally sung by the Levites as they made their way up into the Temple (a flight of fifteen steps recently found by archaeologists on the side of the Temple mount caused great excitement – perhaps this was where the psalms were sung). David describes his dream of making an appropriate resting-place for God. Where the ark rests, so will God's presence be (see Exodus 25:22 and 40:34–35) and there those who love God will shout for joy.

In response, God promises David an everlasting covenant and kingdom for his descendants, with bread for the poor and priests clothed in salvation. David has said that those who love God and do God's commands will shout for joy, and the verb is repeated for extra emphasis in verse 16. The verb *ranah* means singing and joyous tumult – this is a covenant which is a source of delight to those who keep it.

✷ *Come, let us sing with joy to the Eternal and shout out to the rock of our salvation* (Psalm 95:1). *Let delight in God's presence fill our lives.*

David – God's right-hand man

When the people first asked Samuel for a king, it was a judge and strong general they wanted (1 Samuel 8:20). This psalm portrays David as just such a war leader. It makes clear the pathos of war – the 'womb of dawn and the dew of youth' (*yaladtecha*, the Hebrew word for youth, is derived from that for birth). Yes, the people are willing to fight but was it for this that their mothers birthed them?

In David's desire to affirm that he is a priest like Melchizedek (who greeted Abraham with bread and wine when he entered Canaan, blessing and congratulating him on defeating the local kings – see Genesis 14:18–21), we can see potential conflict for control of the nation's religious life. Will kings be religious leaders as well as generals? Melchizedek's everlasting priesthood is not comparable with that of Aaron and his descendants. David hopes to emulate Abraham's victory over hostile kings.

There is a complex wordplay in the last two verses. The Hebrew words for 'nations' and 'corpses' are similar, and, while the nations' heads will be crushed, David's will be exalted.

✳ ***May God who makes peace in the highest realms make peace for us and for all Israel and for all human beings.***

Jewish liturgy

FOR REFLECTION – alone or with a group

● How can we know what it is God wants of us when we no longer have prophets who tell us exactly and reliably what God asks?

● Does God actually want splendid places of worship? Are we adding depth to our prayers by building impressive places to worship? Is it more important to make some of our time holy and dedicated to God?

● How do we judge how much money and time we may put into making our own homes a pleasure to live in compared to the amount we contribute to the place where we worship and to those who have no home?

FOR ACTION

Make a study of the Temple in Jerusalem, finding pictures and descriptions of it in its full glory. Compare the glory of the Temple with some of the great religious buildings in your area, perhaps visiting a few.

LENT – COVENANT
5. Jeremiah

Notes based on the New Revised Standard Version by
Albert H Friedlander

Rabbi Dr Albert H Friedlander OBE is the Dean of the Leo Baeck College and Rabbi Emeritus of the Westminster Synagogue in London. He has been a Fellow of the Wissenschaftskolleg in Berlin, and has been a visiting professor at many European universities. His books in the field of theology and history have appeared in various languages. Currently available are: Riders Towards the Dawn: Christian and Jewish Thinkers after the Holocaust *(Constable, London) and* Out of the Whirlwind: The Literature of the Holocaust *(New York, 1999, revised edition) and his translation of the Five Scrolls of the Hebrew Bible. He is the President of the Conference of Christians and Jews (UK) with the Archbishop of Canterbury, the Cardinal of Westminster, and the Chief Rabbi. He is the Honorary President of the World Conference of Religions for Peace, and co-editor of the journal* European Judaism.

The translation of the Book of Jeremiah used here is based upon the Hebrew Bible, but the notes also use the New Revised Standard Version.

The Book of Jeremiah addresses every community of faith throughout the centuries. It places the vision of God into a world of suffering and war, into a time of destruction when hope seems far away. The prophet struggles with an impossible task: he must present a society of social injustice and selfishness with the awareness that its foundations are crumbling, that their beloved city is doomed, and that a time of darkness and exile lies ahead of them. In a time of confidence he preaches doom; but when despair comes, he presents hope. His own life is under attack; he is, truly, a suffering servant of God.

Sunday April 6   *Jeremiah 7:1–15*
Ritual without sincerity is useless
Jeremiah's 'temple address' came at a difficult time. The good king Josiah had fallen in battle, his successor had been deposed, the current king Jehoiakim was a vassal to Egypt. Could insincere worship in the Temple sustain Israel's faith that they had a covenant with God? Does God dwell in the Temple when it is filled with injustice? The prophet brought them God's word:

Do not trust in these deceptive words: 'This is the temple of Adonai, the temple of Adonai, the temple of Adonai.' For if you truly amend your ways and your doings ... act justly one with another, if you do not oppress the alien, the orphan, and the widow, or shed innocent blood in this place, and if you do not go after other gods ... then I will dwell with you in this place ... in the land ... for ever. *(verses 4–7)*

The sanctuary can become a 'den of robbers' (7:11) in an unjust society. It is easy to worship there and to feel righteous, to lose oneself in ritual and to feel holy. What happens when the worshipper finishes the prayers and steps out into the streets of the city? There, injustice rules the market-place, and one forgets that God is worshipped through ethical actions: the covenant, basically, is a moral code.

✴ ***God, help me to be honest with myself. Let me not see my religion simply as worshipping in your house, meeting my obligations within the ritual. Help me to see that I must reach out to everyone through the ethical actions which make the world the true sanctuary in which God dwells.***

Questions: What was Jeremiah's role in his time? Are there prophets today? Could I be a prophet? How?

Suggestions: Are there committees in your community who work with social issues? You may try to involve yourself in their work. Have you sent a letter to the newspapers?

Monday April 7   *Jeremiah 7:16–26*

False worship breaks the covenant

Religion builds its house as a sanctuary against the false gods in every society. Jeremiah warns the people:

The children gather wood, the fathers kindle fire, and the women knead dough, to make cakes for the queen of heaven; and they pour out drink offerings to other gods... *(verse 18)*

Parents and children are always drawn into the culture of the day, even where it undermines their own religion. The 'Queen of Heaven' was the Assyrian Ishtar, goddess of fertility, and the 'cakes' were probably star-shaped. Wasn't it harmless fun, sharing the ritual of neighbours? 'No', shouts the prophet. 'You do not confuse God here: you confuse yourself. You lose the way of worship, you destroy your faith.' Israel was dedicated to a certain task, to be 'the light of the nations'. False worship can only lead to destruction.

✳ *God, help me to be true to my faith, respecting others, but aware that I must follow the way which has been shown to me by sacred scripture. There are other ways which lead to you, to righteousness, and to my neighbours. As I grow stronger in my own tradition, I will join others in moving towards your kingdom on earth; but help me to be my covenanted self.*

Questions: What are the idolatries of our time? In the media? In business? In my home?

Suggestions: Discuss 'idolatry' with your friends. Do they think of it as a sin?

Tuesday April 8   *Jeremiah 23:1–6*

The coming of the kingdom

When a people lives under oppression, far from God, from itself and its dreams, the prophet comes to remind them of the divine promise:

> And I will gather the remnant of my flock out of all countries whither I have driven them, and will bring them again to their folds; and they shall be fruitful and multiply. And I will set up shepherds of them who will feed them..
>
> Behold, the days come ... that I will raise unto David a righteous branch, and a King shall reign and prosper, and shall execute justice and judgement in the earth. *(verses 3–5)*

Israel still lived in its vision of its covenant and of its role in the divine plan, but despair was at hand. Here, the prophet addresses their needs on various levels. There is the promise that a righteous king will rule them (Hezekiah?) and that their future is bright. Beyond that, there comes the greater dream of the Messiah, the Anointed One, a branch from the root of David – the promise for all of humanity. The biblical vision distinguishes between 'the days of the Messiah' and God's kingdom at the end of days. The better world has to be realised within human history, and Israel can hope that the new king will create a just world in which all can live in peace. It is still a human task. Beyond that there is the ultimate vision of the Messiah, and human hope is built upon this.

✳ *Oh God, we are ready for the coming of the kingdom. May the kingdom be ready for us, speedily, in our days.*

Question: Where do we find the signs of the coming of the kingdom? In ourselves? In our world? In our sanctuaries?

Action: Go to a 'retreat' within your community which strives towards this vision.

The sacredness of kings and priests

Throughout history, religion and politics have often been partners, as the government received support from religious institutions and protected them in return. At times, both forgot that power is abused without the covenantal relationship with God.

> In those days and at that time I will cause a righteous Branch to spring up for David; and he shall execute justice and righteousness in the land.

> For thus says ADONAI: David shall never lack a man to sit on the throne of the house of Israel, and the levitical priests shall never lack a man in my presence to offer burnt offerings, to make grain offerings, and to make sacrifices for all time. *(verses 15, 17–18)*

Jeremiah, the priest of Anathos, saw the wickedness of kings who burned his books, of priests who conspired against him. And he saw the Temple destroyed and witnessed the end of the kingdom. Nevertheless, he asked the people to pray for the rulers in their new place of exile. He prophesied the end of that exile, and saw God's mercy prevailing. In history, the kings and the priests endure in different ways: in government and in sanctuaries; and all remain as part of the vision leading towards the kingdom of God.

✳ *May God, whose kingdom is an everlasting kingdom, bless all of the Royal Family and their counsellors and give wisdom to the government of this country, to all who lead it. May this kingdom find its honour and greatness in the work of redemption and the building of God's kingdom here on earth. May this be the Divine will.* Hebrew Prayerbook

Questions: Is there still sacredness in government? Should there be boundaries between the state and its religious institutions? Why or why not?

Action: Attend a national act of worship like 11 November to understand the role of royalty.

A book of consolation

A message of consolation must be grounded upon the full awareness of the pain which enfolds a people. It is not the vision of the far future which gives comfort, but the knowledge of shared suffering. And so Jeremiah describes a reality which all share:

We have heard a cry of panic, of terror, and no peace.
Ask now, and see, can a man bear a child?
Why then do I see every man with his hands on his loins
like a woman in labour?
Why has every face turned pale?
Alas! that day is so great there is none like it;
it is a time of distress for Jacob; yet he shall be rescued
from it. *(verses 5–7)*

In a curious way, the voices of those who have emerged out of
the fiery caldron of suffering have given most comfort to the
world. Aung San Suu Kyi and Elie Wiesel, both Nobel Peace
Prize laureates, have turned the torture they suffered into
messages of hope for humanity. So, too, Jeremiah suffers with
his people, watches the sacred city and Temple burn, endures
the pain of exile, and can still bring the people the divine message
of consolation:

But as for you, have no fear, my servant Jacob, says ADONAI,
and do not be dismayed, O Israel;
for I am going to save you from far away,
and your offspring from the land of their captivity.
Jacob shall return, and have quiet and ease,
and no one shall make him afraid.
For I am with you, says ADONAI, to save you... *(verses 10–11)*

✳ ***God, let me not enter into the darkness which surrounds all
of us; but let me be aware of the sufferings of those who are
imprisoned and enslaved; and strengthen me so that I may
give them comfort.***

Questions: Have you listened to the testimony of survivors from
death camps and lands of oppression? Can these encounters
deepen your faith – or do they weaken it?

Action: Attend a funeral in your community – or outside it – and try
to give comfort to the family.

Friday April 11   *Jeremiah 31:23–30*

Rebuilding after destruction

In the end, the religious vision suggests tasks set for all of us.
Jeremiah clearly distinguishes between his own dreams and the
word of God which he must declare:

'ADONAI bless you, O abode of righteousness, O holy hill!'
And Judah and all its towns shall live there together, and the
farmers and those who wander with their flocks.
I will satisfy the weary,

and all who are faint I will replenish.
Thereupon I awoke and looked, and my sleep was pleasant
to me. *(verses 23–26)*

Our dreams are needed to restore hope and courage. We can
then remind ourselves of our duties and recognise that each
generation has its own work to do. Jeremiah quotes 'the parents
have eaten sour grapes, and the children's teeth are set on edge'
(verse 29) in order to deny it: 'But all shall die for their own sins;
the teeth of everyone who eats sour grapes shall be set on edge'
(verse 30). The nature of human freedom and responsibility is
placed before us at this point. We do *not* carry our parents' guilt
for all of life – and we must not treat the children of sinners as lost
within the guilt of their family. If we want to build a better world we
have to join our near and distant neighbours in that task. And we
cannot claim God's judgement against all those who displease
us: all of us stand before the throne of judgement.

✳ *God, give me the insight to be aware of my tasks. Let me not*
make my visions absolute truth, but let me rejoice in the beauty
and poetry of dreams. Let me reject the darkness that comes
so often, but let me remember the splendour which is so easy
to forget. All of us are the dreamers of dreams, not just the
music makers. May I remember the wonders I encounter.

Questions: Have we ever treated our own visions and dreams as
divine revelation? Have we accepted full responsibility in a world
where we prefer others to take the risks? And do we ever listen
to the dreams of others and find inspiration in them?

Action: Look for a book in the library which deals with dreams and
religious faith.

Saturday April 12   *Jeremiah 31:31–34*

The new covenant

This text is the heart of the Bible. It is a universal covenant, not
confined by the Temple, the priesthood, or the land. The past is
wiped out, the future has begun. Once written on stone, it is now
internalised into the human heart. It is Jeremiah's greatest
message, the centre of his prophecy:

'Behold, the days come,' saith ADONAI, 'that I will make a
new covenant with the house of Israel and with the house of
Judah, not according to the covenant that I made with their
fathers in the days that I took them by the hand to bring
them out of the house of Egypt; which my covenant they
broke, although I was an husband unto them ... but this shall

be the covenant that I will make ... I will put my law in their inward parts, and write it in their hearts; and I will be their God and they shall be my people.' *(verses 31–34)*

Israel and God are now joined together through eternity. They need not explain it to one another, for the covenant lives within their awareness. The human heart is not made of stone, but can love and reach out towards God and the world. Individual responsibility is here enshrined in the new freedom of serving God. It is a new beginning. 'Covenant' means 'agreement' and this has now been established by God. 'Agreement' is also the meaning of the word 'testament'. The 'new agreement', the New Testament, belongs in this awareness. The New Testament does not cancel out the Old Testament, but all move forward on parallel paths, children of God travelling towards the kingdom. The covenant is written in their hearts, God's greatest consolation in a darkened world.

✳ *O God, we thank you for the covenant which you have placed within our hearts. It links us together as your children; it joins us with our neighbour as we study your Bible. Our knowledge of this bond is suffused by love and gratitude. You are our loving parent, and we will build our lives upon the foundation of this covenant. Give us strength to be worthy of this, your gift.*

Questions: Have we examined the Hebrew word *brith* within the Bible? The covenant made with others, the covenant made with God? How does God's covenant differ from the agreements, the covenants made in life, among individuals? Do nations make covenants? Must we be free and responsible to live within this structure of law?

Action: Discuss 'covenant' within your family. Try to set up an 'agreement' of shared ethical actions within your home.

FOR REFLECTION – alone or in a group
● Go back to some of the questions set during the week and ponder them more deeply.

FOR ACTION
Look up in a concordance the use of the word 'covenant' (*brith* in Hebrew) throughout the Bible and make a study of it.

How much do you know about Jews' understanding of their faith? Contact a local synagogue and find out how modern Jews live out the covenant in your locality.

LENT – COVENANT
6. Jesus

Notes based on the Revised Standard Version by
Sr Margaret Shepherd nds

Sr Margaret is a member of the Sisters of Sion, a Roman Catholic congregation with the special task of promoting good relations between Christians and Jews. She is Director of the Council of Christians and Jews in Great Britain.

'Covenant' is a word pregnant with meaning and has, in our own day, acquired a special importance in the new dialogue between Jews and Christians. Pope John Paul II has spoken repeatedly of God's covenant with his people, the Jews, as 'never having been revoked'. God, ever faithful, does not go back on his word. In both the Hebrew and Christian scriptures, 'covenant' is not definitive or fixed, to be summed up in a simple formula. It can refer to many different things, depending on its context.

Palm Sunday, April 13   *Luke 1:67–75*
The call of a covenanting God

Zechariah's prayer is spoken on the occasion of his son's circumcision, the unique sign of God's covenant with his people, bringing both privilege and obligation: 'Be holy, for I the Lord your God am holy' (Leviticus 11:44). Both the prophet Jeremiah and the author of Deuteronomy speak of the interiorisation of covenant loyalty as 'circumcision of the heart': we must first hear and listen to the word of God before we can do God's will. Luke develops this theme of relationship through Mary's 'fiat' and Zechariah's positive response to God's word. Jesus, true son of the covenant, whose story is fully in continuity with the events and hopes of his people's past, creates a new pattern, a new significance. God always 'remembers his holy covenant' (verse 72).

✳ ***God, ever faithful to your covenant with your people, fill us with your love and help us to listen to you from the very core of our being so that we may respond to you with all our heart.***

Monday April 14   *Luke 22:14–20*
The experience of redemption

The word 'covenant' is common to all versions of the last supper narratives, but mention of the 'new covenant' occurs in only one line of the tradition. From the time of the early Christian communities, any reference to 'new covenant' claimed that the promise of Jeremiah 31:31 of a 'new covenant' had been brought to fullness in Jesus and his atoning death, based on the end of the Jeremiah text: 'For I will forgive their iniquity, and I will remember their sin no more' (Jeremiah 31:34). This promise had been fulfilled in its primary sense with the people's return from exile and the rise of a new community around the temple in Jerusalem. But Christians also see it fulfilled ultimately and uniquely in Jesus, the one who had the Torah written perfectly on his heart. We, too, are invited to share in the strength of Jesus' faithfulness to God's teaching, the Torah.

✳ *God of the covenant, you call us to enter into a close relationship with you. Help us to reaffirm daily our commitment to live according to its demands, assured, even when we fail, of your abiding, constant love.*

Tuesday April 15   *1 Corinthians 11:23–26*

Remember the exodus from Egypt

In this text we are given a fascinating insight into the beginnings of liturgical practice in the church. The meal described here finds its origin in the central importance which meals have always had within Jewish life. The Passover meal, the probable context of the Last Supper, referred to by Paul, recalls God's redemption of his people from slavery in Egypt, making them a free people. This was to lead to the covenant at Sinai when the Israelites pledged themselves to live according to God's law, the Torah, and God promised that they would be his special people, a kingdom of priests, a holy nation (Exodus 19:3–6). At the heart of Israel's understanding of the covenant, an understanding shared by Christians, is a concrete experience, a historical event in which God has been actively involved in the fate of humanity. The covenant at Sinai is integrally linked with the Exodus, which is remembered and relived at Passover. Every subsequent generation of the Jewish community owns this event, this binding covenantal relationship, for themselves. It remains contemporary, active and lived today, not merely a relic of the past. This is equally true for the 'new' covenant in Jesus. Both Passover and eucharist recall a historical event of suffering and deliverance. Both, albeit in radically different ways, offer an experience of redemption and covenantal community, the community of God's people today.

✳ *Our redeeming God, help us to be aware of all that enslaves us, to set out on our own exodus, difficult and painful though it may prove to be. May the words of your prophet, Jeremiah, travel with us: 'Be not afraid ... for I am with you to deliver you' (Jeremiah 1:8).*

Bearing common witness to the God of the covenant

Throughout the Hebrew scriptures there is the significant leitmotif of God 'remembering' his covenant with Abraham (see Exodus 6:5–7 and Leviticus 26:42, 45). In the blessings of the holiness code in Leviticus, statements become transformed into promises looking toward the future. We find echoes of this not only in certain psalms (for example, 105:8, 106:45, 111:5), but also in the phrases of the Benedictus of Luke's gospel. Several promise texts from the stories of the patriarchs in Genesis are recalled in Peter's words to his Jewish audience in Acts 3. He rightly calls them 'sons of the prophets and of the covenant', drawing together the different promise texts in the Abraham narratives of Genesis into one single promise. Paul does the same in Galatians 3:15–17.

Together with our Jewish brothers and sisters, we bear common witness to the God of the covenant. Let us respond to the urgency of this in today's world, which desperately cries out for meaning, courage and hope. Let us acknowledge our joint responsibility for the future, for the next generation, to initiate a new history for the good of all.

✻ *God of promise, thank you that we share with our Jewish brothers and sisters a rich heritage of your promises. Help us to work together with them and all people of goodwill to bring your promises into being in our world.*

Finding our identity

In Galatians 3:6–19, Paul writes of what he understands to be possible under the 'law' and the 'promise'. As often in Paul, his thought process is rather complex and difficult. He speaks of the basic promise made to Abraham long before God gave the law on Sinai, seeing this promise – 'your seed' – as fulfilled in Christ. He argues that the promise also encompasses the law, by using the Greek word for 'covenant', *diatheke*, to mean 'testament', as in 'last will and testament'. Like Peter in Acts 3, Paul brings together the various texts in Genesis referring to the promises to Abraham into one single promise, focusing on the more universal content of that promise, the 'blessing to the nations', as distinct from the particularity of Israel itself. He uses the key word 'law' to refer to everything belonging to Sinai and a second key word '*diatheke*/covenant' as both older than the law and reaching beyond it to the moment of its fulfilment in Christ.

According to the complex thought pattern in this text, Christians do not belong to a 'new covenant' as such but to the 'Abraham covenant', resulting in opposition between those who believe in Christ following the promise to Abraham and those who find their identity solely in the law of Sinai (Galatians 4:22–31). May we recognise in these difficult texts, which point to the historical struggle of Christians for their self-definition in those early centuries, our common root with Judaism.

✳ *Loving God, help us, both Christians and Jews, to live today as partners open to a new relationship with each other. Show us how to be there with each other and for each other.*

Good Friday, April 18   *Hebrews 8:1–13*

God does not abandon those he calls

The letter to the Hebrews sets up a deep opposition between the two 'covenants', without using the actual term 'old covenant'. It says that the 'first' is doomed to redundancy when the 'second' comes. This is very reminiscent of the polemical hyperbole of 2 Corinthians. Hebrews takes the promise of a 'new covenant' from Jeremiah 31:31ff quite literally, drawing a stark conclusion. Talk here of two 'covenants' implies categorically that the 'second' is superior to the 'first', replacing and rendering it obsolete. This is one of several passages in the Christian scriptures and early Christian writings responsible for the 'replacement theology' which has brought bitter consequences in history. It is only in our own day that we have begun to correct this untenable proposition, which has caused deep suffering to the Jewish people during the past two thousand years. It questions God's faithfulness and does not do justice to Paul's more mature and subtle reflections in Romans.

✳ *Let us pray for the Jewish people, the first to hear the word of God, that they may continue to grow in the love of his name and in faithfulness to his covenant.*   *Good Friday liturgy*

Saturday April 19   *2 Corinthians 3:1–6*

I am among you as one who serves

Now God's splendour shines from the 'new covenant', not bringing the 'old' to an end, but resembling the removing of the veil from the normally shining countenance of Moses when he entered the sanctuary. However, Paul's comparison of the 'two covenants' takes second place to this wider theme and is only used to explain the task of the Christian. For all its difficult polemic, the real theme of 2 Corinthians 3 is apostolic service.

What, then, does it mean to be 'ministers of a new covenant'? It points to the depth of service Jesus indicated in his profound gesture in John's account of the Last Supper. When Jesus finished washing the feet of his disciples, he asked them, 'Do you know what I have done to you? … A new commandment I give to you, that you love one another; even as I have loved you, that you also love one another' (John13:12, 34).

✳ *Lord Jesus Christ,*
  Son of the Living God,
  Comforter of widows,
  Washer of feet,
  Show us how to care for each other.
  Teach us to love as you did:
  Unconditionally, unilaterally,
  without fear of favour,
  pride or prejudice.
  Give us open hearts
  and wise minds
  and hands that are worthy
  to serve in your name.   *Sheila Cassidy*, Good Friday People
                                    (Darton, Longman and Todd; permission sought)

FOR REFLECTION – alone or with a group

● Does the reality of being in covenant with God impact on your own life?

● If the covenant God made with the Jewish people has 'never been revoked', what implications does this truth have for Christian self-understanding?

● Would you agree with Bishop Richard Harries in saying that 'genuine dialogue involves not only understanding and affirmation but bringing in to the relationship what is distinct and different'? (From an unpublished paper, quoted with permission in *Sharing One Hope? – The Church of England and Christian-Jewish Relations, A Contribution to a Continuing Debate*, Church House Publishing, 2001)

FOR ACTION

Explore the rootedness of Christianity in Judaism and develop friendship with members of the Jewish community through the Council of Christians and Jews.

THE BODY
1. The risen body

Notes based on the New Revised Standard Version by
I Jason Kioa

*The Reverend Ísileli Jason Kioa is a minister of the Uniting Church
in Australia, serving in the suburb of Canterbury in Melbourne
where he has been for the last eleven years. He is originally from
Tonga but is now an Australian citizen. He is an accredited spiritual
director, graduated from the Melbourne College of Divinity. He is
currently the Chairperson of the Synod of Victoria's Commission for
Mission. Jason has wide experience in cross-cultural ministry.*

There may be questions in some people's minds as to what kind of
body Christ had when he rose from the dead. I am certainly not
going to give answers to such questions in these notes. What I *will*
affirm by faith is that, whatever form of body Jesus took when he
rose from the dead, it will be the same kind of body those who
believe in his death and resurrection will come to share. As we
explore the readings set for this week, we will be engaging in an
understanding of the relationship between the spiritual body and the
physical body. Is there a dichotomy between the two? We'll see!

Sunday April 20 (Easter Day)   *Luke 24:36–49**
You are witnesses!
Being a witness to an event or incident carries with it a lot of
responsibilities. The outcome of a legal dispute can depend on
the witnesses' accounts. I have been recently asked to be a
witness in a court case because of something that I saw take
place. Great store is set on witnesses. Channel 10 News in
Melbourne is called the Eyewitness News, implying that the
cameramen and -women and the reporters are there at the
hotspots whenever and wherever the news breaks!

Luke's account of the resurrection of Jesus in today's passage
is quite comprehensive in its list of witnesses. First, there were
the women at the open tomb, followed by Peter. On that same
day, the two disciples on the road to Emmaus witnessed Jesus as
he broke bread with them. They returned to Jerusalem and were
all sharing their stories, yet still with a sense of fear and
uncertainty. For some the root of their uncertainty was the fact

that they themselves had not seen him, whereas for others – unbelievably – the problem was precisely because they had! They could hardly believe the witness of their own eyes! Jesus then came and stood in their midst, providing the missing link.

The risen Christ continues to be the one who helps us to witness to the truth of his resurrection – in worship, as well as on the roads we travel and in our gatherings and encounters, wherever they may be. He brings peace as we seek to share the truth of what we know – however haltingly – and alleviates our fears and doubts by reassuring us of his reality.

✳ *Risen Lord Jesus, continue to reveal to us your new life, and empower us to see that you are feeding us with your word and sacraments on the roads we travel.*

Monday April 21   *1 Corinthians 15:1–11**

Agreeing to the one truth

It is very important that witnesses give the same account! Many court cases are dismissed and ruled invalid because witnesses are not consistent with their stories. Paul in this passage offers an account of the progression of events that took place at Christ's resurrection, and names the witnesses to those events. The trustworthiness of his account is crucial in proclaiming the truth of the resurrection of Jesus Christ. In making his case, Paul appeals to both scripture and tradition. Yet he adds a new note, indeed, a new witness, in his version of events: his own conversion experience is adduced as another witness to the risen Christ. It is this encounter with the risen Lord that is the basis of Paul's apostleship, and the grounds of his trust in God's grace.

There is something significant for us in this passage. The grace that embraced Paul and made him a witness to the resurrection can also embrace us and invite us in to share his experience of a welcoming, inclusive and forgiving God. Moreover, Paul makes it clear that the whole raison d'être of the church is founded on the veracity of the resurrection. To deny that Jesus was raised from the dead is to deny the credibility of the community of faith, as well as the integrity of the good news that the church proclaims from generation to generation.

✳ *Risen Lord Jesus Christ, as we continue to celebrate the new life that you bring, empower us to be graceful and inclusive, so that others may also come to believe.*

Spirit of God in the flesh

In this passage, Paul is not denying that we, as human beings, are in the flesh, in the literal sense. Nor is he rejecting the goodness of the body *per se*. Indeed, it is a key affirmation of a religion that celebrates Christ's incarnation that God embraces and inhabits all human flesh. Rather, Paul is speaking about the risen life that humans may inhabit because of Christ's redeeming work and his resurrection, and contrasting this condition with the 'fleshly' life that is ruled by sin. The Spirit that raised Jesus from the dead is able to redeem humanity so that, although we still live in flesh, we have been redeemed and set free from the power of sin. Thus we can experience life in all its fullness, even now, as we live in our mortal bodies. The demands and urges of our human desires do not control us. Rather, we follow the gentle breeze of the Holy Spirit whose breath breathes new life into our bodies.

✳ ***Come to us, Holy Spirit, blow your gentle breeze on our mortal bodies and breathe upon us new life.***

Fleeting moments of trust and hope

At this point of the account of Job's struggle, we instinctively feel that he has arrived at some kind of climax. His words have a tone of solace and certainty about them which stands in stark contrast to the misery and agony of much of the book.

Over the years, Christian interpreters have long seen here a positive statement in the resurrection of the body, prefiguring the New Testament witness. Unfortunately, the Hebrew of verses 25b–26a is too obscure to draw any sure conclusions. Nevertheless, we can still learn from the struggles of such a man as Job who trusted in God and expressed the belief that, no matter what might happen to his body, God his Redeemer lives and will for ever live. For Job, that was the thing that really counted. His hope, aspirations and trust would have been in vain if his Redeemer did not, in fact, live.

We can all learn from Job. We know how terrible things can happen to people, similar to the kind of things that happened to Job, without any reasonable explanation. The question of the presence of evil in the world is a continuing issue for us all. The knowledge of and trust in a Redeemer who lives, whilst it may not answer all our intellectual questions about such evils, can nevertheless help us to anchor our faith and hope in something deeper than intellectual understanding.

✳ ***Even if I am drowning in the huge waves of the sea, and all help has disappeared, yet I have faith in my Redeemer who*** *lives, and so I will rest in peace.*   *Tongan hymn*

Thursday April 24   *1 Corinthians 15:35–49*

What about the resurrection body?

Gordon D Fee's commentary on this text suggests that Paul's key concern here is to refute those who deny the resurrection of the dead by urging its absolute necessity if there is to be any Christian faith at all. Everything is up for grabs if there is no resurrection!

Almost certainly lurking behind the denial of those whom Paul addresses is a view of the material order that found the resurrection of material bodies (or dead corpses) to be a doctrine that was utterly unacceptable. In response to such repugnance, Paul insists that the resurrection of Christ from the dead was not the resuscitation of his dead corpse, but the transformation of his physical body into a 'glorified body' adapted to his present heavenly existence. Paul emphasises both the continuity and the transformation of the body, using the analogy of the seed that is 'sown one way' and 'raised another', yet is still the same seed – or body. However, unlike the seed and plant, which have a limited life, the new body which Christ will transform and raise will be 'imperishable', giving Christians the hope of eternal life.

✳ **Lord Jesus, make us witnesses to your resurrection so that our faith is sustained and your glory increased.**

Friday April 25   *1 Corinthians 15:50–57*

Where, O death, is your sting?

When Paul talks of a 'mystery' in this text, he is not referring to something that is currently hidden. Instead, he is referring to what was once hidden but has now been revealed through Jesus Christ. The transformation of Jesus' crucified body into his resurrected and 'glorified' one in his heavenly existence is being revealed continuously whenever we proclaim Christ's death and resurrection.

The other very interesting concept in this passage is the notion of the victory claimed by the resurrection. Death's sting no longer has any bite! In other words, death does not have the last say! The change and the transformation that will happen to both the living and the dead when the perishable transforms into the imperishable and when mortality is clothed with immortality means that death has lost both its victory and its sting. This is great news! This does not negate the reality or the loss of death, but it certainly has a lot to say about death as our last enemy.

This text is often read in funeral services. When these words are read aloud, the sound of them is like the sound of the trumpet that is being blown for victory after war!

＊ *Thine be the glory, risen conquering Son, endless is the*
victory thou o'er death hast won.

Edmond Louis Budry, translated by R B Hoyle

Saturday April 26   *2 Corinthians 4:7–18*

The temporary and the eternal

Treasure in clay jars – or, in other translations, treasure in
earthen vessels – indicates the power of God that is indwelling
the apostles' ministry of preaching and teaching. The power of
God transcends the mortality and limitations of the earthen
vessels, in other words, their mortal bodies. So all the physical
persecutions and rejections these early Christians experienced in
their ministry could not crush the treasure which was sustained
by the power of God inside them. Such treasure is eternal.

Paul makes the same point when he speaks of the outer and the
inner nature. Although the outer nature may be diminishing, the inner
nature is being renewed each day by faith in the risen Lord Jesus. The
use of this language of temporal and eternal draws a comparison
between what these early Christians experienced in their physical
bodies and what they were hoping for in the eternal scheme of things.

Once again, the resurrection of Jesus Christ from the dead allows
the apostles to proclaim with confidence that the treasure God has
bequeathed to humanity in and through the gospel cannot be
destroyed, and that those who serve this gospel are also safe with God
in the eternal realm, whatever may happen to them in this earthly realm.

＊ *Thank you, Lord Jesus, for the treasures within us that*
belong to God. In identifying them, may we be strong to
proclaim your message of renewal to the whole world.

FOR REFLECTION – alone or with a group

● What are the issues that trouble Christians today as they seek
to proclaim the truth of Christ's resurrection?
● How can Christ's resurrection from the dead make a difference
to our worship, our work and our hopes?
● How have this week's readings affected your understanding of
pain and suffering in the world?

FOR ACTION

Write out some practical strategies that will help you to be a more
effective witness to the resurrection life that Jesus gives.

THE BODY
2. The sound body

Notes based on the New Revised Standard Version by
Alison Beever

Alison Beever works as an Anglican priest in the diocese of Exeter where she ministers to the city centre churches of Exeter and is Diocesan Director of Ordinands. As a wheelchair user herself she has a particular interest in how the church responds to people with disabilities. She also works with survivors of sexual abuse.

Running throughout our readings this week is the idea of wholeness, and how the body comes to be 'sound'. In many cases, as we think about the body, what is said of the individual can also be true of our corporate experience as the body of Christ. To bear this mutuality in mind enhances the thinking around each reading, and requires us to move out of the comfort zone of 'me' and 'my' to 'us' and 'our'. There is also another issue running through this week's theme, namely, the tension between the world's view of soundness, healing and wholeness and that of Christians.

Sunday April 27   *1 John 1:1 – 2:2**
'More than myself'

Some months ago Paul was involved in a serious car accident. His friends assumed that, once his injuries were mended, he would be back to the fun-loving, carefree companion they had always known. This didn't happen – Paul just 'wasn't himself'. The effects of the accident were more than physical: Paul's confidence was shaken, he had confronted pain and mortality, and was now living with fears he could barely name. His body was mended, but his 'being' was not yet sound. He had to find his way to understanding his inner self, confront his fears and darkness, and work towards a more complete healing, in which body, mind and spirit worked together to bring him back to 'himself'. Eventually he became more than the 'himself' his friends remembered, as he was changed by his experiences and the time of struggle and reflection.

To be of 'sound body' is one element in the Christian commitment to seeking wholeness. This transcends the physical, needing body, mind and spirit to work together towards the 'more than myself' wholeness of the gospel. In this journey, we experience light overcoming darkness in our lives and find others who are also journeying towards the at-one-ness with God in which true shalom is experienced: a peace which brings soundness not just of body but of being for the individual and the church.

✳ *Lord, help me to become 'more than myself' as I walk in your light.*

Monday April 28   *Psalm 4**

To be gracious in need

Mary recently lost her companion of many years. Strong emotions followed this death: sometimes there was a need to be alone, sometimes there was a desperate need for somebody to speak to. She found many of her friends wanted to rush in 'to make it better', or else avoided her and thus denied the reality of her pain. Such reactions are often found where there is pain, in Christian communities as well as in individual lives. Energy is spent seeking to 'make things better', or in denial.

The psalmist recognises different aspects of need when journeying to wholeness through human experience. First, 'you gave me room when I was in distress' (verse 1). The 'room' required is different for each individual: space in which to feel pain and hurt, to experience it before and within God, to take it into the depths of one's being and find it somehow changed, even redeemed. Then there is a 'graciousness' (verse 1) to one another, the need to respect one's own and others' need for space, and seeking the wisdom and 'graciousness' to know when, and how, to move into another's 'space', so that together we may move towards healing. The person moving towards soundness of body and being recognises the need for space and for graciousness for themselves as well as for others.

✳ *Lord, help me to understand my own and others' needs as we travel together and alone.*

Tuesday April 29   *Acts 4:5–12*

Further on and further in

When I first experienced prolonged severe pain, I wanted something to take the pain away as quickly as possible. I did not want to understand what made up my experience of pain. So, when a colleague asked if I was lonely, he received a rather ungracious reply! Only later was I able to reflect on what contributed to my experience of pain, and recognise that this may include fear and loneliness as well as other neurological, sociological and psychological elements. The body which experiences pain, just as much as the sound body, is affected by the relationship of all parts of our internal being, as well as the world around us and the communities of which we are part.

A 'sound body' is not solely the concern of doctors, self-help manuals, or other medical and social '-isms' and '-ologies'. It can only be sound when elements of our world and being are in a balanced relationship. For Christians this 'soundness' goes still further to the recognition that we only have a 'sound body' – as individuals or as the body of Christ – when we are rooted in Jesus, in whose name we are called to an ever deeper journey to wholeness.

✳ *Lord, in your name help me bring healing to the world and to my community.*

Wednesday April 30   *Matthew 5:27–30*
Inside-out salvation
When I was 4 years old, I remember being told by my mother not to touch a newly baked and decorated cake. She left the room, and I gazed longingly at the cake. As I looked, there was an almost seamless transition from looking to touching … and then to tasting! I don't remember being aware of what I was doing until Mother returned to the room! So Jesus' words of warning have a particular echo for me. Thinking can be all too closely related to acting. Fortunately, my mother's remedy was not as severe as that proposed in this passage.

The extreme remedy Jesus suggests in this passage is not to be taken literally, but is here to shock listeners and readers and compel us to take seriously the 'sin' which comes from the inside out. Jesus' words also shocked his contemporaries – and maybe us too – at a deeper level. Salvation does not rest on wholeness of body, he is saying. An outwardly sound body is not enough. Salvation comes from what is within, from the spirit and not just the letter of obedience to the one we follow.

✳ *Lord, help me to deal with the things I find inside myself, that I might be acceptable to you.*

Thursday May 1   *Matthew 6:22–23*
Give-away mirrors?
'What have you been up to?' Words I heard all too often as a child. The giveaway? 'Guilt's written all over your face.' From inside out, I endlessly gave my 'crime' away as a child. How often then my face reflected the state of my conscience. But our faces do not just reflect this.

'Come on in for a cup of tea and a chat.' That was nearly always Grace's opening to a conversation. Yet the invitation and the welcome didn't just come through her words, or the sight of a fire burning in the hearth behind her. It came from her eyes. In her eyes you could see reflected the depth of her life of prayer with God, and the genuineness of her invitation, which she saw as part of her calling to hospitality and listening.

From guilt to godliness, our eyes can be the mirrors of our souls. They can be lifeless, if we have allowed ourselves to die from the inside. Or they can be glowing with life and the love of life, as we see in the light in a child's face when surprised by something longed for, or in the light in the eyes of a teenager in the throes of new love, or in the old couple holding hands as they walk down the road, occasionally looking at each other.

If our eyes show so much of what is human, how much more will the light of God shine out from us, if that light is within our hearts and is rooted in our being. Do you bear witness to Christ, even in the light of your eyes?

✳ *Lord, may your light shine from my eyes and may my whole being witness to your work in my life.*

Friday May 2   Mark 5:21–34

The touching place

On one stay in hospital my bed was opposite Elsie. Elsie was disturbed and frightened, unable to express what was happening to her. Her husband came in for many hours each day. He spoke very little and 'did' none of those small tasks other visitors bustled around doing. He sat, held Elsie's hand, stroked her face, smoothed her hair. He calmed her and brought a peace deeper than any of her medications, deeper than anything he could express, but a peace which could be seen as Elsie slept quietly, her hand in his. It was as he held her, stroked her and touched her that one day she quietly and peacefully died, helped on her journey to life by the one she had spent so much of this life with.

Touch is the key to today's reading. It acts at many levels, releasing power, bringing soundness of body and healing, challenging a community's practice of exclusion, breaking boundaries and taboos, accepting the outcast.

For the body of Christ to be whole, it has to accept and act on the challenge of touch in Jesus' action. It has to learn from Elsie's husband as well as Jesus – that touch transcends much of our doing and speaking, and that we need patience and wisdom to work for good.

✳ *Teach us, Lord, the value of touch. Give us the wisdom to use this simple gift appropriately and without harm to others.*

Rebel for the cause

I have always been a rebel. As a child I fought my parents' hopes,
rejecting 'pretty dresses' for the blue jeans and T-shirt which gave
me freedom to climb trees and be the person I was inside. As an
adult, I rejected my society's proclaimed norm of marriage and
children, choosing the singleness and celibacy which still give me
the freedom to be the priest and person I believe God calls me to
be. As a wheelchair user, I rebel against the expectation of many
that I will be quiet, be 'done to' and be grateful for it. I choose
instead to live as fully as I can and challenge those expectations
which would limit my life and work. These choices are no longer
simply rebellious. Now they have in them a refusal to be
'conformed to this world' and a desire for transformation, as I
seek to live in the 'glorious liberty' of a child of God.

Many people do not have my freedom to 'rebel' and outwardly
challenge conformity to their world. However, we are all called to
challenge that conformity to this world which limits our life in God,
whether inwardly as we pray and seek the transformation of our
own lives, or through more direct action. If the body of Christ, of
which we are part, is to remain sound and life-giving, the challenge,
transformation and renewal spoken of in Romans must be ongoing.
If we are to have 'sound bodies' in Christ we have to look to our
transformation as a continual process, not a one-off event.

✳ *Lord, help me be transformed to your way, not conformed to*
my world.

FOR REFLECTION – alone or with a group

● What prevents you, or the 'body' of which you are part,
experiencing joy, experiencing soundness of body? What can
you do to change this and move towards life?

● What in your culture and community prevents you
experiencing this? How can you challenge it?

FOR ACTION

Identify one thing locally which, if changed, would bring greater
fullness of life to an individual or group. Take what steps you can
to make those changes.

THE BODY
3. The corporate body

Notes based on the Lutheran Bible (German) by
Antje Röckemann

Antje Röckemann is minister of the Evangelical Church of Westfalia in Germany and works as co-ordinator for women's affairs in a church district in the industrial area of the Ruhr-valley. She is also a breath-therapist and chairperson of the European Women's Synod, as well as co-editor of the feminist theological journal Schlangenbrut.

The readings set for this week, mostly from the epistles, deal with questions and problems arising from the attempt to create a (Christian) community. These questions remain unresolved today and are even more complex in our time, for now we have to deal with the task of creating a one-world community if we all wish to live in peace and justice.

How can the image of the body help us to build a community and to find our own part, as well as task, in it? Does this image still speak to us and is it helpful for the tasks facing us in the 21st century? We shall see!

Sunday May 4   *Acts 4:32–35**
One heart and one soul?
Acts presents itself as a report of the first Christian communities and the spread of the new Christian faith. It is not without its problems, however, as such an account. The first verse of today's text brings my reading to a stop: one heart and one soul (the Greek here is *psyche*); another translation might be life, but definitely *not* mind. Even of the first Christians I cannot believe that! And the story which follows (Acts 5:1–11) contradicts this statement, showing that not everybody followed the ideal set out here – they were *not* all of one heart and soul. The next verse in our passage again arouses my protest. The mention of the apostles – in Acts seen as an exclusive male ministry – introduces a hierarchical and exclusive element into the image of the (comm-) unity. Luke contradicts his own definition of an apostle as a witness of the resurrection (Acts 1:22), since such a definition unequivocally includes women (see Luke 24:1–10, 22–24).

Today's passage raises the question of who has been excluded in the account of the sharing of goods (verse 32) and graces (verse 33). Upon whose invisibility is the unity of the community here created? There is no mention in this passage of the conflicts which we know from the rest of Acts certainly were present in the early Christian communities – conflicts connected with diversity, with different origins and with different interests. At the same time, even if the picture here is not entirely historically accurate, it represents the desire to overcome a patriarchal-hierarchical society, the longing for solidarity and the same chances to be given to all. We may embrace that desire today.

✳ *Blessed be our struggle for justice and solidarity. And may those who take responsibility be blessed with understanding and kindness, and those who are overlooked be blessed with courage and power.*

Monday May 5   *Psalm 133**
Living together – in unity?

The psalm states – as many others do – its authorship by David. This is interesting, especially as David did not behave in a very brotherly fashion! As other brothers in the Hebrew scriptures also did not – for example, Cain and Abel, and Jacob and Esau.

Verse 1 gives me enough food for thought about the past and present history of my own country: the murder of Germans by Germans in the *Shoah* (Holocaust); the betrayal by members of the church of church people who were, according to the Nazi ideology, Jewish or 'half-Jews'; anti-Semitic and racist transgressions in recent years; and the infringements of the rights of Muslim neighbours who are generally suspected of being terrorists since 11 September 2001.

The comparisons in verses 2 and 3 widen out my thoughts. The anointing of the priest Aaron (see Exodus chapters 29 and 30), which enabled the people to fulfil their religious commitments, and the dew which is essential for the fertility of the land – these images describe the spiritual and material necessities of a people. They thus invoke the necessary conditions (or perhaps the consequences?) of living together in peace, unity and good-neighbourliness.

✳ *God of hope, help us to celebrate the times and occasions when our living and working together is successful, in our families, parishes, communities and countries. Help us also to notice and be aware of the concessions and steps towards us which others make.*

Unity at all costs?

The epistle to the Ephesians was written at the end of the first century. It is probably not by Paul himself, although the author uses the pseudonym 'Paul' to claim the authority of the well-known apostle. (This was a common practice in the ancient world.) The letter presents 'Paul' as a preacher to the Gentiles who are 'fellow heirs, members of the same body' (3:6) as the Jewish Christians. This is the background to chapter 4, which is written to remind the Ephesians that both Jews and non-Jews belong to the same community. The emphasis on this theme is clearly due to tensions which were existing within the community, and the strong note of unity stressed in verses 1–6 can be read as an attempt to influence the disputing members.

The distribution of God's grace is attributed to Christ (with a quotation from Psalm 68:18 – compare the context in this psalm), followed by a list of the ministries to which different members are called (verse 11), paralleled with a description of the saints and the community (verse 12). The community is seen as the body of Christ, with Christ as the head.

The relation between head and body is formulated in more detail in Ephesians 5:23, where the relation between man and woman in marriage is compared to the relation between Christ and the church. The historical impact of this text assigned a subordinate role to women both in private life (marriage) and in church life. This became obvious to me in a speech made about this text some years ago which focused uncritically on the notion of the 'perfect man' as the aim of Christian discipleship. Personally, I don't wish to change my sex in order to follow Christ, and I do not want to be a member of a community which is hierarchical by definition!

✳ *God of many names, strengthen our efforts to share our different gifts and our different backgrounds so that we may enrich our community.*

Equality with consideration of diversity

Here we have the central text which is usually quoted when the image of the church as the body is considered. Paul develops this image for a particular community – the very heterogeneous community of Corinth, a Greek port which attracted many different groups. The body (the community), he suggests, consists of several members, which all together form the body of Christ. Explicitly mentioned groups are Jews and Greeks, slaves and free people (verse 13). This verse is similar to Galatians 3:28, but without the mention of 'male and female'. Nevertheless no sexual divisions can be found in Paul's account of the church and the distribution of the charisms (gifts) which begins chapter 12. (Whilst Paul does not completely overcome the patriarchal divisions of the society of his time, he does on occasion glimpse and even require an equality of the sexes, such as in Galatians 3:28 and 1 Corinthians 11:11f.)

Paul's understanding of equality here differs from the Ephesians passage (which was written some decades later) and also from the description in Acts. His refusal of hierarchies is accompanied by a perception of real differences. The required honouring of the weakest members reminds us of the commandment in Exodus 20:12 and Deuteronomy 5:16. In the Jewish understanding, honour means not simply some kind of attitude, but the requirement to provide tangible economic support. Accordingly, Paul finishes his account of the need to honour the weaker members of the body, in verse 25, with the demand to care for one another.

In verse 26 Paul expresses the radical idea that the exclusion of particular individuals or groups is something that will affect the whole community. Translated into our times this means that racism, sexism and exploitation of whatever form are central issues for the whole church. We cannot be the body of Christ if we ignore the sufferings and oppressions of our brothers and sisters caught in structures of injustice.

✳ *Creator God, let me acknowledge and appreciate the parts others play in the building of the body of Christ, as well as acknowledging and appreciating my own part.*

Thursday May 8   *Romans 12:3–8*
Mutuality instead of hierarchy

While Paul is in Corinth he writes his letter to the community of Rome where he knows some members well (see the greeting list in chapter 16). Here he is addressing a Christian community living at the centre of power in the *Imperium Romanum*. I read his letter as an essay about God's justice which takes care of the excluded – women and the poor – under the political and economic conditions of the Roman Empire. In chapters 12 to 15, he is concerned to give concrete instruction to Christians finding themselves in such a situation.

With body (verse 1) and mind (verse 2) they are to carry out the justice of God in the community. Nobody should place herself or himself over anyone else (verse 3) – and also nobody should subordinate himself or herself to anyone else, because the body of Christ is formed by all together taking mutual care and responsibility. The individuals are members of the body and therefore dependent on each other. This results in the demand for mutual respect. Corresponding to this is Paul's insistence that the ministries are not arranged hierarchically, but that different charisms and gifts should be equally valued. Thus the Christian community is to overcome the hierarchical society of the Roman Empire and its asymmetrical relations.

✳ *Caring God, help us to realise the political and economic conditions in which we live. Show us how to take care of the body of Christ and our own bodies. And do not let us cease in our efforts for justice.*

Friday May 9   *1 John 4:7–16*

Love as the basis of action

1 John is included amongst the New Testament epistles; however it is really no letter but an essay. The term love (in Greek, *agape*) is used almost to excess: eighteen times in ten verses! Central to our text is the affirmation of the love of God to humans and the whole world. Hence it follows that the relationships of members of the community are to be determined by love.

What is meant here is not romantic love but an active doing, a very concrete commitment to one another including the preparedness to lay down one's very life (1 John 3:16).

The author understands love as an attitude which marks out the Christian. From this, everything else follows, including order in the community, even though 1 John does not deal with this in detail because of the writer's expectation of the end of time (1 John 2:18).

✳ *Loving God, let your love for us be the perspective with which we regard our life together – both in small and in great matters – and help us to change it for the better out of love for you and our neighbour.*

Saturday May 10   *1 Corinthians 11:17–29*

Celebrating the body of Christ appropriately

In Corinth there was a conflict when the community came together at the celebration of the eucharistic meal. Paul intervenes here with sharp words. The community meal presupposes the holiness of the congregation, and this includes social justice among themselves (verses 22 and 29).

The text gives us an idea of the way in which the early church celebrated the Lord's Supper. It was a solemn dinner with a liturgical framework, like Jewish celebration meals. Part of the meal was the benediction over bread and wine (verse 24), which was shaped by the memory of the martyr death of Jesus. The full and equal participation of women at the festive meal was natural, since no distinction based on gender existed.

The memory of this early practice stimulates us to examine the practice around our meals and tables, both at church and at home. It can also inspire us to overcome the hostility to the body and the dualisms in our traditions which have separated out body from spirit and claimed that the body and its needs, including eating and social justice, are less important than so-called 'spiritual' matters. Paul gives no grounds for such thought, for he insists that the body of Christ is celebrated in and with real flesh-and-blood bodies that eat and drink and have their own needs, and must behave with respect for material things.

✳ *Blessed be our eating and drinking that nourish our bodies, please our souls and strengthen the solidarity among us.*

FOR REFLECTION – alone or with a group

● How is the body of Christ, as an image for the church, linked with the flesh-and-blood bodies of women and men?

● There are many employed and volunteer co-workers in the church. Are all involved in decision-making in your church? What about the cleaning staff, for example?

● When was the last time you appreciated diversity and differences in a group? What is your normal reaction to conflicts and differences of view?

FOR ACTION

Write down some of your gifts/charisms – at least ten. Your list could include playing with children, being good with numbers, having a capacity to encourage others and so on. As a result of becoming aware of your own gifts, seek to be attentive to the gifts of other people you meet this week. Tell them of the gifts you recognise in them.

Do some gentle stretching exercises to become aware of your own body and how all its parts work together. What does this tell you about the working of the body of Christ?

THE BODY
4. The mystical body

Notes based on the New Jerusalem Bible by
Joseph G Donders

Joseph Donders, a Dutch priest of the Society of Missionaries of Africa, is Professor of Mission and Cross-cultural Studies at the Washington Theological Union. He was formerly head of the Department of Philosophy and Religious Studies and Chaplain to the Catholic Students at the State University of Nairobi, Kenya.

The word 'mystical' in the term 'mystical body' is confusing. It sounds like a contradiction, like 'a deafening silence'. How can a body, a material reality, be at the same time mystical? A famous theologian and liturgist was once seen pounding his hand on the table, telling his listeners, 'Just forget about that "mystical" in the term "the mystical body of Christ". We *are* his body!' Yet there are good reasons to continue to use the term 'mystical' for the body we form with him. We are incorporated in him, the *Risen* Lord.

Sunday May 11   *Ephesians 5:25–33*
Taken up in a process
Paul explains that Christ looks after the church and feeds it because he and we belong together: 'We are parts of his body.' He then uses that insight to explain the relation between a husband and his wife. A husband relates to his spouse as Christ to the church. He then draws a conclusion: 'Wives should be subject to their husbands as to the Lord in everything.' He says this in a cultural context where wives and children were considered men's property, and where men ruled their families.

Paul's comparison seems to overlook the fact that while Christ is the head of the body, both men and women are equally members of that body. Their common membership entails equality: an equality that was new in those days, and had to be worked out. Paul indicates how to work towards such equality: by loving each other, just as Christ loves all the members of his body.

This is not the only case where Paul indicates a Christian attitude that is given as a task to be realised. He taught that in Jesus Christ slaves and masters are equally members of Christ's body. Yet the abolishment of slavery took Christianity almost twenty centuries!

✵ All-loving God, renew in us your Spirit so that we may live our convictions more faithfully!

Monday May 12   *Colossians 2:9–12*

Embodied in Christ

Walter Brueggemann, a prominent Bible scholar, castigates Christians for often telling a reduced or shortened story when describing their faith and consequently themselves. This is something that happens when you tell a story again and again. Something overwhelming has happened to you. At first you can't even tell the story, but after some time you do it better and better, leaving out some details and overstressing some others. You now know how to tell the story! Brueggemann suggests that this happened to our Jesus story. Too often it is reduced to merely three items: firstly, fall; secondly, redemption; thirdly, life hereafter.

Those three insights are true, but they are not the full story! Our text speaks of something that is overlooked in that kind of summary. It tells us not only that in Christ divinity lives in all its fullness in bodily form, but also that 'we find in him our own fullness'. We are taken up in him! In our baptism we were buried with him, and in him we have been raised up, joining him with all those others in his life!

✵ Dear Lord Jesus, help me to grow more aware of your life-giving presence in me and in those I am living with. Let my life and my attitudes reflect yours!

Tuesday May 13   *1 Corinthians 15:50–57*

Belonging together

Nobody knows who wrote the following prayer but it is attributed to William Penn (1644–1718). It expresses the deeply human intuition that we belong together, and that death does not really separate us. 'We give back to you, Father, those whom you first gave us. You did not lose them in giving them to us, and so we do not lose them in their return to you.' We continue to belong to each other.

It is like a plane that takes off, disappearing in the sky over the horizon. It grows smaller and smaller and goes out of sight, and we say: 'There they go!' But elsewhere others are waiting and they say, 'Here they come!'

Paul reveals to us the roots of this insight. We are woven together in the risen Lord. It is at his return – when the final trumpet will sound -- that we all will change and realise in a new and definite way that we are together in him.

We have not yet arrived at that final point in time. Yet our belief in that togetherness in Christ should be our compass and guide in life.

✳ *Loving Father, who bound us all together in Jesus Christ, your Son, renew in us your Spirit, so that we may live the truth of our connectedness in life and in death.*

Wednesday May 14   *Matthew 25:31–45*

From Jesus' point of view

Children will sometimes stand on their heads to have a new look at the world. In his book on Francis of Assisi, G K Chesterton suggested that Francis did the same.

It is helpful to try to do something like that in our own lives, seeing things upside down and turning them around. We could do it with Matthew's description of the last judgement. Reading this text, we usually conclude that we should see Jesus in the poor. It is true, we should do that.

Turning the passage around, we can come to a different understanding. The story does not only tell how Jesus relates to others, the downtrodden. It also explains how Jesus relates to us. Anything done to us is considered by Jesus as done to him. Anything denied to us is considered by Jesus as denied to him. He identifies himself with us, with you and with me.

'Identifying' is maybe not even the correct expression. Rather, it is as we are together with all others that we are in him, and he in us! Let us not regard this merely in a kind of general sense, but grasp its truth in a deeply personal way. Let us recognise just how close Jesus is to us, and how close we should be to him.

✳ *Lord, let me abide with you!*

Thursday May 15   *Matthew 26:26–29*

This is my body

Jesus had taken charge of their Passover meal that night. He had asked his disciples to reserve a table. But once at the table he went further than just having the Paschal meal.

Though a meal – especially in the evening – always brings people together, it does not really make the partakers one. That night Jesus wanted to show that he was one with them, and they with him.

Matthew explains how, while they were eating, Jesus took bread, blessed it, broke it and gave it to his disciples, saying: 'This is my body'; and taking a cup, he blessed it and handed it to them, saying: 'This is my blood'. The reality signified at that moment brought them all together in him.

The time I realised this best was during the Second World War, when in occupied Holland some German soldiers came to our parish celebration on Christmas night. We, who were in those days real enemies, parishioners and soldiers, knelt next to each other to receive Christ's body and blood.

Though we were not at peace with each other in the world in which we lived, we were at peace with each other in his body and blood.

✴ *Lord Jesus, help us to remember how you brought us all together into your one body.*

Friday May 16   *1 Corinthians 6:12–20*

Temples of the Holy Spirit

In 1985 an American monk, Thomas Merton, left his monastery to do some business in Louisville, Kentucky. Walking through the shopping centre, at the corner of Fourth Street and Walnut Street, he was suddenly overwhelmed by the realisation that all the people around him were the temples Paul wrote about in his letter to the Corinthians, temples of the Holy Spirit.

All of a sudden he realised that he 'loved all those people. That they were mine and I theirs, that we could not be alien to one another even though we were total strangers.'

In his book *Conjectures of a Guilty Bystander*, he described his experience: 'Then it was as if I suddenly saw the secret beauty of their hearts … the person that each one is in God's eyes.' And he added, 'If only they could all see themselves as they really *are*. If only we could see each other that way all the time. There would be no more war, no more hatred, no more cruelty, no more greed … All the darkness and cruelty of life would vanish completely.'

Rather humorously, however, he foresaw one possible problem: if we really saw each other like this, we would have a tendency to fall on our knees in front of each other!

✴ *O God, break down the barriers that divide us!*

Discerning the body

The people around Jesus, women and men, had eaten with him before the last supper. At that last supper he deepened the meaning of their eating together, when he took the bread and the wine, offering them a 'sharing' in his body and blood.

Paul reminded the Corinthians of this tradition, which he himself had received from the Lord. He did this because he had heard stories about how the Corinthians celebrated the Lord's Last Supper. They did it in the context of a larger meal, where some had plenty to eat, while others were left hungry. He wrote to them, 'When you meet [like that] it is not the Lord's Supper that you eat.'

The consequences of being at table with Jesus are enormous. They are of a global and cosmic scale with all kinds of social, ecological and economic ramifications. They are so great that hardly anyone has been able to live those consequences to the full.

Yet being at table with him assures us of the final outcome, and it gives us the strength to do what we can to further God's Reign, the reign of justice and peace.

✳ *Lord, you lived and died among us to gather into one the scattered children of God. Help us to join your mission among us.*

FOR REFLECTION – alone or with a group

● Paul criticised the way the Corinthian community celebrated the reality of Christ's body. What would he say about its celebration in the community you belong to?

● What does it mean to you to belong to the 'mystical' body of Christ? Is the word a help or a hindrance?

● What are the consequences of being at table with Jesus for your local church community?

FOR ACTION

Join the Sunday worship in a parish or community that is not yours, to show that you belong together with them and they with you.

THOSE IN AUTHORITY
1. Under the authority of God

Notes based on the Revised Standard Version by
Maxwell Craig

Maxwell Craig, a minister of the Church of Scotland, has served parishes in Falkirk, Glasgow and Aberdeen. From its launch in September 1990 to December 1998 he was General Secretary of ACTS (Action of Churches Together in Scotland). In 1999 and 2000, he served as minister of St Andrew's Scots Church in Jerusalem. He is now chairman of the Scottish Churches Housing Agency and a director of the Scottish Refugee Council. He is a member of the Iona Community; and a chaplain to the Queen in Scotland.

Authority is a concept that is under close scrutiny today. Teachers, parents, policemen, magistrates, even ministers of religion have been placed in positions of authority, and find themselves targets for questioning: 'Who gave you authority over me?' Did they choose to follow careers that would give them authority over people? If they did, perhaps that fact alone should disqualify them. And yet we need people in authority. Our society would soon drift into chaos without them. But to whom are they accountable? That's the question this week's notes will try to answer.

Sunday May 18   *John 19:1–11*
Authority is accountable

Pilate was in a pickle. As governor of the Roman province of Palestine, he was arbiter of its justice. Roman justice could certainly be savage, but it did try to honour its laws. A man from an obscure part of his province had been brought before him; the charge was based on religious grounds which Pilate neither understood nor accepted as valid. Yet the last thing he wanted was a riot. His personal ambition would not allow him to have to send reports of trouble in what was proving to be a troublesome province. He could find no fault in Jesus, but to release him would risk a riot. 'I have the power to release you and to have you crucified,' he said to Jesus, who replied that his power had been given him 'from above'. Did God give Pilate his power over Jesus? Yes – and no. Yes, in the sense that God wills that his creation is ordered and that means levels of authority within each nation. No, in that God did not induce the Emperor to appoint a man who could be blinded by personal ambition. Pilate's authority was subordinate – he was accountable, but failed to recognise to whom he must give an account of his stewardship.

✳ *O Christ, the master carpenter, who at the last through wood and nails purchased our whole salvation, wield well your tools in the workshop of your world, so that we who come rough-hewn to your bench may here be fashioned to a truer beauty of your hand. We ask it for your own name's sake.*
A Celtic prayer

Monday May 19   *Psalm 96:1–13*
Fear of the Lord
Are we afraid of God? Should we be? When I went to work in a parish in Aberdeen, I discovered that the motto of the University, which was near neighbour to my parish, was 'The fear of the Lord is the beginning of wisdom' (Psalm 111:10). Psalm 96 is a song of praise, which claims that 'our' God, the God of his chosen people, is indeed Lord of all peoples and of all the earth. Praise and adoration run through every line of its verses – until the fearsome promise of verse 13: 'For he comes to judge the earth'. Is this what causes a whisper of fear to swell into a cadenza in our ears? Whatever subordinate authorities we may fall heir to, in our families, in our local communities or even on a wider scale, we shall answer for our exercise of them to the God who made us. Fear is not a noble motive, but the fear of God is of a different order. It reminds us that we are accountable not just to electors, who can be cajoled by spin, but to the One who knows us through and through – and will still use his righteousness and his truth when he judges us.

✳ *Lord, you know us, you know our frailty. We confess that we have not used the gifts you have lavished on us for the benefit of those whose lives touch ours. You've given us neighbours; we've run a mile from loving them. You've given us Jesus, your beloved Son, and we've run a mile from following him. Forgive us, we pray; and when we stand before your judgement seat, we pray that Jesus will stand beside us. We ask it in his name.*

Tuesday May 20   *Joshua 1:1–9*
Subordinate leadership
The book of Joshua tells the story of Israel's entry into the Promised Land. But this book poses a problem. It appears to

warrant and to bless the brutal conquering and destruction which fill its pages. It seems a world away from the God and Father of our Lord Jesus Christ, with his message of love and of forgiveness. More precisely, it suggests to modern Israelis that the whole land of what was Palestine is theirs by right, to the exclusion of its indigenous Palestinian population. The truth is that this book was written centuries after the events it describes; insofar as it is history, it is a history written by the victors, with an eye to what succeeding generations might make of their inheritance. But these opening verses do contain genuine religious truth. Now that Moses was dead, Israel needed a leader – and Joshua was to be that leader. These verses make it clear that Joshua's leadership was conditional: he was to remain constant to the law of God. He was accountable not only to the people he was leading, but also to God, who had given him his orders and had promised to be with him.

✸ *Holy Spirit of God, we pray that you will guide our living and enliven our serving; give us thoughts higher than our own thoughts, prayers better than our own prayers, that we may spend and be spent in his service, whom to serve is perfect freedom.*

Wednesday May 21   *Ezekiel 34:1–10*
Leadership failure
Can there be any more damning rebuke than the one Ezekiel delivers to 'the shepherds of Israel'? In ten trenchant verses he strips them of all credibility as leaders of their people. They have been charged with the responsibility of 'feeding' the people. They have chosen instead to feed themselves. One of the most important tasks for any leader is to care for those least able to care for themselves – the weak, the sick, the crippled: these the shepherds have failed in their hurry to feather their own nests. The passage carries the very clear message that authority, however absolute it may appear, is always subordinate to the authority of God. The priests of Israel were becoming a caste apart. This was the source of Ezekiel's anger. It's an anger we see in many nations today, where leaders are quick to ensure their own wealth, whether that can be afforded by their people or not. When a footballer or a pop-idol can command absurdly high wages, the temptations for those who hold the levers of power become great. Ezekiel's words are plain: if you fall for that temptation, God is against you.

✳ *O God our Father, we are tempted to seek better conditions for ourselves, forgetting the needs of those who are homeless, or in poverty; we pray that your blessing will embrace them and touch their lives. And we pray for all those set in authority over us, Members of Parliament, Government ministers, company directors, that they may bear the needs of the poorest in their hearts and in their deciding.*

Thursday May 22   *Ezekiel 34:20–31*

No one shall make them afraid

God's judgement makes us afraid. Does it? If you believe that God is our judge, as Ezekiel certainly did, you have good reason *not* to be afraid. Ezekiel's message is that God cares for us. Yes, he will judge us when we make life difficult for other people. But he has made us a promise which can lift us out of the constant competitiveness of modern life. There is a common conviction that we have to do the other person down, if we are to get on. That is not God's way. He sees all his people as a flock of sheep. He will provide a bountiful earth to meet our needs; he will appoint a caring shepherd to sort out our differences; and he will be our judge. But with God's everlasting arms always around us, we shall have nothing to fear. That's God's promise. He doesn't promise an easy ride; nor does he promise us seventy years of healthy life. But his covenant will not fail us, either in this life or in the life to come. That's why nothing need make us afraid.

✳ *O God our Father, we know the things we're afraid of, the thousand and one dangers of a hurrying society. Lift us above our fears, that we may sense the mercy of your enfolding presence and the majesty of your holiness. You have made your purpose clear in Jesus, your Son; help us to follow his way, speak his truth and live his life. For his sake we ask it.*

Friday May 23   *Psalm 97*

The Lord is king

Royalty gets a bad press in these democratic days. Is kingship something we want to say about the God who made us? Is a royal palace the place where Jesus can feel at home, Jesus who was born in a stable and had nowhere to lay his head? The psalmist ascribes kingship to God because it was the highest metaphor he could find in the armoury of his language. Our everyday language can't cope with the majesty of the living God. That's why we have to use poetry and metaphor. The king, in the psalmist's day, was the one who had supreme authority over all the minor authorities who plagued the lives of ordinary people. Royalty in our society may not have such supreme authority, but the metaphor of God as king may still hold.

The theme that runs through this psalm is the note of rejoicing. We're glad that God is our ultimate authority, holding sway over all the bounds of earth and sea and sky. We're glad because, at last, there is One with whom the buck stops. So many of our leaders claim, whatever complaint we may make, that it is not their fault. God does not dodge our complaints about our hurts; he loves us and will judge us – both as Father and as King.

✳ *Lord Jesus, you've taught us to pray 'Our Father', yet we know that God is Lord of all the earth. You've taught us to think of you as our friend – and yet we call you Lord. Give us grace to accept what you've taught us; and to be glad that there is one who is truly King of all kings. We ask it in your name.*

Saturday May 24   *2 Corinthians 13:1–13*
The purpose of delegated authority
Paul ends this 'severe' letter, as it has been called, with a reference to the source of his authority. That source is not his own commitment to the faith, it is not his personal charisma, nor his undoubted eloquence. His authority springs from the Lord himself, and is given for a clear purpose – to be positive in building up the body of Christ. He has seen and been informed of plenty in the Corinthian church which requires to be torn down; but all of that is left to the judgement of God, who is the supreme authority. Paul is given authority to teach the truth of the gospel, with all its edifying grace. My experience of the ecumenical movement has taught me that so many of our fractured churches concentrate on the alleged follies of brother and sister Christians, rather than on the things which build the church, such as the forgiving spirit which refuses to judge, the loving grace which accepts the person who is different. Paul recognises that his authority has clearly defined limits; it is delegated from the authority of the Lord himself.

✳ *Lord, help us to see our place within the continuing purpose of your Kingdom, so that when we're given authority, we may not claim that authority as absolute. You alone are God, and your authority remains supreme. So we come into your presence in humility, seeking your forgiveness for the many times we've claimed too much for ourselves, in Jesus' name.*

FOR REFLECTION – alone or with a group

● Is it helpful to talk about fearing God, when fear is such a bad master?

● If God is the supreme authority, how does that affect our day-to-day living?

● Do those who have been given authority in our society recognise that their authority is subordinate?

FOR ACTION

Do your best to ensure that, in the areas of your life where you have been given authority over other people, you exercise it acknowledging that you are accountable to God as the source of all delegated authority.

THOSE IN AUTHORITY
2. Good rulers and bad rulers

Notes based on the New Revised Standard Bible by
Juanita D Paniamogan

Juanita (Neneng) D Paniamogan is a church and development community worker connected with the United Church of Christ in the Philippines (UCCP) and working in Mindanao. She has been a visiting tutor with the Development Studies Course at the University of Birmingham and the United College of the Ascension (1997–2000). She is active in social issues, particularly concerned with women, ecology, justice and peace and development work.

Rulers have been called by various names by different people based on their experiences of being ruled. In our country, we have rulers whom we call '*tuta*' which is a Tagalog word meaning 'puppy'. These rulers do not think of the people's aspirations but follow instead the dictates of foreign rulers and their own selfish interests. Sadly, we have few rulers who uphold the welfare of the common people. But rulers are not only the elected or appointed ones, there are also many 'rulers' in our homes, in our churches and in the various organisations we are involved in. We are all rulers at some time, somehow, even if we do not always recognise it. We all have the potential to be good or bad rulers. The call to be a just ruler is a call to all of us.

Sunday May 25   *Psalm 72:1–20*
Like rain on the fields

This is a very beautiful prayer for rulers, especially in these times when many of them seem to do the reverse of what is being prayed for here. Indeed, our rulers today need just this kind of prayer from all of us.

The good ruler makes decisions in favour of the poor and the deprived. The just ruler sees to it that every one of his or her people is given equal opportunities to grow and bloom. They help see to it that the fields produce sufficient for all the people and no one goes hungry. We should pray especially for the rulers in our country, as well as in other countries, who may well forget who brought them to power and to whom they are accountable. In many places today, rulers have become victims of greed and enrich themselves at the expense of others, securing themselves through loans and guns and enjoying themselves with every luxury and comfort. They have forgotten the ordinary folk on the farms, in the factories, in the market-places, on the seas, in all the different workplaces where the wealth of the land is made.

But we are all 'rulers' too, in the various contexts where we may exercise influence. How do we fare as 'rulers'? Do our thoughts and actions consider what is good for the poor, deprived and struggling? Have we become like rain on the fields for others?

✳ *O God, you are our ruler and guide. Govern our motivations and aspirations with your justice and righteousness so that our lives may reflect your being. Make us good and just 'rulers' wherever we may be.*

Monday May 26   Micah 3:1 – 4:4

Neither shall they learn war any more

Good rulers work for peace! Human history shows that war has destroyed millions of people and made many lands desolate. We have only to think of Nagasaki and Hiroshima in Japan, Vietnam, Iraq, Kuwait and Afghanistan – and there are many more. These wars manifest how rulers manage conflicts. They would rather resolve disagreements by arms than through dialogue and negotiation. Our own country, the Philippines, has been and is still experiencing war. Our rulers have opted to use weapons of death rather than digging down deep into the real cause of conflicts. While our people clamour for rice instead of bullets, our rulers have wasted meagre resources to kill the people in their attempts to achieve peace. It is very sad to see these resources used to kill rather than build people's lives.

While rulers at the top act like this, how about us in our homes and workplaces? Are we using peaceful means to resolve conflicts? What kind of parents, spouses and workers are we? Would we rather use dialogue and face-to-face negotiations or character assassination, backbiting, and harassment to solve our conflicts, enrich our relationships and create a climate of respect, equality and justice?

✳ *God of peace, forgive us for attempting to resolve conflicts through violence. Give us patience and creativity so that we can face 'unpeace' with your wisdom, love and understanding. Make our rulers realise the value of people over things and their own self-centred interests. Give us your peace – both inside us and around us.*

From darkness to light

People in all societies long for a leader who can make changes in their lives. Certainly in our country, election time is always an exciting time not only because many good and bad things happen but because this is the time when people hope that things can be different. They have a hope that their basic needs can be met and opportunities for growth and development can be provided by the rulers. But rulers come and go, enriching themselves whilst the poor are made poorer. Verses 6 and 7 in today's passage enumerate the qualities of a true leader – such a leader will be a messiah or saviour who will deliver the people from want, oppression and exploitation. This, too, had been the dream long held by the Israelites. The words in this text have, of course, been long linked with Jesus the Christ, the Messiah who fully lived out the qualities of a good leader.

Those of us who can vote must exercise our right to do so. We thus play our part in choosing from amongst the candidates the best leader who can make possible the changes which ordinary people aspire to. And each of us is once again reminded to look at ourselves and reflect on how we use the power we have to make a way for those who are lost and to provide light for those in darkness.

✴ *Powerful God, you have shared your power with us through your Holy Spirit. Help us to enable others to regain their power instead of keeping all the power to ourselves.*

What it means to be ruled

I am personally uncomfortable with the word 'ruler' because I usually associate it with oppression, exploitation and abuse of power. This may be due to our experience in the Philippines as a country which has been ruled in the past by the Spaniards, Americans and Japanese and continues in the present to be so ruled, albeit now with a different face. Moreover, as a woman living in a patriarchal society where men rule over women and the affairs of the state, I remain uncomfortable with the word.

In today's passage Samuel clearly describes to the people the implications of having a king. This picture continues to be true in many ways today. Our own ex-president and his family were at one time the richest persons in Asia, if not in the whole world. This happened when more than seventy per cent of our people wallowed in dire need and poverty. Such a picture of abject poverty sitting alongside extravagant wealth is true in many parts of the world where the rulers and their friends hold a greater share of the wealth of their country, living luxurious lives and using their power to amass more and more to themselves.

Those of us who are given the right to choose our leaders can learn from these verses. We can choose those leaders who will go beyond their selfish interests to consider the plight of the majority of the people and who will work to make life better for all. Each of us, too, has a kind of power which we can use either to enrich ourselves or to empower others. We each must choose which of these ways we will go.

* *O God, you listened to the demand of the people to have a king and you allowed them to bear the burden of their choice. Help us today to choose leaders who can make a difference to the poor. Enable us to use our own power to unleash power in others so that they do not allow their rulers to exploit them.*

Thursday May 29   *Revelation 13:1–10*

The patience and faith of believers

The book of Revelation is one of the most difficult books in the Bible, and this passage illustrates the difficulties. Bible scholars suggest that the seven heads of the beast symbolise the Roman emperors. In particular, the head which has received the mortal wound is understood to refer to Nero, who persecuted many Christians. Yet, after the description of the suffering and torments of the saints, the last verse challenges and encourages believers to persevere and not to lose hope.

The picture described is one of violence. It can be compared with our world today where many endure violent situations – at home, in the workplace and in their community and nation. A wife is battered by a husband who thinks that because he is the man of the house, he can have whatever he wants. A daughter is sexually abused by her father because he is the head of the household and he can do anything he likes with his children. A man is bullied by his employer but afraid to tell the authorities in case he loses his job. A woman worker is forced to choose between getting laid by her boss or being laid off from work. Where is God in these situations?

Our text paints a grim picture of the aggression of the powerful and the hopeless life of the 'ruled'. But verse 10b encourages us to press on, to persevere and to continue hoping and believing that even in such terrible situations God is still at hand.

* *Caring God, help us to know your presence in times of helplessness. Give us hope and wisdom so that we can be courageous and stand firm.*

This calls for wisdom
The number 666 is one of the most celebrated and controversial symbols in Revelation. I am amused that some people identify this image with the head of one of the major church denominations today! Some of them are very convinced of this truth, as if they were there when John wrote his strange book. Yet as we said earlier, it seems much more likely that the wounded beast refers to Nero, perhaps the most evil of the rulers of the Roman Empire who demanded loyalty and worship from all subjects on pain of death.

The text describes a picture in which the followers of the beast are utterly subservient, or made so by those in power. This rings true with situations today in which rulers employ all kinds of tactics to deceive the people, making promises and offering miracles, exerting pressures and sanctions, or threatening death to those who attempt to 'subvert' the will of the powers-that-be. For example, I am appalled by the effects of globalisation among the farmers, the fisherfolk and the ordinary people of the third world. There have been beautiful promises made by our leaders (who became spokespersons of international trade) in order to persuade the people to 'go global'. But, in reality, international trade has only benefited those with the opportunities and means to avail themselves of its technology and so, once again, the rich have been enriched and the poor disempowered. Whether we are the powers-that-be or the subjects, we all need God's wisdom to discern God's will and purpose in our lives and the events in our world.

✳ *God of wisdom, enable us to see beyond present realities, especially when things seem to be rosy for us. Encourage us to seek what is true, just and right for all people, rather than what is pleasant for ourselves and our group. Help us to use our power to enable others to see their worth and potential.*

A call for endurance
Ultimately, justice will prevail. In many cases, the poor, needy and powerless are deprived of their fair share of wealth and opportunities. The rulers take all the resources for themselves, use their position to enrich themselves, their families and friends, and to ensure their position is maintained in high places. Yet the seeds of destruction are often present within such exploitation and justice

finally wins out. Our country has seen two of its rulers plummet to their downfall after amassing so much wealth while watching the majority of the people become poorer. Those who protested against the injustice experienced torture and death at the hands of the powerful, yet were ultimately proved right. These 'martyrs' stood firm in their desire and efforts to make change, to transform the status quo, to reverse the relationships and social dynamics.

The picture being described in these verses gives us hope that, ultimately, those who abuse their power, including those who allowed themselves to be used, will receive their just punishment. Those who persevered and remained faithful to God, who stood firm against all forms of lies and unrighteousness, will receive their rewards.

This passage challenges us to pursue justice, peace and abundant life for all. It calls us to use whatever power we have, wherever we are, to empower those who are marginalised and deprived. It invites us to encourage each other to persevere even in the midst of persecution and social pressure, so that all people and the whole creation can live with meaning and joy.

✴ *Enable us, God of love, to persevere in working towards the realisation of your will for our lives and for the whole world. Strengthen us when we are weary, pull us up when we fall along the way, give us a push when we hesitate, inspire us with hope and determination to go on. For we know that we are not alone, and that you are always with us.*

FOR REFLECTION AND ACTION – alone or with a group

● Identify people you consider good and bad rulers in your history and in your present context. What made them good or bad?

● What power do you have in what contexts? How you are using that power in relation to the people around you?

● Share experiences of powerlessness with one another. How does it feel to be powerless? What could have been done to empower you?

● Find ways to encourage and enable your present leaders and rulers to do their job well. Write to them, or find other means of representation to communicate to them the things you think they need to be doing for the good of all and the things they need to stop doing.

THOSE IN AUTHORITY
3. Duties of those in authority and of those under authority

Notes based on the New Revised Standard Version by
Pauline Webb

Pauline Webb has held office as Vice-Moderator of the World Council of Churches' Central Committee and as Vice-President of the Methodist Conference. In her retirement she still chairs several committees – as President of Feed the Minds, of the Society for the Ministry of Women in the Church and also of the World Conference on Religion and Peace. She is herself a Methodist local preacher and a religious broadcaster.

The word 'authority' comes from a Latin word meaning 'to cause to grow' or 'to originate'. To be entrusted with authority means being given power over others in such a way as to require obedience and so to enable them to grow in responsibility and self-control. It could be argued that the aim of all true authority is to make its exercise unnecessary. The authority of a parent is fully discharged when a child reaches maturity. The authority of a state has no need to be enforced so long as its citizens behave in a socially responsible and orderly manner. The ultimate authority is the sovereignty of God, the originator of all life, whose power, as Jesus demonstrated, is exercised through a love that dares to liberate rather than dominate the creation.

Sunday June 1   *Mark 10:32–45*
Humble service

The person to whom the highest authority is entrusted in Britain is known by the title 'Prime Minister' – that is, the 'first servant', not only of the crown but of the people too.

This concept of service as the proper exercise of authority stems from the words of Jesus, repeated in several places in the gospels, that he himself came 'not to be served but to serve'. Unlike the political rulers of his time, his followers are told to use whatever power they have over others not to boss but to serve them. It is significant that Mark places this important saying in the context of Jesus' conversation with the apostles as they follow him on the way to Jerusalem. Despite the fact that Jesus has made it clear that his way of obedience is a way that leads to self-sacrifice, James and John still express ambitious hopes that one day they will be raised to important rank in the courts of heaven. There is nothing wrong in being ambitious to hold office, whether it be in the church, in the realm of politics or in the world of work, so long as we see that office as giving us a greater opportunity for serving others rather than expecting them to serve us.

✳ *Servant Lord, show me how to use more effectively at home, at work or in the community whatever power I have to serve the needs of others.*

Monday June 2   *Matthew 22:15–22*
Hall-marked currency
In the debate that raged for many years about the introduction of the euro as a common currency for the whole of Europe, one of the questions frequently being asked in Britain was about whose image should appear on the coins. For British people, only the sovereign's head could give the stamp of authority to the currency. If that were to be removed it would be seen as a challenge to the nation's sovereignty. Similarly, Roman emperors emphasised their authority over their subject peoples by impressing their image firmly on the currency. The word used of the image in Greek is *ikon*. It is the same word used later in the New Testament when human beings are described as bearing on their own lives the image of God (Colossians 3:10). However much power the secular authorities might claim over the material aspects of our lives, regulating how much money we must contribute to the common purse, no emperor can exercise authority over our true selves. We bear on our souls the hall-mark of the divine Sovereign, the only authority to whom we should pay total tribute.

✳ *Eternal God, you have impressed your image upon our lives. Help us to know our true value, and whilst paying our dues in the kingdoms of this world, help us to value above all the treasures of your Kingdom.*

Tuesday June 3   *1 Peter 2:13–17*
Discerning obedience
These words were originally written to a minority community of Christians living in Asia Minor who were highly suspected by the public authorities of being a subversive group. There was even

the threat of persecution in the air. The writer reminds Christians that they are not called primarily to be trouble-makers but to live as good citizens, not under compulsion, but by free choice. Their respect for all people as well as their love for their Christian community will make clearer to others what the message of the gospel really is. Their obedience to God carries with it allegiance to such laws of the land as promote goodness and restrain evil.

Such willing obedience should not be unquestioning. A couple of years ago a sister in the Benedictine Order was at first forbidden by the Vatican from participating in an international conference discussing the ordination of women. The Superior of her Order courageously responded that in the tradition of the Benedictines, the vow of obedience required also the ability to discern the rightness and appropriateness of the order given. The sister was allowed to attend.

✳ *Liberating God, teach us willingly to take upon ourselves the yoke of obedience as good citizens, but grant us also the gift of discernment to distinguish between just and unjust requirements and show us how to seek their amendment.*

Wednesday June 4   *Romans 13:1–10*

Strong government

Even secular authorities have a power delegated to them by God, in order to ensure that there is an ordered environment, protected from the effects of unbridled human selfishness. St Paul, living under the Roman Empire, argues that therefore such civic authorities must be obeyed, so that the community might live in peace. Strong government has divine sanction because the alternative to it is anarchy. William Tyndale, in his treatise on *The Obedience of a Christian Man*, wrote: 'It is better to have a tyrant for a king than a shadow – for a tyrant, though he do wrong unto the good yet he punisheth the evil and maketh all men obey. A king who is soft as silk shall be more grievous to the realm than a mighty tyrant.'

The alternative to tyranny is not weak but strong government. Christian resistance to civic authorities can be justified only where more humane, more just, more responsible government can be put in their place.

✳ *Pray for all who hold authority under God in the State and in the local community. Pray particularly for those people who*

*live under oppressive regimes that they may be given
wisdom and courage in resisting and replacing them.*

Thursday June 5   *Ephesians 6:10–20*

Strong resistance

Earlier in this letter the writer has advised Christians to be
obedient to those set in authority over them, in the home or the
workplace. Now he goes on to affirm that he is convinced that
whoever might appear to be governing our lives, in the form of
earthly rulers, the real battle is not with them but with spiritual
forces of evil which seem to have usurped God's power and
taken over control of the world. Therefore we must resist them
with more than political or military weapons. We have to take on
that whole armour of God that was described by the prophet
Isaiah (Isaiah 59:17) as he depicted God's determination to
establish justice in the world. It is the whole armour, the 'panoply',
designed both for defence and for attack. It will shield us against
the tempting tricks used by evil powers and also equip us to take
initiatives in proclaiming God's word and will for the world. Note
the emphasis on verse 10 and in verses 13 and 14 on the need to
be strong – not relying on our own strength but on the strength
which comes from God and enables us to resist even powerful
opponents.

✳ *Righteous God, help me to keep my spiritual armour in good
repair, so that I may stand firm in the integrity of faith,
upholding the truth of the gospel and not succumbing to the
lure of secular values. For the sake of your kingdom.*

Friday June 6   *1 Peter 5:1–11*

Gracious oversight

Leadership always carries great responsibility. Even chairing a
committee can make great demands on one's integrity. You are
entrusted with a position of privilege which you can use either to
further your own ends or to enable others to grow in responsible
participation. I remember once being advised when in the chair to
keep alert to all that was going on around the table as well as to
the agenda actually tabled on it! In any group of people there can
be those vying for power whilst others may be so timid that they
can too easily be crushed. Peter's advice to leaders in church
affairs is that they themselves must practise the kind of strong
humility which combines courageous faith with generous

compassion. Moreover they must help people to keep a right sense of proportion, comparing their own priorities with the problems faced by members of God's family in other parts of the world. Above all they must learn never to rely on their own strength but on the grace and mercy of the God who has called them into leadership.

✳ *Pray for all committee meetings associated with your own church, that they may become occasions of spiritual blessing and that all who attend them may grow in mutual trust and understanding and in shared commitment to the cause of Christ.*

Saturday June 7   *John 13:1–17*

Accepting service

Imagine entertaining a great celebrity to dinner in your home. You would go to great lengths to prepare the meal in the kitchen, and serve it in an orderly dining room.

Then suppose the guest at the end of the meal insists on donning an apron and doing the washing-up! Your first reaction would be one of reluctance to accept such menial service from one who deserved great honour. It is always hard to accept service from others, especially from those of whom we feel unworthy. Jesus' gracious humility humbled the apostles and made them more aware of their own unworthiness.

In his remarkable libretto to the opera entitled *The Last Supper*, composed by Harrison Birtwistle, the poet Robin Blaser sets the feet-washing story in a modern context. He imagines the dialogue that might have taken place, as Jesus described the kind of dust each disciple carried on his feet, needing to be cleansed. He reminds the disciples of 'the poor, still with us, unremembered dust', 'the State confused with God – the sacrifice of millions on the altar of the Future', 'the dust of unmournable wars and killing fields'.

Each of us has walked through dust of one kind or another. Let us in humility receive the cleansing that Christ stoops to bring us.

✳ *Be my servant, Jesus, and make me clean and humble enough to serve others.*

FOR REFLECTION – alone or with a group

● A popular hymn speaks of loyalty as 'love that asks no question'. Have children any right to question parents, or citizens any right to question civil authorities?

● Is civil disobedience ever justified? What conditions would you lay down for it?

● What is the difference between being humbled and being humiliated? What do we learn from Jesus' example about the nature of true humility?

FOR ACTION

Undertake one action supporting someone who lives under an oppressive regime – for example, writing to a political prisoner, welcoming an asylum-seeker or joining in a protest demonstration. Consult Amnesty International for advice.

BIBLE EXPLORATION
SEARCHING STORIES

● Explore stories and story-telling in Luke's gospel

● Look at the stories of our faith

● Connect our own stories with God's stories

● Studies of five Bible stories: Emmaus; The good Samaritan; The woman bent double; The two sons; The widow and the judge; Zacchaeus.

● Workbook for 7–11-year-olds; Study Guide for leaders, house groups and Bible study groups.

Workbook UK price £3.75
Study Guide UK price £6.50
(prices include postage and packing)

 CHRISTIAN *education*

Order through your IBRA representative, or from the appropriate address on page 303.

THE PENTECOST POST: BIBLICAL LETTERS
1. Mind the gap

Notes based on the New Revised Standard Version by

Edmund Banyard

Edmund Banyard is a minister and a former Moderator of the General Assembly of the United Reformed Church. He has written both plays and devotional material and for many years edited All Year Round *for Churches Together in Britain and Ireland.*

We would not be using these notes if we were not conscious of the value of a daily Bible reading, but it is still possible to misunderstand and draw wrong conclusions from what we read. The passages selected for this week remind us that things are not always what they seem at first sight and that short passages need to be understood in their context and ultimately in the light of the central gospel message. Should the people of God try to keep themselves apart from the world? What does the passage from Esther really say about the position of women? Was the building of the first Temple a glorious unqualified work for God? These are just some of the questions we shall be facing in the next few days as we seek to 'mind the gap'.

Sunday June 8   *Jeremiah 29:1–9*

Seek the welfare of the people you live amongst!

In Psalm 137 we hear the anguish of an exiled people: 'By the rivers of Babylon … we wept when we remembered Zion' and the cry 'How could we sing the Lord's song in a foreign land?' Understandably there were those who fanned the flames of bitterness, hatred and religious fanaticism and tried to stir up rebellion. It is against this background that Jeremiah writes telling the exiles to accept the situation in which they find themselves and to become integrated into the community.

Jeremiah is not suggesting that they abandon their faith. On the contrary he urges them to pray to the Lord, not only for themselves, but for the welfare of the city in which they live, telling them that from now on their lives are inextricably bound up with the lives of all the people around them.

Welcome or not, this is surely a message for the people of God to take to heart in every age. If God is truly the God of all, then there is no place where the Almighty is not present and no people for whom the Almighty does not care. Thus, wherever we find ourselves and however much we might wish we were somewhere else, without losing our Christian identity we need to look for ways in which we can serve the Lord within the community. 'Let your light shine before others, so that they may see your good works and give glory to your Father in heaven' (Matthew 5:16).

✱ *Lord, bless me, I pray, and help me to share your blessing with those I shall meet this day.*

Monday June 9   *2 Chronicles 30:1–12*

It's not enough to have good intentions

In an earlier period than Jeremiah, Hezekiah was a reforming king who had the intention of purifying and restoring the worship of God in the Temple that it might once again become the religious focal point for the peoples of Israel and Judah.

There was however a disappointing response from the people at large, the reason probably being that this centralisation and reform of ritual worship would inevitably mean the sweeping away of many local shrines. No doubt the nature of the worship offered at these places varied immensely and was often of a dubious nature, but it was to these local shrines that people related and they didn't want to lose them.

Hezekiah had the best of intentions, but that in itself is not enough. Even when we believe things are badly wrong and feel that we should urgently set about putting them right, we need to show understanding and listen to the aspirations and fears of others. It could even be possible that our ideas and plans, however brilliant and however well intentioned, are not the best way of serving the kingdom of God in this particular place at this particular point in time.

✱ *Lord, give me the patience and the understanding to listen for what you may be saying to me, particularly through other people when, in trying to serve you, I come up against frustration and disappointments.*

Tuesday June 10   *2 Chronicles 2:1–17*

What makes a 'holy place'?

Today we go even further back in time to the reign of Solomon and the building of the first Temple. There was a tremendous sense of achievement when it was completed. But it had also meant heavy expenditure and forced labour, and may well have left a legacy of discontent and sown the seeds from which came the later break-up of the kingdom.

Today the Temple site is one of the sources of tension in the Middle East. It is occupied by a great Mosque while Jewish worshippers are reduced to gathering at the 'Wailing Wall'. We may not speak lightly of other people's holy places and what they mean to them, but we can properly ask what our own attitude to 'holy places' should be.

For the most part we worship in buildings inherited from earlier generations so it is not a question of whether we should have a cathedral or a community hall. We should however remember the words in verse 6: 'But who is able to build [God] a house, since heaven, even highest heaven cannot contain him?' This is repeated in the dedication of the Temple (6:18). God does not need a house made with hands. Would you agree that the building we meet in for worship is not holy in itself, but only in so far as what happens within it gives glory to God?

✳ *Help us, Lord, wherever we may gather with our brothers and sisters in Christ, to hallow that spot by truly worshipping you in spirit and in truth.*

Wednesday June 11   *Esther 1:16–22*

Don't get it wrong!

What do you make of this passage? Is the thought for the day to be: 'Every man should be master in his own house'? The answer of course has to be a resounding 'No!' We are back in the period of the exile and today's reading is really only setting the scene for what is to follow later in the Book of Esther.

The king is feasting with his courtiers. The wine has flowed freely and he is described as being 'merry' (verse 10). In this drunken state the king sends a summons for his queen to come and be displayed as he might display a horse, a work of art or any other of his possessions. When Queen Vashti refuses to appear, the king is far from merry and she is deposed. This is the background against which Esther is chosen to become queen in place of Vashti. When the time comes, Esther will take the great risk of approaching the king unbidden, as dangerous as not responding when summoned, but in so doing she will be able to save her people from destruction.

This passage serves as a reminder of the injustices against which many have still to struggle today. I doubt whether Vashti could be claimed as a pioneer of women's rights; she may just have thought she had more hold over the king than proved the case. Nevertheless she was abominably treated. Esther is seen as a heroine because she, a young woman, took her life in her hands to reveal an evil plot and achieve a great victory against the plotters, all men, in what was overwhelmingly a man's world.

✳ *Enable me, O Lord, to recognise and oppose any forms of injustice and oppression in the society of which I am a part.*

Thursday June 12   *2 Kings 5:1–8*
Not in the circles of power
It is so easy to jump to the wrong conclusions. An Israelite girl who has been captured and is now a slave in Aram tells her mistress that her husband's leprosy might be cured if only he could see the prophet in Samaria, the territory from which the girl had been taken. The woman is sufficiently impressed to encourage Naaman, her husband, to make the journey and put the girl's words to the test. Naaman, being the king's right-hand man, seeks and gets his master's approval before setting out.

So far so good. Now the trouble starts. The king of Aram assumes that if such a mighty healing can be effected in Israel then it must come at a high price and that the king of Israel must be in control of the operation. The king of Israel however is distraught when Naaman arrives laden with costly gifts and asks for healing. It doesn't occur to him that Naaman is genuinely seeking help; instead he assumes Aram is creating an excuse to embark upon further hostilities. Thus another little war, with both sides feeling affronted, might well have broken out if Elisha hadn't intervened.

Elisha is important and influential in the Bible narrative, but that doesn't mean that he moved in the recognised circles of power; God's most active and effective servants seldom do.

✳ *Remind me, Lord, when I need reminding, that you are most likely to be found working in the world through men and women who seldom seek the limelight.*

Friday June 13   *1 Kings 21:1–11*
Not the whole story
This is a thoroughly unpleasant story or rather, as with other readings this week, part of a story. Ahab wants to extend the grounds of his palace and so makes Naboth what he considers to be a very reasonable offer. Naboth, however, is well aware that his family has farmed this particular plot for generations and is

unwilling to part with it. Unable to get what he wants, Ahab sulks. Hearing what has happened, Jezebel, the stronger character, contrives to have Naboth judicially murdered so that Ahab can claim the land as forfeit. The leaders of Naboth's community, through weakness and fear, do as Jezebel tells them and so Naboth is killed.

We could point to all too many modern parallels where the powerful ride roughshod over the powerless, all too many instances of those who might have made a stand failing to do so because they want a quiet life. Are we then to say, 'Well, life has always been like that and it always will be'? That would be to ignore what follows when Elijah appears and pronounces the judgement of God.

✳ *I thank you, Lord, for the knowledge that whilst you are a loving and compassionate God you are also a God of justice.*

Saturday June 14   *Nehemiah 6:1–9*
No easy calling
In most of our readings this week we have been looking at things which are not quite what they seem at first glance, but here the situation is grimly straightforward. This is part of the account of the return from exile and the rebuilding of Jerusalem. Surely it should have been a great and joyous adventure. We may think of how chapter 40 of Isaiah looks forward to this return: 'Comfort, O comfort my people, says your God ... the uneven ground shall become level and the rough places a plain. Then the glory of the Lord shall be revealed.'

Nehemiah returns to the ruined city, however, facing not only a daunting rebuilding task but also the opposition of those who have no desire to see Jerusalem rebuilt and who will do anything they can to stop it happening. Thus, looking back to chapter 4, we read (verse 18) that 'each of the builders had his sword strapped at his side while he built'. In addition, as we have read, Nehemiah is having to counter false charges of rebellion.

Nehemiah, however, carries his work through to its conclusion. If there is something worth doing, something good, something which we believe serves the purposes of God and helps some of his people, then it is worth doing whatever difficulties lie in the way.

✴ *Lord, grant me the strength and the will to carry on and not give up when I meet real difficulties in undertaking the work which you have given me to do.*

FOR REFLECTION – alone or with a group

● Would you agree or disagree with this statement: 'It is when we are prepared to read the Bible critically, and even to question some of the things we find there, that we are most likely to hear the word which God has for us today'? If you disagree, what other statement would you want to put in its place?

FOR ACTION

Join a class at your local college or university to study some aspect of the biblical texts more critically. Or read a challenging book on biblical study.

THE PENTECOST POST: BIBLICAL LETTERS
2. Broadcast news

Notes based on the New Revised Standard Version by
Barbara Calvert

Barbara Calvert is a Methodist local preacher living in Paisley, Scotland, where her husband, David, is Superintendent minister of the Ayrshire and Renfrewshire circuit.

She taught RE in secondary schools in Gloucestershire and Herefordshire for ten years. Then, before moving to Scotland, she worked for Christian Aid as area co-ordinator for the three counties of Gloucester, Hereford and Worcester. Her work with Christian Aid has taken her to Israel/Palestine, Uganda, Haiti and Jamaica. Now she is writing and working locally to raise awareness of justice and peace issues in the church and community.

All the New Testament documents are literary forms of broadcasting the good news about Jesus Christ and life in the kingdom of God. Sometimes this good news is expressed in letters, such as Paul's letters to 'his' churches; but the good news is also expressed through what we call the 'gospels', for 'gospel' means good news. As we read these selected passages, we ask ourselves, 'What is the good news that we are trying to broadcast to people in our contemporary world?'

The Christian church is not only an instrument of broadcasting the gospel; it also has the task of building bridges within communities and between peoples of different churches, faiths and philosophies. We can't broadcast news without building bridges. The readings which illustrate the bridge-building work of the church challenge us to search for appropriate ways of building bridges today.

Sunday June 15   *Romans 1:1–7*
Who are we?
My youngest daughter enjoyed French and German at school and was always enthusiastic about school exchange programmes. Preparation to visit someone she had never met was very important. Letters were exchanged giving information about herself, her family and her interests. Discovering common interests boded well for a successful exchange.

In his letter to the Romans, Paul is planning for a visit to people he has never met. First he gives information about himself, 'a servant of Jesus Christ, called to be an apostle'. Then he explores the common ground, their shared faith, by quoting a simple credal statement which Christians in Rome would recognise.

When we moved from Gloucester to Paisley in Scotland, I had to give up my job of area co-ordinator for Christian Aid. At first, without this role in the workplace, I found it a bit difficult to say who I was. My identity had been very much tied up with my work. What I discovered mattered to the people I had never met before was not my work but the fact that we shared a common faith.

If we are to be involved in broadcasting the good news, it is our faith that is important, our identity as followers of Christ. Paul does not begin his letter to the Romans by stating that he is a tent-maker!

✴ *We proclaim: we are followers of Christ.*

Monday June 16   *Revelation 1:9–11*
Sharing our news
John wants his message to be heard, so he begins by carefully preparing the ground: I am one of you; I am John your brother. But then John goes deeper: Like you, I have been persecuted for my faith; we have a common experience of suffering.

In February 2000, the annual floods experienced by Mozambique were particularly bad. The water covered vast areas of land, washing away homes, schools, hospitals and roads. People gathered on roofs in the hope of rescue. Once the floods had subsided, one of the most urgent needs was to get seeds in the ground to prevent the disastrous floods being followed by widespread hunger. Christian Aid was able to make a rapid response through its long-term partner in the area, the Christian Council for Mozambique.

Later that same year, parts of Britain experienced the worst floods in living memory. Homes, churches, schools and businesses were flooded. Many people were unable to return to their homes for months. Christian Aid received a letter from the Christian Council of Mozambique: 'Having suffered through destructive floods here, we know how traumatic this calamity will be for those affected in many ways … Though our organisation and our country lack financial resources to send you, please be assured of our sense of kinship with you at this time. Know that our prayers are with you daily…'

✴ *We proclaim: solidarity with all God's people.*

Establishing networks

As Christians we belong to a worldwide network of churches. From each other we gain strength and encouragement. On a visit to the Holy Land a few years ago, many of the Palestinian Christians I met used the expression 'dead stones and living stones'. The 'dead stones' are the religious sites in the Holy Land that thousands of Christians from all over the world flock to visit each year. The 'living stones' are the Palestinian Christians who feel forgotten but, at no small cost, maintain a Christian presence in the Holy Land. The Palestinian Christians long to be recognised as part of the network of the worldwide Christian community.

In today's passage we see Paul beginning the task of establishing a network of churches. He asks the churches in Corinth to collect money for the poor in Jerusalem. He encourages them by telling them that he has already given the same directions to churches in Galatia. Already we have a network forming from Galatia to Corinth to Jerusalem.

Today Methodists throughout the world celebrate the 300th anniversary of the birth of John Wesley. He, too, knew the importance of establishing a network. Members were put into classes; churches were organised into circuits, each belonging to the Connexion.

✴ *We proclaim: membership of a worldwide church.*

Developing community

In 1999, a group of people from churches in Gloucester went to Haiti. One hot afternoon we met under the shade of a mango tree with a group of women who lived in an impoverished rural area near the small town of Petit Goave. Two years earlier they had all 'put their heads together' and thought, 'What can we do?' With a small loan from the Haitian Methodist Church funded by Christian Aid, they set up a Women's Community Bank. Each of the women started their own very small business: one sold oil and coconuts, another fruit and vegetables. These tiny schemes provided vital income for their families. The women met together each week and paid back a small amount of the loan. Then the women would sing and pray together, enjoying one another's company. They were a supportive community. When they told us their story, they asked us to sing to them. Our two groups had totally different experiences of life, different histories, and no common language. But that afternoon, through simply sharing something of our story in laughter and song and prayer, there was a oneness between us.

Christ breaks down the walls between all people and God has 'a plan for the fullness of time, to gather up all things in him'. Paul is broadcasting the good news of oneness between Jew and Gentile. What does the good news of oneness mean in today's world?

✳ *We proclaim: oneness with all God's people.*

Thursday June 19   *Galatians 4:8–11*

Becoming more fully human

Recently I spent a week on Iona. The theme for our week was 'Walking the Tightrope'. We tied a 'tightrope' around the pillar of the chapter house and across to the window catch. During the course of the week we developed the idea of the Christian life as walking the tightrope – keeping in balance the material and the spiritual. As we journeyed along the tightrope we gained inspiration and insight from the story of Moses travelling out of Egypt through the wilderness. Who, we asked, are the Hebrew slaves making bricks without straw in today's world? And we were reminded of the all-important command not to look back, an imperative if you are walking the tightrope!

In today's passage Paul is pleading with the Galatians not to turn back. 'You were enslaved … how can you turn back again?' Don't fall back into religion, he says, worrying about fasts and special days. Retain your freedom in relationship with God.

The Iona Community too does not believe that people are brought to Iona to be changed into 'religious' people, but rather to be made more fully human. This is the news broadcast today from Iona, a tiny, remote island in the inner Hebrides.

✳ *We proclaim: our God-given humanity in all its fullness.*

Friday June 20   *Mark 1:1–15*

No secrets

At home, we have a yellow star-shaped candle. Tied round it with raffia is a hand-written label: 'Jamaica AIDS support'. We bought the candle from the Lifeskills candle-making workshop, hidden round the back of a community centre in Kingston, Jamaica. We had visited the hospice where patients suffering from HIV/AIDS-related illnesses are cared for. Like the candle-making workshop, the hospice is largely hidden from view. Jamaica AIDS support is working against the stigma attached to the disease.

In Malawi, Susan Cole King, before her untimely death in 2000, had been working on HIV/AIDS education. At first the church had not wanted to know but Susan's tireless persistence had eventually brought them round. Susan wrote, 'The first response of Christians to AIDS is to reach out with compassion and acceptance, as Christ did, to offer care and whatever healing is possible.'

In the prologue to Mark's gospel, the voice from heaven declaring 'You are my Son' is heard only by Jesus. But the reader overhears the voice and is let into the secret. Mark's gospel goes on to tell the story of people discovering who Jesus is. Then the good news of the kingdom of God is broadcast to all – kept secret from no one.

✳ *We proclaim: the good news of the kingdom of God.*

Saturday June 21   *Romans 15:14–21*
Personal encounters
'No one forgets a good teacher' was the slogan for a recent teacher recruitment advertising campaign. If we think back to a good teacher, it will not be for the facts they taught us or for the knowledge they imparted that we remember them, but for the person they were or the passion with which they taught their subject.

Paul was a passionate teacher of the gospel, never to be forgotten. 'I make it my ambition to proclaim the good news … "Those who have never been told of him shall see, and those who have never heard of him shall understand."' To fulfil his ambition to broadcast the good news everywhere, Paul went on long and dangerous missionary journeys. He established communities of believers and networks of churches, and he nurtured the young churches through letters which both taught and encouraged. But Paul is not content with writing a letter to the Romans. 'I desire, as I have for many years, to come to you' (verse 23). Distance learning is all right, but there is nothing like the personal presence of a teacher!

And so Christ came into the world. And it is by our personal presence that we too share the good news.

✳ *We proclaim: Christ in our world today.*

FOR REFLECTION – alone or with a group

● What is the good news that we are trying to broadcast to people in our contemporary world?

● What are some of the different ways in which this can be done?

● Where do we receive good news from others?

FOR ACTION

Write a letter or send an e-mail sharing good news with someone or some organisation in another part of the world. Ask them to share some good news with you.

3. Bridge-building

Sunday June 22   *Philemon 17–22*

Crossing the bridge

Some years ago, over a matter long since forgotten, I remember remarking to a school colleague, 'It's the principle that counts'. 'No,' he replied, 'Principles, principles, what do they matter? It's people that count.'

Paul is pleading for Onesimus whom he is sending back to Philemon. He asks Philemon to forgive his runaway slave, Onesimus, and welcome him back as a brother in Christ. Philemon could have replied, 'It's the principle that counts. Onesimus ran away; he must be treated as a runaway slave and punished.' We don't know how Philemon responded to Paul's request. What we do know is that Paul was asking Philemon to reach much higher than the letter of the law (a principle), and respond with the spirit of forgiveness and love.

In this, Paul is acting very much in the spirit of the teaching of Jesus. Almost every day there is an opportunity for us to do the same. And could it be that, through the bridge-building efforts of Paul, the 1st century bishop of Ephesus, named Onesimus, was once this young runaway slave?

✳ *Make me a captive, Lord, and then I shall be free.*

Monday June 23   *Titus 3:8b-15*

Bridges of action

The needs of the world, whether local or global, can seem overwhelming. A survey carried out by Christian Aid in the 1990s, called *The gospel, the poor and the churches*, interviewed people from a wide variety of congregations in Britain about their attitudes towards poverty. The survey found that people approached the enormous scale of poverty in the world by falling into two camps: the passive coper and the active coper. Passive copers tended to bury their heads in the sand because they believed that the problems of the world were so overwhelming that there was nothing they could do. Active copers got stuck in: praying, caring, fund-raising and campaigning, believing they could make a difference.

One minister I knew had her own personal motto which she displayed all over the place – in her office, on the lectern and in the back of her car. It read 'Just do it'! In this letter to Titus, the writer twice exhorts the people to 'Just do it', to devote themselves to good works. 'Just doing it' is often the way to build bridges with those who are uncertain about the effectiveness of the Christian faith. They are enabled to respond when they see love in action.

✳ *Ours are the feet with which he is to go about doing good.*

Tuesday June 24   *1 Corinthians 5:1–5*

Open the bridge

Today we have the church burying its head in the sand. Paul has heard that a man in the church in Corinth is living with his father's wife and is incredulous that the church has put up with it. Why hadn't the church taken any action? Perhaps it was easier to pretend they didn't know what was going on.

Today the church is being urged to take action over one issue which for too long it has ignored – violence against women. In 1998 in Harare, the World Council of Churches held a festival to mark the end of a Decade of Churches in Solidarity with Women. At that festival, women who had suffered different forms of violence within the church spoke out with courage and called the global Christian community to account. The church could no longer pretend it didn't know what was going on. Now all churches are being encouraged to look openly and honestly at the issue of violence against women.

Overcoming violence in all its forms involves building bridges. It is a peace process, a process of non-violence, but it is not about doing nothing. Bridge-building requires action and the active participation of us all. Overcoming violence against women is now one of the projects contributing to the World Council of Churches' Decade to Overcome Violence (2001–2010).

What other problems within our own church communities have we buried our heads in the sand over for long enough?

✳ **_Make me a channel of your peace._**

Bridge supports

Fund-raising is a curious activity. One type of fund-raising involves organising events such as concerts, charity dinners, fashion shows or sponsored walks. Often participants join in because they are attracted to the activity and may not even be very aware of or interested in where the money is going. In fact, I was once invited to a three-course Lent lunch! It was a sumptuous meal and each year the event was very well supported by the people of the village, raising a huge sum of money for the charity involved. But at the lunch I was told not to talk too much about the work of that charity because it might put some people off coming!

Paul shows that he is involved in another type of fund-raising in writing to the Corinthians. He explains the need, cites the example of others who had given so generously, and encourages them to respond as an act of faith.

Fund-raising can raise large sums of money but it can also build bridges of mutual support and love between people. Paul did not seek to raise funds for the saints at Jerusalem without also raising awareness of their needs. There's a challenge for us!

✳ **_Yours are the eyes through which is to look out Christ's compassion to the world._**

Prayer as a bridge

'Absent in body; with you in spirit.' How often have we said those words ourselves or been strengthened by them?

During the apartheid years in South Africa, Desmond Tutu said: 'Your prayers have been for us … like a ring of fire protecting us from our enemies and giving us a place to stand.' Nelson Mandela, too, frequently commented on the huge difference it made in their long and painful struggle simply to know of the solidarity of people from around the world, absent in body but with them in spirit.

Daily we are faced by situations of suffering around the world. Our prayers can seem inadequate, but what a difference it makes if we know more about the people and their situation. Then we can pray not just *for* the people but *with* them. Try starting a prayer with the words 'I pray *with* …'

In today's passage, Paul is encouraging Christians in Colossae whom he has never met. However, he knows a lot about them and therefore can say genuinely that he is *with* them in spirit. Paul encourages the Colossians to remain firm in their faith in Jesus Christ whom they have 'received' (verse 6). Absent in body; with you in spirit.

✳ ***I pray with…***

Friday June 27   *1 Thessalonians 3:6–10*
The bridge in person
Occasionally, in my teaching days, I would go into the staff room for the lunch break to find all the tables covered with displays of books. Representatives from book publishers were at the school to encourage busy teachers to buy their books, knowing that they were far more likely to make a sale if they spoke to us in person than if they simply sent a catalogue.

Today we read that Timothy has just returned from Thessalonica. It wasn't possible for Paul to go to Thessalonica himself at this time so he sent Timothy as his personal representative. Paul is greatly encouraged to hear first-hand accounts of the faith and love of the Thessalonians and that they remember him kindly. This is an example of Paul's careful oversight in nurturing young churches. Timothy visits; Paul follows up the visit by writing a letter; and he tells the Thessalonians of his longing to see them face to face.

We have no letters from Christ; in fact we have no writing of his at all. But Paul was following in the footsteps of the one who came in person, whom we long to see face to face and whose representatives we are called to be.

✳ ***Christ has no body now on earth but yours.***

Saturday June 28   *Colossians 4:15–18*
The post bridge
Many of Paul's letters were written using an amanuensis, a letter-writer, as is clearly the case in his letter to the Colossians. Paul

employed every means at his disposal to spread the gospel. He personally went on missionary journeys; he trained others in this same work; he wrote letters of teaching and encouragement, often employing an amanuensis. Each one of these approaches helped Paul to get the message of the gospel across.

The speech-writers of political leaders today also play a vital role in getting the message across. Good speech-writers will be gifted with a certain intuition that enables them to express the thoughts and ideas of the politician in a way that will go down well with the public. The job involves both understanding the mind of the politician who is to give the speech and being sensitive to how the message might best be expressed. A good writer has an invaluable part to play in the life of leading politicians. But how often do we hear, in a tone of admiration, a report that the politician has abandoned his/her speech and is now speaking in his/her own words? Words spoken from the heart may not be so clever or so eloquent but they speak of sincerity and passion. And so Paul closes his letter to the Colossians with these words: 'I, Paul, write this greeting with my own hand. Remember my chains. Grace be with you.'

✳ *O for a heart to praise my God.*

FOR REFLECTION – alone or with a group
● When have you 'heard' the good news being broadcast most effectively? What made it effective?
● Can you identify areas of life where bridge-building is needed? How can you play your part in such bridge-building in the community?

FOR ACTION
Identify areas in your own life where there are opportunities for broadcasting good news and building bridges. Seek ways in which you might do this.

SIMPLE GIFTS
1. Free spirits

Notes based on the New Revised Standard Version by
Helen Julian CSF

Helen Julian is an Anglican Franciscan sister, living in Somerset in a community house whose main ministry is hospitality. She is the author of Living the Gospel: the spirituality of St Francis and St Clare *and also writes for* New Daylight.

Being a 'free spirit' sounds very attractive. It brings visions of doing just what I want, when I want. But this isn't the kind of freedom which God offers. God's gift of freedom is both much more deeply rooted, and much more demanding. It's the freedom to be single-minded in God's service, to be liberated from anything which prevents that – even if sometimes we'd rather not. Though it is indeed a gift, it's one which we have to grow into, learn to desire and develop the skills to co-operate with.

Sunday June 29   *Luke 9:57–62*
Strange freedom

Surely this is no way to treat volunteers? Two of the three anonymous would-be disciples offer freely to follow Jesus. Instead of welcoming them, he gives them a stark warning about the cost of what they are volunteering to do. And it's no different with the person whom Jesus calls. There is no time even to fulfil the sacred duty of burying a parent. The demands of the kingdom are so urgent that they must have absolute priority.

This is freedom of a kind, but it's freedom with a high price tag. But Jesus asks no more of his followers than he does of himself. He is 'on the road', going towards Jerusalem, though his preaching is being rejected by the Samaritan villages he passes through, and he knows that death waits for him in Jerusalem. He is free enough to do this, and he offers the same freedom, with the same price, to his disciples.

We don't know how the would-be disciples responded. We can hope that they grasped the offer of life, leaving behind the deadness of life without Christ. Knowing our own response to the demands of discipleship may put a question mark over that hope.

Following Christ offers us freedom, but it's a strange freedom for which we need to develop the taste.

✱ *Jesus, set me free to follow you whatever the cost.*

Monday June 30   *Psalm 77:1–2, 11–20*

The world set free

It's easy to turn inward when life is hard and nights are dark. The psalmist doesn't succumb to this temptation, but instead, day and night, relentlessly seeks out God, refusing any other comfort.

The comfort which does finally come emerges from remembering what God has done in the past, not just for the one who prays but for the whole people. It comes from remembering what kind of God Israel worships, a God of holiness and wonders, who uses his power to liberate.

There is a freedom in turning away from my own concerns to contemplate the bigger picture, to remember *our* story, not just *my* story. The God who can make the deep tremble and the earth shake can surely cope with my problems! And equally he can cope with my complaints and my crying.

Because God is who he is, we can be free to be who we are, to be real before God. We can cry out for our liberation from all that binds us, knowing that this is what God desires for us, as for the whole creation.

✱ *Almighty, Liberator God, continue your work of bringing freedom to a world which desperately needs it.*

Tuesday July 1   *Galatians 5:1, 13–18*

Freedom to be slaves

Why would anyone not want to be free? Paul's exhortation to the Galatians in verse 1 seems very strange.

Perhaps it makes more sense in the light of verse 13. If our freedom is in order to 'become slaves to one another' it becomes a little less desirable! However this 'slavery' is tempered by the warmth of love and mutual service. We are not set free in order to do exactly what we like; the yoke of the law, of slavery, is taken off, in order that we may freely take on the yoke of Christ (Matthew 11:29).

And then, there can be a security in the law, in knowing exactly what to do in any circumstance. The life of freedom, in which we live and walk by the Spirit, requires a constant attention to the Spirit's whispers and leadings.

I know for myself the temptation to say to the leader of my community, 'Oh, you decide', rather than go through the long and sometimes painful process of the whole group listening to one another and trying to come to a common mind. The freedom in the Spirit of this epistle is no soft option.

✴ *Christ, help me to stand firm in the freedom you bring, and to freely choose the yoke you offer.*

Wednesday July 2   *Deuteronomy 16:1–4*
The afflictions of freedom
God is free to choose where his name dwells, that is, where he is to be found and worshipped. Because we are made in his image, he therefore offers freedom to his people too. For the Israelites, this meant first of all freedom from outward slavery, and this is not to be underestimated. The story of the Exodus has inspired many in their fight for freedom.

But God offers also a more interior freedom, perhaps signified in the unleavened bread. Following the instruction to leave behind the leaven of their old life and not to store up the leftovers of the evening meal would give the people a chance to grow in their trust that God would provide in the future, as he had done in the past.

But the unleavened bread of liberation is also the bread of affliction. As we've already seen, freedom is often a double-edged gift. In the wilderness the people came to look back with longing on their slavery in Egypt, where at least they had plenty of varied food. They grumbled against God, and against Moses. Offering freedom will not always make us popular.

✴ *God of the Exodus, give us courage to travel into the freedom you offer, and not to look back.*

Thursday July 3   *Psalm 16*
Choosing other gods
Freedom and choice are today's 'gods' for many people, including Christians. Choice is the ultimate good – parental choice of schools, patient's choice of treatment, choice of TV channels, choice of church. The promise of freedom is used to

sell and to persuade. More money and more things mean more freedom and more chances to exercise choice.

But 'money can't buy me love' and it doesn't buy freedom either. The other gods are illusory and can't ultimately deliver on their promises.

The psalmist by contrast is entirely focused on the one true God, accepting him as Lord and turning away from anything else which seeks to claim his allegiance. And as with all true, life-changing choices, this one choice precludes others. In my choice of life in a religious community, I said no to marriage and children. Another chooses to pursue their creative gift, accepting that by that choice they turn their back on security and wealth.

These choices may seem a denial of freedom, but in reality they bring us to genuine freedom, as we serve the one true God whose 'service is perfect freedom.'

✳ *Protect me, O God, for in you I take refuge. You are my Lord; I have no good apart from you.*

Friday July 4   *1 Kings 19:16, 19–21*

Called into freedom

There are echoes here of the passage from Luke 9: there the one who wants to say goodbye to his family is not allowed to; here Elijah does allow Elisha to do so. But it was a dramatic farewell, which may not have comforted Elisha's family much! He burnt his bridges very thoroughly – there was to be no going back.

The call of God may cut across family ties and loyalty. St Clare, an early Franciscan saint, left home secretly in the middle of the night in order to follow her vocation to follow Christ in the way of St Francis. Although God always allows us the freedom to respond or not to his call, it can feel as though there is no choice. 'Here I stand,' said Martin Luther, 'I can do no other.' But the call of God is always into freedom, into the freedom to be who I am created to be. My own call into religious life, with its vows of poverty, chastity and obedience, seems to limit my life. But I know that in fact it has opened up freedom to grow and change which I could have had in no other way.

✳ *God of vocation, help me to hear your call into deeper freedom and to respond whole-heartedly.*

Becoming God's family

'God has no grandchildren' goes an old saying. Each of us must come into relationship with God in our own right, not because of our ancestry. And no one can by right claim to be mother or brother or sister to Jesus. Only those who do God's will are accepted into that close and intimate relationship. But that in itself is an amazing claim – that we can be so closely related to God, the creator of the universe, in Christ.

It is a claim that made a deep impact on St Francis. He wrote passionately about how glorious it was to have a heavenly Father, how beautiful to have a Spouse in Christ, and how sweet and desirable to have Christ also as brother. He also wrote about how we can become mothers to Christ, when through love we carry him within ourselves, and give birth to him through the working of the Holy Spirit in our lives.

As we saw at the start of the week, God's freedom is costly. It demands a willingness to give up many things which are good in themselves. But what he freely offers in response is so precious that the price seems small.

✳ *Father, Brother, Spouse, draw me into relationship with you.*

FOR REFLECTION – alone or with a group

● Where might God be calling you, individually or as a group, to a freedom which you don't want to accept?

● Can you think of an event in your past which seemed a disaster at the time but became a means of liberation?

FOR ACTION

What small action can you take today to begin to liberate yourself from something which holds you back from the freedom which God offers? And alongside that, what small action can you take which will help to free another person or group from 'slavery'?

SIMPLE GIFTS
2. Bare essentials

Notes based on the Revised Standard Version by
Peter Privett

Peter Privett is an Anglican priest who has been a teacher, parish priest and Diocesan Education Adviser. He is also a textile artist who now works freelance, leading workshops, retreats and educational events.

The hot air balloon is losing height.
There is so much clutter in the basket.
What might need throwing overboard to enable survival
    and rescue?

This collection of readings invites us to penetrate into the
    heart of things.
It is a challenge to examine what is essential.
When the chips are down,
what is most necessary for life?

It seems to be part of the reality of the human condition
that we find ourselves cluttering and layering up more
    distractions,
building up protective layers
that keep us immune
from the reality of human pain and ecstasy.

What can be discarded and removed?
What can take us back
to naked essence,
return us to divine grace?

The story of faith reveals that the process is difficult
and sometimes painful.
Letting go is not easy,
clinging is easier.

Carl Jung told the story of a minister who sought counselling. He advised him to spend time alone with himself each day. Some time later, the minister reported that he had listened to his favourite music and read poetry. Jung reminded him of the original instruction. The minister replied, 'I couldn't possibly be with myself like that.' Jung replied, 'If you can't, then how do you expect others to be with you?'

To the heart of the matter
   Paul understands the importance of bare essentials,
   and wants to direct us to the reality at the heart of everything –
   to the heart of the universe, the heart of creation, the heart of
      being –
   to the Christ on the cross.

   Here is one who has been stripped bare of everything,
   who encounters the essentials of living.

   Here is one who understands what it is to be stripped of
      everything –
   friends, security, clothes, dignity,
   and, if Mark's gospel is taken seriously,
   even God.

   The discussion throughout the letter to the Galatians
   focuses on the issues that arose
   from Judaism and early Christianity attempting to live
      alongside one another.
   It focuses on a very male and paradoxical argument about
      circumcision.

   On one level, the discussion is about the removal of
      protective layers,
   in this case penile skin.
   What happens in reality is the opposite.
   Layers of theological protection are built up
   and these lead to division and dysfunctional community.

   There is a challenge here
   to examine how we use our religious practices to avoid the
      realities of life
   and how they sometimes become protective layers that
      obscure our vision of God.

✳ *New Creation,*
   call us into a community of fellowship, a new Israel,
   a community that is committed to a spirituality of letting go.

Essential discipleship and mission
   The call to discipleship and mission is one that is committed
   to a spirituality of letting go.
   It is one that lets go of individualism,
   in favour of companionship and mutuality,

and one that lets go of security of knowledge,
in favour of vulnerability and weakness.

The call to discipleship is a recognition of another's
  humanity.

The disciples are called to discard, not accumulate,
to let go of the clutter and concentrate on the bare
  essentials.
They go with only themselves.
Their task is to listen to the other,
to offer peace, wellbeing and blessing.

They are called to a ministry of stillness, continuity, and
  stability,
a ministry of 'staying with' and 'getting to know',
a source of healing,
a sign that the kingdom is close.

It is a ministry that understands the meaning of hospitality,
that banquet can happen when the simplest of foods is shared.

It is an understanding of living in the light of giving and receiving,
of a mutuality of living.
It is an understanding of our common humanity.

Essential discipleship is one that gives delight and joy
and even dangerous and deathly influences are put in their place.

Essential mission is one that embraces a spirituality of letting go.

✳ *For the encounters today –*
for those I listen to –
for those I eat with –
for those with whom humanity is shared,
thanks be to God.

Tuesday July 8   *Mark 14:51–52*
Essentially flesh
  A life-drawing class model knows about the spirituality of
    letting go.
  I attended such a class a few years ago,
  where the model had literally let go of her clothes.

  She was essentially bare.

  In her late fifties, and breaking all the stereotypes of
    contemporary beauty,
  she stood still for an hour and a half,
  for a class of twenty people.

The ample folds of her skin and the scar of her caesarean
    operation
proclaimed a deep humanity.

What was even more overwhelming
was the fact that she so entirely inhabited her body
and was so secure in her physicality.
There was no smuttiness here,
but an unconditional offering of a human being
in all the beauty of her vulnerability.

The nakedness of the Bible passage isn't quite like this.
The nakedness is not offered, but enforced,
and is met with shock by the young man.
Perhaps there were ribald comments from the soldiers
and mocking laughter as the youth ran away.

However, both artists' model and the unnamed young man in Mark
remind us that we are carnal creatures,
creatures of flesh –
'the Word became Flesh'.

The artists' model taught me that bodies matter.
They need to be loved and inhabited,
not hidden away with feelings of self-loathing and
    embarrassment.

A spirituality of letting go may mean
that I learn to love the doctrine of the incarnation,
which proclaims that
bodies matter,
all bodies –
those with blemishes,
those without parts,
those of all ages, colours, and sizes…
even mine.

✴ *In my flesh shall I see God.*
What does 'being exposed' mean?
What do I cling to that covers me up?

Wednesday July 9   *Psalm 123*
Look up – let go
    A movement from downwards to upwards looking
    may also reveal the spirituality of letting go,
    the spirituality of bare essentials.

The language of movement permeates the psalm –
eyes move from being cast down to being lifted up,
hands move to remind servants of their position,
souls move from acquiescence to shouts of primal questioning.

There is a movement from being passive to being active.
The cry of pleading, the primitive cry for release,
the shout of necessity,
    'Have mercy',
enables a movement upward.

This ability to look up means that other possibilities are
    achievable.
The ability to look up is also prophetic,
for it enables a wider vision,
a wider perspective to be taken,
to see one's own context within a bigger picture.

At the end of the psalm,
the one who has been in a subservient position
is able to name and give voice to an intolerable condition
and to know that it is intolerable.

The essence of the situation is named.
The upward movement of the eyes,
the 'Have mercy'
joins the sound waves and pulse of eternity.
The call from one fragile being
into timeless eternity
lets go of oppression
for a life of possible liberation.

✳ *Lift my eyes today that I may look up to see the world in all
its fullness.*
Join my eyes with the eyes of others.

Thursday July 10   *Isaiah 66:10–14*

Dance with the child

If you have been in a position of oppression for some time,
it's often difficult to see that freedom is possible.
The psychology of oppression often leads
to amnesia of being, of identity, of future freedom.
The prophet's task is
to restore memories of freedom, wellbeing and identity,
to bring again into consciousness the bare essentials.

This prophet uses language that brings into remembrance

the beginnings of our human nurture.

We are reminded of our infant dependence, of our oral
  sustenance.

Psychologists remind us that
in the nursing relationship more is being met than physical
  sustenance.

It is the gaze of the eyes,
the warmth of the countenance,
the comfort and warmth of the cradling arms,
the smell of the breast,
and the heartbeat of the adult
that sustain and nourish inner and outer feelings of wellbeing.

The passage abounds with the language of abundance and
  fullness,
of fecundity, of security and delight.

Sustenance, intimacy, and a sense of wellbeing
enable an outward dance of relational love.
From the hip and the knee,
the smiling, giggling, eye-dancing child
reaches out to the world
so that all may be included in the dance of connection.

The prophet calls us to a spirituality of letting go our adult
  postures
to revisit the dependence and delight of childhood,
with the assurance that it's not too late to start.

✳ *Life-giving God, divine child,*
  reawaken the child in me
  so that we may dance to the pulse of love.

Friday July 11   *2 Corinthians 12:1–10*
Risky business
  The spirituality of letting go can be a risky business,
  especially when you're under threat,
  at the centre of personal criticism,
  feeling hurt, or having your role and work questioned.

  It is thought that the underlying material
  in this second letter to the Corinthians
  is Paul's response to criticism of his mission and himself,
  a response to a group questioning his status and credentials.

  When faced with a similar situation, a popular response is
  to go on the defensive,

promote our success,
prove our credentials,
reiterate our status,
and outspin the 'spin doctors'.

The ecstatic experience that Paul quotes
could be used to silence the critics,
in a playground cry of,
'My ecstatic experience is more ecstatic than yours!'

The 'thorn in the flesh'
brings us back into the harshness of reality,
back from the flight of ecstatic fancy.
It is a reminder that for much of the time
we live with our flawed humanity
and the flawed humanity of others.

The 'thorn in the flesh',
the frailty and weakness of human experience,
brings us back to what is essential:
and for Paul this is the letting go,
the abandonment of the selfish ego
into the experience of divine grace...

✳ *In the muddlesome reality and unsortedness of life,*
in agony and ecstasy, in unknowing and perplexity,
in hurt and deceit, in weakness and insults...
'My grace is sufficient.'

Saturday July 12   *Mark 15:33–37*

Bare essentials

Jesus lets go
and utters the chilling cry of abandonment on the cross –
'My God, my God, why have you forsaken me?'

The cry brings us to the bare essentials,
not just of human living,
but of creation and eternity itself.

The cry and the darkness
return us to beginnings –
to the primal source,
to the primeval chaos where darkness moves once again
    over the waters of the deep, to the primal absence, the
    primal silence,
and the intensity of nothingness –
the very bareness of essence.

The cry is at the intersection
where eternity and humanity meet –
the intersection of bareness,
the intersection of essence.

At this profound moment of connection,
a human response is one of disconnection,
of perplexity, and crass misunderstanding.
The talk of the bystanders
is literally at cross-purposes.

It is the ultimate moment
of being utterly stripped to bare essentials,
no defences are offered, no guarantees given.

The enormity of this truth is too enormous,
too bare to contemplate.

Our human defences want to say
that it couldn't possibly be like this,
but the reality proclaims that
there are 'no handles on the cross'*,
no defences, no guarantees.

The awe,
fullness of the cry,
is that the divine is here.

Of this, is God.

The phrase is taken from the title of Kosuke Koyame's 1976 book.

✳ ***Pray in silence.***

FOR REFLECTION – alone or with a group

● What might we let go of?
● What are the divine bare essentials?

FOR ACTION

Create a list of all the things that go to make up your life – home,
work, food, people, leisure, ideas, qualities and so on ... Build as
full a picture as you can. Write them individually on small pieces
of paper or card. Group the bare essentials.

SIMPLE GIFTS
3. Look right in front of you

Notes based on the New International Version of the Bible by
Evelyn Cresswell

Evelyn Cresswell is a former teacher who has worked in various contexts of social change, ranging from clubs undergoing immigrant influx in Britain to working in South Africa with the courageous prophet, Rev Dr Beyers Naude, to change at grassroots the political mindset by demolishing apartheid's false biblical foundations. She continues to write and works now within communities in Zululand.

The title of this week's notes may imply that it is easy to see what is right in front of one, but once I walked right up to my daughter before she recognised me because she was expecting to meet someone else. Generally, we only see what we are looking for, and so we can miss what is right before us and obvious in its own right. This poem of Christopher Fry's is suggestive:

> Thank God our time is now,
> When wrong comes up to face us everywhere
> Never to leave us 'til we take
> The biggest stride of soul man ever took.
> Affairs are now soul size,
> The enterprise is exploration into God.
> Where are you making for?
> It takes many thousand years to wake, but will you wake
> for pity's sake?

The Old Testament prophets engaged with their present. Do we? Are we sufficiently 'awake' and free from stereotypical ways of seeing to actually notice what is really happening before us? In our contemporary preference for activism we are challenged to find new ways of waiting on God so that we will not be blind to what God may be making obvious to us in our 'now'.

Sunday July 13   *Deuteronomy 30:10–14*
Who and where am I?

As I read this passage I am reminded of the many who go off on their own spiritual quests, in the spirit of Western individualism, seeking places and persons that will help them become more 'spiritual'. 'Spirituality' has become a modern buzz word, and the spiritual path is increasingly sought. This passage reminds us that spirituality can never be thought of as a personal acquisition leading us to focus on ourselves. The purpose of growing more spiritual is to connect us more effectively with others.

The Deuteronomic writer here anticipates Jeremiah 31:33, with its promise of God's law being written in the human heart, when he says: 'The word is very near you; it is in your mouth and in your heart so that you may obey it' (verse 14). How we speak to our neighbours and how we express our attitudes from our hearts towards them either creates or destroys community. Likewise, the attitudes and actions of nations and corporate bodies towards one another can make or mar world community. The movement of the Old Testament is to promote an ever-widening view of community and responsibility towards others, through Isaiah and Jonah to Jesus who said, 'I have other sheep that are not of this sheep pen. I must bring them also' (John 10:16). Jesus fulfilled the law by incarnating it, and establishing a new vision of community. Are we ready to think fundamentally about our attitudes to others and about our own practice of mission in the light of Jesus' own methods of carrying out God's mission?

✴ *May the words of my mouth and the meditation of my heart be pleasing in your sight, O Lord, my Rock and my Redeemer.*   *Psalm 19:14*

Monday July 14   *Colossians 1:15–20*

Who is Jesus Christ today?

How hard it must have been for those first Christian writers to try to express the meaning of Jesus Christ in the fullness of his humanity and the 'nothingness' of his Godhead (Philippians 2:6–8). Today's reading is one such attempt, presenting Christ as the 'image of the invisible God'. How can we understand such theological language today? Perhaps by recognising the paradox that we come to 'fullness' only through 'emptiness'. Calling Jesus the 'firstborn over all creation' implies in Jewish tradition that he was an offering, as all 'first fruits' were offered to God. Being born 'in human form', he was subject to death because that is the human condition, but the way in which he met and faced his death, as the culmination of his whole life's offering, meant that he became 'the firstborn from among the dead'. When we too are 'born again' into God, we also are freed from making death the end of our living, whether this is manifested in a fanatical pursuit of life-extending medicine or in other ways of self-protectiveness. We can live a more outgoing faith-filled life because we are no longer preoccupied by our own physical demise. The second birth is our entry into new life with him who holds all things together (verse 17) in total respect for man and nature. Such life transcends the natural order and creates in us the joy of being reconciled to all things (verse 20) through Christ.

✳ *Lord, help us to live our lives freed from the fear of death.*

Tuesday July 15   *Psalm 19*
Voiceless language
Was there ever a more graphic text to help us human beings recognise that we are not 'the whole' as we so often assume ourselves to be in our imperialistic attitudes and judgements? This psalm opens our eyes to the majesty of all that is not ourselves, as we stand in awe before the power and magnificence of creation: 'The heavens declare the glory of God' (verse 1).

How much account do we take of that which is right in front of us? Do we allow natural beauty to speak to us as the psalmist allowed the sun to speak to him, suggesting the strength and purpose of a bridegroom who has everything to live for, and is full of joy because of all his responsibilities?

The psalmist has the wisdom to know that the Creator can speak to us through nature as one of his many options in communicating with us. Feeling awe before the natural order is a far cry from simply using nature as a foil to our own jaded spirits, a sort of escape from ourselves. We are not nature worshippers, as the psalmist reminds us when he describes the ordinances of God as 'more precious than gold' and 'sweeter than honey' (verse 10). He concludes by asking that God keep him 'innocent of great transgression'. And there is no greater sin than the presumption of limiting God to our own perceptions of him and constraining his activity by our partial understanding of how he may choose to communicate with us.

✳ *For I know my transgressions, and my sin is ever before me.*
Against you, you only, have I sinned.   *Psalm 51:3–4*

Wednesday July 16   *Luke 10:25–37*
Who is our neighbour today?
Christians have, over the years, tended so to literalise this parable that they may have confined its meaning. It has become

an exemplary tale about helping those we perceive to be in trouble, especially those who are strangers to us. It makes us feel good to be of help and use to others, and there is nothing wrong with that. But there is more to 'passing others by'. For example, how does 'looking at the world in front of us' connect with our changed world demographics in respect of our immediate neighbours, who often belong to other faiths? Do we engage with them at all? It was the religious priorities of the first two passers-by that kept them from expressing compassion beyond the bounds of their own immediate communities. To move beyond those bounds represented exposure to risk in every possible way. In what ways do our religious or denominational strictures inhibit us from 'being neighbour' to those from other faith groups?

Or another possible reading. This parable simply features 'the robbers' as props in the story, so we tend to ignore the question of how we may victimise people today or how we may set people up to be victims. We have become habituated to recognising ourselves only in the role of 'helper', since this fits nicely with our 'Christian image' of ourselves. But in so doing, what do we leave out of our Christian awareness?

✳ *'O Lord, you have searched me and you know me ... See if there is any offensive way in me, and lead me in the way everlasting.'*   *Psalm 139:1, 24*

Thursday July 17   *Psalm 25:1–10*

Put on the spot

The Psalms reflect the personal as well as communal journeys of those who have come to God in former times, including their wrestling with the issues that bothered them. They are very immediate texts and so we can often identify with them. We may also allow them to speak for us on occasion.

Lord, you stand right in front of me. In repeating this psalm, I am exposing myself to you and to your perspectives. I see your compassion and your mercy as you look at me in faith and hope, seeing in me all that I am called to be. 'In you I trust, O my God.' In you I find my joy and affirmation. 'I lift up my soul.'

God sees the truth in the human heart, whatever its condition or situation. Is it so for me too as others stand before me? Am I truly born into God's kingdom of faith and hope and love, or is my own righteousness and the maintaining of it the real issue for me? Can I affirm the faith and goodness of others as Jesus did, wherever he found it, whether they were of his own tradition or not?

✳ *'Show me your ways, O Lord,*
teach me your paths;
guide me in your truth and teach me,
for you are God my Saviour,
and my hope is in you all day long. '   **Psalm 25:4**

Friday July 18   *Amos 7:7–9*

Have we lost our prophetic concern for our nation?

Writ large in this passage is the fact that Israel was a community of faith. It mattered how the whole community expressed its faith in God. In them, God was honing an instrument to witness to his purpose of salvation for all people. Elsewhere in scripture it is said, 'And David shepherded them with integrity of heart' (Psalm 78:72). Here we have a similar expectation of God's chosen: 'Look, I am setting a plumb-line among my people Israel.' Amos had found the people had strayed from the true, and were no longer a nation of integrity. As Christians today, have we succumbed to a comfortable and undemanding individualism which leaves out of account a care about our total community and the impact of faith within the wider world and on our fragile universe? How false was so much Christian insistence that religion should keep out of politics in an apartheid-ridden South Africa! Ask yourself, how deeply do I care about the integrity of my government, and how committedly do I pray for it myself and also with others?

✳ *'May the Lord not be angry, but let me speak just once*
more. What if only ten can be found there?' (Genesis 18:32).
Lord, let me never tire of the work of intercession you have
given me.

Saturday July 19   *Luke 10:21–23*

Having a child's heart

How I love that inversion of the expected world order that we find in Isaiah's prophetic vision of a new order on earth, beginning with the phrase, 'The wolf will live with the lamb' and concluding with, 'and a little child will lead them' (Isaiah 11:6). It is echoed here in Jesus' words of joy that God has revealed his truth to 'little children' and hidden it from 'the wise and learned'. One of the characteristics of children is that they recognise genuineness when they encounter it, and are spontaneous in their response to it. The 'wise and learned' may be laden with vested interests. They may be so locked into their own thinking as to be incapable of recognising truth when they meet it in an unexpected context. Have I perhaps turned my faith into a prison of mental security to keep me inside, and, inevitably in the process, kept others out?

✳ *Open my eyes, Lord, and empty my heart of its self-concern, so that I may be ready to recognise you when you make your visitation.*

FOR REFLECTION – alone or with a group

● Have the rapidity of change, the growing confidence of secular society, and the changing perceptions of the church, eroded our confidence in Jesus Christ, the Saviour of the world?

● How can we help to prepare our local church to be ready to receive 'the world'?

● How deeply committed am I to 'letting go and letting God'?

FOR ACTION

Prayer is the greatest faith action there is, for it is the practical acknowledgement that this is God's world. Pray with renewed commitment for some specific situation in your own context or in the wider world, and be open to allowing your prayer to prompt you to action.

SIMPLE GIFTS
4. Open doors

Notes based on the Revised English Bible by
Jim Cotter

Jim Cotter writes and publishes (as Cairns Publications), and focuses the new Small Pilgrim Places Network, caring in particular for its pilot project at Llandecwyn, near Harlech, in North Wales. He is an ordained member of the Church in Wales, and enjoys friends, theatre, music, and hills.

There is a small church two hundred metres above a beautiful estuary on the north-western coast of Europe, where people have been buried in its *llan* or 'enclosure' for two and a half thousand years, but where few people now live within range. Can it find a new life as a small pilgrim place offering hospitality for quiet prayer and thoughtful conversation? When and how can its doors be open for simple gifts? When and how can yours – in church, in home, in heart?

Sunday July 20   Luke 10:38–42
Kitchens and schoolrooms

Cooks are usually hospitable people. Even if they are fierce about not having intruders in their kitchen, they are glad to see guests enjoying their meals around the table. The true 'hearth' of many a home is the kitchen. The kettle is usually not far from boiling, and many a troubled story has been told as host and guest share a warm drink. Some cooks have even trusted me with the vegetables to prepare, while giving me a cup of tea and sitting me down at a table out of harm's way. There is a clear – if invisible – boundary between territories. The kitchen door may be open, but while the cook bustles, the helper had better sit still in one place. That is the world of Martha.

But something more is afoot in this story. At the time of Jesus, the teacher and the taught were invariably men, and a 'lesson' would take place in spaces exclusively male. There was a strict, permanent, and visible boundary. There was no open door here. However, Jesus was very good at opening previously shut doors. No room where he was present ever had a closed door. So it was typical of him, and revolutionary for his society, that a woman should be 'sitting at his feet': a comfortable, intimate, relaxed place. It was as specific as a seat at a kitchen table, but much more challenging. Disturbing indeed to the boundary setters in any society.

✳ *Pray for cooks and teachers, for guests and pupils, for open and generous minds and deeds.*

Monday July 21   *Colossians 1:24–28*

Open-heart surgery

Think back for a moment to yesterday's reading. For Mary a door was opened of heart and mind and will. Thereafter, she may have shut that door from time to time, for sleep, for privacy, for confidentiality, for recovery, but never permanently. An irrevocable change had taken place. The Spirit that moves through lives affected by Jesus is always gently but insistently opening those doors.

The gospel is always about open secrets, not closed ones. It may be a mystery deeper than any of us can fathom but its message (and its practice) is not exclusive to an inner elite. It is for everybody. It may not be easy to put into practice, but it is not complicated. Even if God's purposes are at times obscure to us, if we focus mind and heart on the way of Jesus, a 'wealth of glory' (verse 27) will be opened up to us. The catch is that we have to be as open and vulnerable as was Jesus if we are to recognise this 'open secret' in all its glory.

The hardest part is to open the doors of hearts and lives to share in the world's suffering. To do this is both for the sake of the gospel and for the living of the gospel. We are called to live every moment in conscious open-heart surgery. The wonder is that as we take on the burdens of others, and as other people take on ours, we find a deep mutual joy welling up within and among us. In everyday terms, my neighbour's shopping bag is lighter than my own.

✳ *Pray for the opening of closed hearts, for a willingness to bear one another's burdens, and for the grace to allow others to share ours.*

Tuesday July 22   *Psalm 24*

Who exactly enters the great doors?

Who precisely are the great west doors of cathedrals and palaces opened for? In this psalm we are given the picture of a ceremonial entrance by a warrior king returning victorious to his court. So God is depicted as a king of glory entering the doors of his dwelling place. Who is outside cheering his progress? Who is inside acclaiming his victory? Would the walking wounded be on the inside? Let alone the severely disfigured? And the prisoners of war?

Is Jesus such a king? Does he not open the doors to the stigmatised, the foreigners, the soldiers, the enemy, indeed to all who accept his invitation to the party? Does he not welcome first and let the food and the drink and the stories and the laughter dissolve the enmity and the separation?

The challenge is this. If a group of people (a church?) does this kind of thing day in day out, they will get into trouble. They will find themselves outside the charmed circles of those with ecclesiastical or political power who by definition keep their doors firmly closed.

✳ *Pray that those who are never invited to banquets will find glory in simple meals with whoever happens to be there.*

Wednesday July 23   *Psalm 15*

Open for justice?

It's all very well. Open doors! Really open for everyone? For anyone? What about those who do not have clean hands and pure hearts? Those who lie and cheat? Those who are malicious and gossipy? Those who charge interest and let others get deeper and deeper into debt? Surely justice demands they be kept out?

I think the next question is this. Do you know of anyone who has never done such things? And do you know anyone who has never done anything but these things? In theory there could be. In practice I have yet to meet one. And if you argue that there are indeed very virtuous people, then what about the systemic decisions made on their behalf by governments and banks? We are all caught up in the structures of injustice (sin), and if the door is closed against one it is closed against all.

Then the question becomes, How do we move, how are we drawn, towards personal and corporate life which is more virtuous and just? I think I am most likely to be changed by someone who welcomes me rather than by someone who shuns me, someone who bears the cost with me of helping me to change – and of waiting until I am prepared to do so. Is not that the character of the God of Jesus?

✳ *Pray that we may grow in our capacity to welcome and in sharing the cost of putting things right.*

Closed doors
Amos is perhaps the fiercest of the prophets. His words sear the wealthy. He thunders in the name of the God of justice, a God whose word cannot be heard (maybe cannot even be uttered) where there are gross inequalities of income and unfair distribution of resources. Verses 5 and 6 focus sharply on those who cannot even rest and enjoy a festival without counting the hours before they can open again for the business of gain by fraud.

Perhaps it is only the poor who really know how to party, who know the mutual giving and receiving in relationships of trust. They are able to relax and enjoy themselves without looking over their shoulders with suspicion and calculation or looking around the room to see what contacts will be useful to cultivate.

The homeless and the destitute look from the cold dark street into the warmly lit restaurant or dining car. The doors are closed and guarded. It is the very opposite of open doors welcoming all and especially sundry to the banquet of God. The trouble for the defended and wealthy is that they won't feel at ease with the company and the seating arrangements. They will exclude themselves. Even open doors cannot make them cross the threshold.

Maybe those inside will risk coming outside again to draw the cold-hearted in.

✳ *Pray that the wealthy may recognise that the outcasts are the only ones who can save them.*

Open hand
What a contrast in tone and atmosphere to that of yesterday's reading! Here is something altogether more poignant and intimate. It speaks of all who have ever loved, who have longed for the beloved, but somehow have missed the moment. The door of the heart is opening but there is something that prevents total trust and abandonment. And it is often a banal something. We wait a few minutes, dithering. We prefer comfort and security to risk. I'm all warm and cosy in bed, and now he comes knocking at the door.

Try an experiment. Make a fist with one of your hands. Let it stand for a closed door. Gradually open your hand to its fullest extent. Let that stand for an open door. Move between the two extremes. What is it like to have your hand half open, ready at a moment's notice to close or open? Then think of the person you love most. Which way is your hand moving? The open hand is of course the hand that is vulnerable and has to trust. It is also more alive.

✳ *Pray for those who automatically close their hands because of past betrayals.*

Saturday July 26   *Genesis 18:1–10*

Open to strangers

Here is a good test of open doors and hearts. How welcoming are you to the unexpected visitor, especially to the stranger? Do you drop everything, even to your inconvenience? Yet, in a tribal desert society, it is a strict law – not least because you do not know when you will need such hospitality yourself.

The story alerts us to the truth that visitors, especially strangers, bear gifts, sometimes to the host's great surprise. Not least do messengers from God. The least likely candidate for angel probably is one. And the host is the one who has the cooking pots handy to share a meal.

We are back to Martha and Mary. The exchange across open doors is the liberating and healing word and touch which take place at the meal with whoever happens to be sitting on either side of you around the table. In the ministry of Jesus, when that exchange takes place, there indeed is the Kingdom of God.

✳ *Pray that we may be alert to the gifts of strangers.*

FOR REFLECTION – alone or with a group

● Try the fist/open hand exercise again, preferably with others. Share the stories that come to mind.
● How many doors and chests do you lock, and why? Is it right to lock away secrets – in chests or in hearts?

FOR ACTION

Do something practical to make your home, your church, your office, your farm, your community centre, more welcoming to strangers.

1 & 2 CHRONICLES

Notes based on the Hebrew Bible by
Jonathan Magonet

Jonathan Magonet is Professor of Bible and Principal of the Leo Baeck College, a Rabbinical seminary in London. His books on biblical subjects include A Rabbi Reads the Psalms, The Subversive Bible *and* From Autumn to Summer: A Biblical Journey Through the Jewish Year *(SCM). He runs an annual Jewish-Christian Bible Week in Germany.*

The Book of Chronicles records the history of Israel from the period of the united monarchy under King David and King Solomon through the division into Northern and Southern Kingdoms, the destruction of the former and the end of the latter, the Kingdom of Judah, when Jerusalem fell and the people were taken into exile in Babylon. Unlike the Books of Samuel and Kings, on which the Chronicler's account is largely based, the author is less interested in the human drama and more concerned with the history of the Temple and other religious institutions.

In preparing these notes, I have tried to allow the biblical text, in its original Hebrew and with its very particular literary style and religious concerns, to speak for itself. This sometimes takes us to unexpected places and leaves us, the readers, with the responsibility of trying to understand the message, or several messages, it is offering. Jewish tradition suggests that though we do not always have to agree with the biblical text, we do have to let it challenge us.

1. David's kingdom established

Sunday July 27   *1 Chronicles 10:1–14*
The old order changeth...

We enter the world of the Chronicler at a dramatic moment of change. Saul, the tragic first King of Israel, dies at his own hand on the battlefield. The full tale of Saul's rise and fall is found in the Book of Samuel. But while the Chronicler will turn to Samuel for this and later chapters, the rest of Saul's story is absent here. Only his death is recorded and the disposal of his body. Added to the account in Samuel is a phrase that his entire household died with him, an exaggeration, but a way of signing him out of history.

Whereas in Samuel the whole story allows us to draw our own conclusions about the significance of Saul's life, the Chronicler adds two concluding verses to sum it up: Saul's death was a punishment from God for rebellion or disobedience. Clearly the Chronicler has his sights set on David as the central figure in his own religious understanding. But nevertheless it is painful to read of a lifetime summarised in such a devastating way. Saul deserves a better epitaph as the first 'messiah', the flawed but nevertheless anointed King of Israel.

✳ *Remember us for life, our Sovereign, who delights in life.*
Traditional Jewish prayer

Monday July 28   *1 Chronicles 11:1–9*
The king is dead, long live the king
Our chapter omits the intrigues, assassinations and other extraordinary events, amounting to civil war, that followed Saul's death. Instead the tribes gather to David in Hebron, his first capital, the place where the patriarchs were buried, establishing his link with Israel's history. Then, in a formal ceremony, the elders make a covenant with David and acknowledge what is already, in fact, a reality: that he is king over the whole of Israel.

Again, as if it is self-evident, we learn that David moves to capture Jerusalem. It is certainly a shrewd political step, since the city stands outside the territories of any of the tribes, a neutral place from which to rule a still divided nation. But it is more than this for the author of Chronicles: it introduces the place where the Temple will one day stand. In the process of capturing it we meet Joab, already a significant figure in David's rise to power in the fuller account in the Book of Samuel, and he will come to play a major, if challenging, part in David's story. But, for this triumphant beginning, the problems recorded in Samuel disappear as David steps onto the stage, the ideal king.

✳ *May the hope of Zechariah one day truly be fulfilled: that Jerusalem will be called 'the city of truth'.*
Based on Zechariah 8:3

Tuesday July 29   *1 Chronicles 12:23–40*
David consolidates his power
The previous passages have listed in detail the soldiers who rallied to David at various stages in his earlier days when he had to flee from

Saul. Now also they support him at the time of his election as king. If the elders gave him his political credentials, the support of the warriors of the different tribes gave him a necessary military credibility.

Such passages serve as a reminder that when the Israelites had demanded that Samuel give them a king, one of their reasons was to protect them from their enemies. Military strength would be a major factor in determining the survival of this nation as it struggled to establish its place amongst the different local kingdoms and alliances. The numbers, which are vast, may be exaggerated or rely on a numbering system that was no longer understood – the word *elef*, translated as 'thousand' may instead have indicated a unit of some sort.

The text emphasises that amongst those who joined David were members of the tribe of Benjamin, Saul's family. This reinforces the view that David was the true choice for the entire nation, something acknowledged even by the family of his former enemy.

✳ *May the will come from you to annul wars and the shedding of blood from the universe, and to extend a peace great and wondrous, in the universe.*   *Nachman of Bratslav*

Wednesday July 30   *1 Chronicles 13:1–14*
The use and abuse of religion
In the parallel account in the Book of Samuel, David's military battles with the Philistines are recorded before the story of the ark. Here David's concern with fulfilling a religious task is given priority. By summoning all of Israel to join him at this moment – again something not recorded in Samuel – the Chronicler completes his account of the support that David has for his actions from the political, the military and now the religious leadership.

But the ark is not an object to be taken for granted. Its power derives from God and if mishandled there are consequences. (In the Book of Samuel the ark is described as the 'ark of God' [in Hebrew, *elohim*] when it is powerless, or 'the ark of the Lord' [in Hebrew, *YHWH*] when God acts through it.)

A rabbinic commentary is highly critical of David for loading the ark on a cart. Did he not realise that in the wilderness period it was carried on the shoulders of the Levites?! But what do you expect from someone who could be so casual about religious formalities as to say (Psalm 119:54): 'Your laws have been my songs in the house of my wandering'?

✳ *Judge of all the earth, as we try to make the world religious, guard us from making our religion too worldly.*

Who is in charge, David or God?

The Chronicler now picks up the episode recorded in an earlier chapter in Samuel of David's defeat of the Philistines. It links with the previous chapter through a word-play. The Hebrew verb *paratz* means 'to break through' or 'break out'. In verse 11 David says, 'God has broken through my enemies like water breaks through', hence the name of the place *ba'al-peritzim*, 'master of breaking through'. In the previous chapter the same word *paratz* is used of God: literally 'breaking through a breaking' against Uzzah for touching the ark, and hence the name of the place *peretz uzzah*, the 'breaking through of Uzzah'. The same God who had 'broken through' against Uzzah, thus defeating David's purposes, was now clearly 'breaking through' on David's behalf.

The Chronicler adds a sentence to the end of the 'Samuel' version, about David's growing reputation and the Eternal bringing 'the dread of him' on all the nations. The Hebrew is ambiguous about whether the 'him' to be dreaded is David or God. But the theme takes us back to the original conquest of the land. Their success was not because of David's military prowess but because God was controlling events.

✳ *'Not to us, Lord, not to us, but to your name give authority,*
   for your faithfulness and your truth.'   Psalm 115:1

David, the 'sweet singer of Psalms'

The Samuel version merely records that the ark was carried to Jerusalem. This version introduces a formal role for the Levites who carried it on their shoulders just as they had done in the days of Moses when they transported it through the wilderness. Here David is portrayed as someone deeply concerned with the proper religious rites, a very different view of him from that in Samuel. It appears to be part of the Chronicler's concern to establish a continuity between David's desire to create the Temple and Solomon's eventual fulfilment of that desire, both actions demonstrating the king as spiritual leader of the people.

The remainder of the chapter has David appointing the Levites as singers and musicians who sang and played before the ark as it was carried to Jerusalem. Again this fills out in considerable detail something that was only briefly mentioned in Samuel. It establishes the role of the Levites in the Temple and probably reflects practices and traditions of the time of the Chronicler. It also reinforces David's reputation as a composer of psalms and a musician. He is the one who oversaw the development of this element of Temple worship.

✻ *'May the fame of God's glory be blessed for ever and God's glory fill all the earth... The prayers of David son of Jesse are completed.'*   Psalm 72:19–20

Saturday August 2   *1 Chronicles 16:1, 7–22*

The lessons of a song of praise

The song of praise to God, sung by Asaph and the musicians, is absent in Samuel. It is an amalgam of two other psalms (105:1–15 and 96:1–13) with additional sentences from Psalm 106:1, 47–48.

A couple of minor changes alter the emphasis. Psalm 105:8 reads, 'He (God) is mindful of his covenant for ever', while the Hebrew text of Chronicles (though not in all the translations) contains a command to Israel, 'Be mindful of his covenant for ever.' Similarly a line is added, not present in Psalm 96, which intrudes between calls on heaven and earth, the sea, fields and forests to rejoice in God, 'and let them say among the nations: "The Lord reigns"' (1 Chronicles 16:31).

The end of the 'psalm', verses 35–36, asks God to gather the people from amongst the nations; this could well reflect the post-exilic origins of the psalm and Chronicles itself. So it is tempting to read something into the additions. The first is a call of reassurance to remember that God's covenant is eternal, despite all the tribulations they have had to face. The second asserts God's rule over all the earth changing a poetic expression into a universal hope.

✻ ***Guardian of the covenant, remember your covenant with us, as we remember our covenant with you.***

FOR REFLECTION – alone or with a group

● By concentrating on the religious aspects of David's life the Chronicler omits his personal strengths and weaknesses, struggles and failures. Does this do justice to David?

● Does it help or hinder us in understanding our own religious struggles?

2. Succession

Sunday August 3   *1 Chronicles 17:1–16*
David is not the one to build the Temple

David's desire to build a home for the ark echoes faithfully the version in Samuel (2 Samuel 7), with at least one minor exception. When David presents his ideas to Nathan, the prophet immediately agrees. It turns out that he is wrong, a reminder that the personal opinions of biblical prophets are no more likely to be correct than those of any other person. It is the word of God that is of ultimate significance.

The text of 2 Samuel 7:4 contains an oddity. Between the opening words, literally, 'It was in that night' and the continuation, 'it was the word of the Lord to Nathan, saying', there is a gap in the Hebrew text. The masoretic notes (the technical instructions for the scribes on how to write the text) state: 'There is a break in the middle of the verse'. This dramatises Nathan's misreading of the situation. But the rabbinic tradition, which loves to fill in such gaps, has God wake Nathan up with the words: 'You know what an oath-maker David is! Before you know it he'll vow not to eat anything till it's built! Get back there and stop him!'

✷ *Help us keep all the promises we make to others; forgive us for the failed promises we make to you alone.*

> *Based on the Jewish* Kol Nidre *(All vows)*
> *prayer of the Day of Atonement*

Monday August 4   *1 Chronicles 21:1–7*
Deconstructing 'satan'

Between the Books of Samuel and Chronicles there has been a spiritual sea-change. The author/s of Samuel have no problem ascribing to God the responsibility for 'enticing' David into doing the census (2 Samuel 24:1). The Chronicler introduces the figure of satan as an intermediary.

This Hebrew word needs some explanation. As a verb it appears in the Bible when an angel prevents Balaam from cursing Israel (Numbers 22:22). There it means 'to get in someone's way', to be an adversary. However, in Balaam's case its role is to prevent him doing something wrong. Here too the satan deflects David from his path, though in this case by encouraging him to do something wrong. In the Book of Job the satan has a specific identity within the divine court amongst other angelic beings.

In Jewish tradition the adversary is the one who tempts us in this life and is our prosecutor when we stand in judgement. But it is not some evil being or force independent of God. A rigorous monotheism cannot extricate God from all aspects of what happens in the world or separate God from the human experience of suffering.

✱ *Source of all life, remove the temptation that awaits us, and the guilt that lies behind us.*

Based on the Jewish evening prayer

Tuesday August 5   *1 Chronicles 21:8–19*

Disturbing images of God

What is wrong with conducting a census? Joab appears to reflect a deep concern within biblical culture about counting people – though there seems to have been no problem when Moses did so in the Book of Numbers at the beginning and again at the end of the wilderness period.

One explanation of this passage is indeed based on the difference between it and Moses' counting. Moses specifies males from the age of twenty years upwards, and this relates to the immediate military needs of the people as they prepare to face the new dangers before them as an emerging nation. But Joab is to count all the males able to 'draw a sword' (2 Samuel 24:9) which would effectively include those much under the age of twenty, thus condemning the next generation to military adventures as David expanded his empire.

So why does God, even through the agency of the satan, entice David in this way? Like God's acceptance of Abel's sacrifice but not Cain's (Genesis 4:3–5), and God's attack on Moses on his way back to Egypt (Exodus 4:24–26), the biblical authors are prepared to offer glimpses of mysterious, disturbing and challenging dimensions of God, who cannot be taken for granted.

✱ *Help us accept the teaching of Isaiah: 'For my thoughts are not your thoughts, nor my ways your ways – an oracle of the Lord. For as high as the heavens over the earth so are my ways above your ways and my thoughts above your thoughts.'*

Isaiah 55:8–9

Wednesday August 6   *1 Chronicles 21:20 – 22:1*

Jerusalem between faith and politics

Jerusalem was the city of the Jebusites before David conquered it. It already had a long history as a religious centre, for Abraham had exchanged blessings there with Melchizedek, 'King of

Salem', the priest of El Elyon, the Most High God (Genesis 14:18–22). David is clear that such a significant place, that God has indicated cannot be acquired either by conquest or as a gift, must be paid for at an appropriate price.

The transformation of Jerusalem from a political capital into the spiritual centre of the nation, the future site of the Temple, is bound up with David's experience of awe and fear at the sight of the angel with the drawn sword. Nevertheless there is a tension in this vision, which hints at both the power and the tragedy of Jerusalem down to the present day. Some of the psalms make a distinction between 'Zion', the spiritual centre, and 'Jerusalem', the centre of political and national life. But with its intoxicating mixture of spiritual passion and political or national pride, this 'city of peace, shalom', continues to challenge and even to destroy all who seek to claim possession of it.

✴ *Let us pray for the peace of Jerusalem; may those who love it be at ease. May there be peace within its walls, tranquillity within its homes.* Based on Psalm 122:6–7

Thursday August 7 1 Chronicles 22:5–13

David, the shedder of blood

Once again the Chronicler omits all the intrigues and struggles for power to be found in the earlier accounts, this time in the first chapters of the Book of Kings. Solomon is already the chosen successor and David offers him guidance, especially regarding the building of the Temple.

Why was David himself unable to build the Temple? When Solomon discusses the matter with King Hiram of Tyre (1 Kings 5:17), he explains that David was so engaged in wars he did not have time to undertake such a major building activity. Perhaps Solomon was being diplomatic in talking to an outsider. But here David is more explicit. He is a man who has shed blood, and it is not for such a man to build a religious sanctuary. Instead, the building will be completed by a son born into a situation of peace, shalom, as the name 'Solomon', *shlomo*, indicates.

A rabbinic comment links this to an earlier commandment about the building of the altar (Exodus 20:22). It should not be built with stones hewn by an iron tool because 'the altar is created to help prolong life, but an iron tool, like a sword, shortens life'!

✴ *May the words of Isaiah be fulfilled: 'They shall turn their swords into ploughshares and their spears into pruning-hooks. Nation shall not lift up sword against nation, never again shall they train for war.'* Isaiah 2:4

David introduces Solomon

The story of Solomon's succession reaches its climax as David presents him before a public assembly of the leadership of the nation. The Chronicler is particularly interested in the religious structure of the nation, so he puts the initial emphasis on Solomon's task of building the Temple that David was not allowed to undertake.

David links his own selection as king back to the choice of the tribe of Judah for leadership and hence forward to Solomon, his son. But all depends on their loyalty to God's commandments if they are to continue to possess the land, with the Temple as the enduring sign of God's presence.

David's frustrated wish to build the Temple in his own lifetime led to a rabbinic legend that impudent people used to go to David's window and call out: 'David, David, when will the Temple be built? When will we be able to go to the House of the Lord?', implying the time would not come until after David's death! But David suppressed his anger and instead wrote a psalm which he hoped he could one day sing (Psalm 122:1): 'I rejoiced when they said to me, "Let us go up to the House of the Lord."'

✷ *Source of our life, help us turn our frustrations into*
opportunities, our anger into creativity.

The king is dead, long live the king!

Once again the Chronicler has glossed over a series of challenges to Solomon's succession that are graphically recorded in 1 Kings 1—2. The version in the Book of Kings describes Solomon as simply obeying his father's dying advice and wishes. Nevertheless, Solomon acts with ruthlessness in removing a potential rival to the throne in his older brother Adonijah, and the latter's supporters amongst the military, priestly and prophetic leadership. All of which becomes the bland statement here: 'All the leaders and all the army commanders and also the sons of King David pledged allegiance to Solomon the king' (1 Chronicles 29:24).

The problems that Solomon had to confront were part of the public record and well known. As in the Chronicler's reworking of the material on David, the focus in this account is on the king's reign itself and not on the personal life of the king. Instead of the tabloid version we have a document that focuses on the achievements of David in establishing the political and religious foundations of the state which are then brought to completion by his son Solomon. Their private lives are subsumed to their public achievements on behalf of God and the people.

✳ *You who know the secrets of all flesh, may our private truth and our public actions never be too far apart.*

FOR REFLECTION – alone or with a group
● Why is the Chronicler so committed to the centralisation of Israel's worship in the Temple in Jerusalem?
● How do we separate the spiritual aspects of Jerusalem from the political and other dimensions that have turned the 'city of peace' into a cause of bloodshed from biblical times till today?

3. Solomon

Sunday August 10   *2 Chronicles 1:1, 7–12*
The wisdom of Solomon
Solomon's modest request for wisdom is granted and much more as well. A rabbinic parable explains that Solomon's request was like that of a counsellor who had been raised in the court of the king. The king said to him, 'Ask whatever you want from me.' The counsellor thought, 'If I ask for silver and gold, that is all I will get.' So he thought: 'I will ask for the hand of the king's daughter, for that will include everything.' So Solomon asked for wisdom, for that included everything.

The first book of Kings (3:16–27) records the famous story of the two women who came in judgement before Solomon. Each had given birth to a child but one had died, and each claimed the living child was hers. When Solomon threatened to cut the child in two so that they could share it, one agreed but the 'true' mother said: 'Give her the living child but do not kill it.' Solomon awarded the child to her.

Even the wise Solomon could not have known who the physical mother was, nor could this test reveal it. His wisdom lay in awarding it to the one whose instinct was truly maternal.

✳ *Judge of all the earth, may we always get the balance right between the judgement of the law and our human needs.*

187

Solomon acknowledges David

The building of the Temple is complete and with due fanfares, ceremonies, processions and singing it is dedicated. The Chronicler has emphasised throughout that Solomon was finishing the work started by David his father. Nevertheless, a rabbinic legend suggests that Solomon might have tried to claim too much of the credit. The story goes that when Solomon tried to bring the ark into the Holy of Holies the gates refused to open. So he tried quoting Psalm 24:7, a psalm of David: 'O Gates, lift up your heads! Up high, you everlasting doors, that the King of glory may enter.' They asked, 'Who is the King of glory?' and he replied, 'The Lord, strong and mighty' (Psalm 24:8). The gates did not respond, and Solomon tried again: 'O Gates, lift up your heads! Up high, you everlasting doors' (Psalm 24:9). Again they asked, 'Who is the King of glory?' and his answer, 'The Lord of hosts, he is the King of glory', still did not satisfy them. Only when he mentioned David his father was there an immediate response: 'O Lord God, turn not away the face of your anointed; remember the good deeds of David your servant' (2 Chronicles 6:42).

✱ *You who are called 'the king above the kings of kings': may the good deeds of King David inspire us, and may we learn the lessons of his failures.*

Centralising worship in the Temple

Solomon's speech purports to quote words that God has previously said to David. But the passage that appears to be the source, in 2 Samuel 7:6–17, has a very different emphasis. There, God had challenged David by saying, 'In all the time I have accompanied the children of Israel in their wanderings, I never asked any of the leaders to build me a home!' True, that was a rhetorical ploy to stop David from building the Temple, but Solomon has inverted it to mean, 'but now I have indeed chosen such a place, and appointed such a leader', that is, Solomon himself.

Precisely because the Temple was a radical departure from Israel's earlier nomadic experience of God, Solomon has to create this authorisation for what he is doing. A few chapters earlier we read that Gibeon was the place where the ark was located, and where Solomon had his vision of God. Samuel used to serve in the Temple at Shiloh, and David once took refuge with the priests of Nob, another shrine. Alongside the language of prayer and exhortation there are some diplomatic moves here as Solomon establishes the legitimacy of his rule and this new central place for the cult, the Temple.

✱ *'The earth is mine alone, and you are only tenants with me'* (Leviticus 25:23). *May we learn to distinguish our desire for the spirit of a holy place from our greed to own the real estate where it is located.*

Wednesday August 13   *2 Chronicles 6:12–21*

Solomon's prayer at the dedication of the Temple

Solomon's prayer is very carefully constructed but one can hear behind his words some of the issues he is addressing. For example, his insistence that the whole universe is not large enough to contain God, let alone this 'house' (verse 18), is both a modest statement about his achievement (while at the same time pointing to the magnificence of the Temple!) and an answer to those who might mistakenly imagine that God would indeed, like the idols of other nations, 'live' in this Temple.

Having established the relationship he would like to have personally with God, he offers the same to his people. Despite the formality, even correctness, of his words, Rashi, the celebrated mediaeval Jewish commentator, detected a hint of a more private pain when Solomon adds: 'to hearken to the cry and to the prayer of your servant' (verse 19). The word 'cry', *rinnah*, usually means a shout of joy, but sometimes it refers to a cry of distress (1 Kings 22:36; Lamentations 2:19). Hence Rashi's remark, 'Anyone who flees in distress will not pray but express his cry in secret.' That is the cry that God alone hears.

✱ *May God always hear the unspoken words of those who flee in distress, and may we always respond to their needs.*

Thursday August 14   *2 Chronicles 7:11–22*

The covenant with God and its conditions

God appears again to Solomon at night and responds positively to his prayer. He accepts Solomon's theological assumption – that natural disasters are evidence of God's displeasure because Israel has failed in some way to live up to their covenant with God. Nevertheless there is always the possibility of *teshuvah*, literally 'turning', turning away from wrongdoing and back to God, 'repentance' on their part, at which point God will forgive them and remove the threat. However it is noteworthy that whereas Solomon has spoken of natural disasters, drought, locusts and pestilence (2 Chronicles 6:26–28) and also man-made ones like combat with an enemy, God only refers to removing natural ones: 'I will heal their land' (verse 14).

So the option of exile from the land through enemy actions remains as an ultimate punishment if the Israelites break the laws of the covenant and serve other gods. It is worth recalling that a covenant is effectively a kind of contract between two individuals or groups, though what binds them is also a sense of mutual love and loyalty. Nevertheless there are terms and conditions attaching to both partners in such a contract and inevitably there are also penalties for breaking it.

✳ *Our Father, our Sovereign, remove pestilence, sword, famine, captivity and destruction from the children of your covenant.*
   Traditional Jewish Prayer for the Day of Atonement

Friday August 15   *2 Chronicles 9:1–12*
The Queen of Sheba
Solomon's encounter with the Queen of Sheba is the source of innumerable legends. But the biblical account is tantalisingly incomplete. What were the riddles she posed to him (verse 1) that he answered so well? Both the Jewish and the Muslim traditions fill the gap by offering sample questions that she posed. For example: 'A wooden well with an iron bucket, which draws up grains of sand and pours out water – what is it?' Solomon's correct answer is 'a tube for applying mascara' – the iron bucket is the applicator, which draws the powder (grains of sand) from its container, the 'wooden well'. But if it gets in the eyes they water.

The legend of Solomon's wisdom led to the tradition that he composed three books, but in what order? In one version, as a young man in love he wrote the Song of Songs. In middle age he wrote Proverbs, and when he was old and world-weary Ecclesiastes. But another version reverses this. Only a young person could write a book as cynical as Ecclesiastes! In middle age he did indeed write Proverbs. And when he was old and nostalgic he wrote Song of Songs!

✳ *Blessed are you, our Living God, Sovereign of the universe, you have given a share of your wisdom to those in awe of you.*
Jewish prayer on seeing people with religious knowledge and wisdom

The folly of a king

Beneath the surface of the Chronicler's view of the seamless continuity between David and Solomon there are any number of problems. That Jeroboam is in exile in Egypt is a brief reminder of an earlier potential rebellion that Solomon suppressed (1 Kings 11:26–40). Now, at this delicate moment of the succession, old concerns about the previous regime need to be addressed.

Rehoboam makes such an elementary political mistake that even the biblical view that God caused it so as to fulfil the prophecy about Jeroboam, mentioned in 1 Kings 11, is hardly credible.

The Hebrew text is quite scornful about Rehoboam's youthful advisers. The term 'elders' means literally 'elderly men' as well as those with wisdom and authority within society. In stark contrast Rehoboam's companions are literally called 'children'. Their childishness is revealed by their advice.

In such traditional cultures age is recognised as the source of wisdom, a view maintained by rabbinic tradition: 'If youngsters tell you to build and elders tell you to demolish, obey the elders and do not obey the youngsters, for the building of the youngsters is in reality demolition and the demolition of the elders is in reality building' (Babylonian Talmud Nedarim 40a).

✳ *What can we say before you, for in your presence are not the powerful as nothing, the famous as if they had never existed, the learned as if without knowledge and the intelligent as if without insight?*

From a Jewish morning prayer

FOR REFLECTION – alone or with a group
● What is the relationship between wisdom, which includes secular knowledge and intellectual thought, and the 'truths' of religion?
● Solomon built the Temple, but was judged for bringing foreign cults into Israel through his marriages and political alliances. How should we judge his achievement?

---

4. The divided kingdom

Sunday August 17   *2 Chronicles 12:1–16*
Living with political realities

This chapter establishes the *realpolitik* that will form the background for the history of the two kingdoms. For they lie along the key trade route between the 'superpowers' of their day, Egypt to the south and Assyria/Babylon to the north. Their independence is always affected by the rise and fall of those empires and the degree of control each will exert in turn. A rabbinic tradition (Babylonian Talmud Pesachim 119a) details these recurrent changes, as follows.

The treasures of the Temple and the king's house, which Shishak removed back to Egypt, were actually the booty that the Israelites had taken from the Egyptians during the exodus (Exodus 12:35–36). But this wealth had originally come to Egypt when Joseph gathered moneys from people who came there to buy grain during the years of famine. In turn these treasures were taken from Shishak by the king of Ethiopia, but then regained by King Asa of Judah (2 Chronicles 14:13). Judah lost them to the Arameans, who lost them to the Ammonites, and they fell again subsequently into the hands of Judah who lost them to the Assyrians who lost them to the Babylonians, who lost them to the Greeks and finally to the Romans!

✳ **Blessed be God who has no fault and no forgetfulness, who shows no favour and takes no bribe. You are righteous in all your ways and living in all your deeds.**

From the Jewish daily morning service

Monday August 18   *2 Chronicles 15:1–9*

The struggle for a people's soul

The Chronicler expands a few verses in 1 Kings (15:9–24) about King Asa to three chapters (14–16). The emphasis is upon themes common to the book, including the recurrence of divine prophecies and the view that loyalty to God, through the correct ritual and liturgical acts, leads to material success. Moreover Asa's policies and the resultant prosperity serve to attract back those of the other tribes who had seceded with Jeroboam to the Northern Kingdom, thus partly restoring the intact nation of the past.

On the negative side, throughout the book, the Chronicler is concerned with the rise of idolatry, even though by his own time the forms described here had long since disappeared. Idol worship was introduced by Solomon, who built altars in Jerusalem to the gods of his wives. It was made worse by the next generations of kings, Rehoboam and Abijah, being purged by Asa, only to be reintroduced later.

The great gathering in Jerusalem in the third month (verse 10) would coincide with the festival of Shavuot, 'weeks', the commemoration of the giving of the Torah, the divine teaching, on Mount Sinai and the entry into the covenant with God.

✳ *Lord, our God, we put our hope in you. Soon let us witness the glory of your power when the worship of material things shall pass away from the earth and idols shall at last be cut off.*

From the Jewish daily prayers

Tuesday August 19   *2 Chronicles 20:1–30*

God as Sovereign over all nations

The previous chapters have established Jehoshaphat as a 'good' king, a worthy successor of his father Asa, continuing his policy of keeping out idol worship in Judah. As a politician he seems to have attempted more problematic alliances with successive kings of Israel, on one occasion becoming involved in a dangerous military adventure (chapter 18). Here he is confronted by several local enemies, only to be rescued by his continuing faith in God.

The chapter is full of echoes. Jehoshaphat stands in the Temple evoking Solomon's prayer at its dedication, seeking the help from God that Solomon had called for. The enemies, Moab and Ammon, are traditionally part of Israel's family, even if in a rather scandalous way, since they were born of Lot, Abraham's nephew, and his two daughters after the destruction of Sodom. But they were also Israel's enemies during the wilderness period, a memory that Jehoshaphat also evokes.

Again the Chronicler reinforces a theme that has already appeared (2 Chronicles 15:5–6), that God is the ruler of all the nations of the world, determining their destinies. Therefore such military threats must have meaning within God's plan for Israel, if they can but fathom it and respond as God wishes.

✳ *May the day come soon when the world will be set right by the rule of God and all humanity shall speak out in your name.*

Jewish daily prayer

Wednesday August 20   *2 Chronicles 26:1–23*

The daily struggle to survive

Though King Uzziah tends to blend into the list of Judah's kings, he evokes a particular memory in certain Jewish circles. The pioneering generation who helped create the modern State of Israel at the beginning of the twentieth century were deeply engaged in agriculture, draining mosquito-ridden swamps and clearing rocks from potentially fertile land. One thing that sustained them was finding biblical passages that echoed their experience. Some they turned into songs. One such was based on Uzziah's building projects: 'Now Uzziah built towers in Jerusalem ... and he strengthened them. And he built towers in the desert and he hewed many cisterns' (2 Chronicles 26:9–10). Each time around, the words are sung faster and a tone higher, an impossible Hebrew tongue-twister. The song reflected their desire to reclaim the land, but also the need to find water and concerns about self-defence and security.

Behind the Chronicler's customary interest in whether Uzziah was a 'good' or 'bad' king we have a stark reminder of the precariousness of life in biblical times, a society dependent on rain and a good harvest for survival in a world under constant threat from the unstable regimes and marauding tribes of the region.

✳ *May we never be in need of the charity of others nor their loans but dependent on your hand alone which is full, open, holy and ample; so shall we never lose our self-respect nor be put to shame.* From the Jewish grace after meals

Thursday August 21 *2 Chronicles 33:1–12*

King Manasseh repents

Manasseh is the archetypal 'bad' king of the Bible. Indeed because of his sins Jerusalem would one day fall.

The rabbis pondered his repentance. When Manasseh realised how serious his situation was, he remembered a verse his father used to read to him: 'When you are in distress, and when all these decrees have come to you, in the end of days you will return to the Lord your God and listen to the divine voice. For the Lord your God is a merciful God, who will not turn you adrift and will not destroy you, and will not forget the covenant of your fathers that God swore to them' (Deuteronomy 4:30–31). But he prayed on the basis that if God answered him, well and good, and if not, then all gods were alike.

The angels blocked up the windows to prevent the prayer reaching God, saying: 'Will you accept the repentance of someone who worshipped idols and erected an image in the Temple?' But God replied: 'If I do not accept him in repentance, I am locking the door before all repentant sinners!' What did God do? He dug a tunnel for Manasseh under the Throne of Glory!

✳ *Reach out to our minds so that your being fills us with awe; pierce our hearts so that we love you – then we shall return to you, both in truth and with a perfect heart.*
From the Jewish prayers for the Day of Atonement

The scroll in the Temple

The discovery of the scroll in the Temple, identified with either the whole or large parts of the Book of Deuteronomy, clearly had a major impact. It is seen as triggering Josiah's great reform, the third recorded by the Chronicler (after that of Asa in 2 Chronicles 15:8–15 and of Hezekiah in 2 Chronicles 29).

Why did the people go to Huldah? The question assumes that it would have been more 'natural' to go to a male prophet, like Zephaniah, Jeremiah or Ezekiel who were around at this period. So ingenious solutions are offered by the rabbis: Jeremiah was too young at the time, and the others were too radical to be asked. All of which is to ignore the fact that any number of other 'professional' prophets could have been chosen.

Perhaps Huldah was simply the right person at that historical moment. The fact of her being a woman fits in with previous biblical examples where women played a crucial role at a transitional moment, like the Hebrew midwives, Moses' mother and sister and Pharaoh's daughter at the time of the exodus. Significantly Hannah's prayers for a son (1 Samuel 1–2) ushered in the monarchy, whilst now Huldah's prophecy was to mark its end.

✳ *Let us no more talk with haughty pride,*
Let no arrogance leave our mouth.
For the Lord is an all-knowing God
Who weighs our deeds.

Based on Hannah's prayer 1 Samuel 2:3

A future and a hope

The closing chapter of Chronicles draws the story to the inevitable end that the writer has predicted. With hindsight the Chronicler has placed a particular interpretation on this history, from the triumphant start with David and Solomon, through the division of the kingdoms and the ups and downs of successive kings, judged by their loyalty to God alone, through a particular form of worship centred on the Temple in Jerusalem.

The Book of Kings ends on a slightly hopeful note with the fate of King Jehoiachin in Babylonian exile. Chronicles likewise ends in an upbeat way with King Cyrus of Persia's wish to rebuild the Temple in Jerusalem. These same verses will reappear at the start of the Book of Ezra , which records the actual return from exile.

Despite what has happened in the past, the future remains open. The destruction of Jerusalem and the Temple is not the end but only a stage, however disastrous, in Israel's ongoing relationship with God. So the last gift of the Chronicler is the hope, however grim the situation, of return to God, of restoration and renewal. It is a hope that must be earned.

* ***May all come to accept the duty of building your kingdom so that your reign of goodness shall come soon and last for ever.***   *From the Jewish daily prayers*

FOR REFLECTION – alone or in a group

● Behind the emphasis of the Chronicler on the 'religious' interpretation of Israel's history is the reality of international politics, alliances, border disputes and wars that successive generations of Israelite leaders had to address.

● Does the Chronicler's approach help or hinder us in confronting these issues today?

● In what way are these stories of a world long since disappeared of use to us in today's seemingly very different world?

FOR ACTION

The Temple is no more, but Jerusalem remains the site where Jews, Christians and Muslims are caught up in struggles over the religious, political and national significance of the site where it stood. It is easy to take sides but if conflicts are to be resolved, and not simply aggravated, people have to try to understand the complex claims and counterclaims, but above all the significance of the place for all three faiths. A good project would be to study the history of Jerusalem as a shared enterprise together with people of all three faiths.

INTERNATIONAL BIBLE READING ASSOCIATION
1020 Bristol Road, Selly Oak, Birmingham, Great Britain B29 6LB

ORDER FORM – For 2004 Books

Please send me the following books:

Name: _____

Address: _____

_____

_____ Postcode: _____

*To qualify for 2004 books at these special IBRA readers' prices, this order form must be used (photocopies not accepted). Your order will be dispatched when **all** books are available. Mail order only.*

Code	Title of Book	Quantity	Unit Price	Total
ZYW31	Words for Today 2004		£6.75	
ZYL32	Light for Our Path 2004		£6.75	
ZYF0897	Finding Our Way Together Book 1		£8.00	
ZYF0910	Finding Our Way Together Book 2		£8.00	
ZYF0938	Finding Our Way Together Book 3		£8.00	
ZYF0974	Finding Our Way Together Book 4		£8.00	
ZYF0897-SET	Finding Our Way Together series (4 BOOKS)		£25.00	
ZYD0989	Discovering Christ *Advent & Christmas*		£8.00	
ZYD0994	Discovering Christ *Ascension & Pentecost*		£8.00	
ZYD0999	Discovering Christ *Lent & Easter*		£8.00	
ZYO0990	Online to God		£6.25	
ZYL0781	Living Prayers For Today		£15.50	
ZYM0902	More Living Prayers For Today		£15.50	

❏ I enclose a cheque (Payable to IBRA)	Total cost of books
❏ Please charge my MASTERCARD/VISA/SWITCH	UK postage included Overseas – add £3.00 airmail per book
Card No: _____	
Issue No (Switch): _____	Donation to International Fund
Expiry Date: _____	TOTAL DUE
Signature: _____	*Payment in **Pounds Sterling**, please*

The INTERNATIONAL BIBLE READING ASSOCIATION is a Registered Charity

International Bible Reading Association

Help us to continue our work of providing Bible study notes for use by Christians in the UK and throughout the world. The need is as great as it was when IBRA was founded in 1882 by Charles Waters as part of the work of the Sunday School Union.

Please leave a legacy to the International Bible Reading Association.

An easy-to-use leaflet has been prepared to help you provide a legacy. Please write to us at the address below and we will send you this leaflet – and answer any questions you might have about a legacy or other donations. Please help us to strengthen this and the next generation of Christians.

Thank you very much

International Bible Reading Association
Dept 298, 1020 Bristol Road
Selly Oak
Birmingham B29 6LB
Great Britain
Tel. 0121 472 4242
Fax 0121 472 7575

Charity Number 211542

THE TWELVE
1. Called

Notes based on the New English Bible by
Bernard Thorogood

Bernard Thorogood served as a missionary in the South Pacific for 18 years and then in 1970 became General Secretary of the London Missionary Society/Council for World Mission. From 1980 to 1992 he was General Secretary of the United Reformed Church, with much ecumenical involvement. Now retired, he lives in Sydney and is a minister in the Uniting Church in Australia.

The first apostles were just an ordinary, assorted group of men, not especially learned or wise or holy. But Jesus called them to be with him and they had the courage to say 'Yes'. They became foundation people because they were wholly convinced that Jesus was the gift of God present in human life, the one servant Lord who showed the mind and heart and healing power of God.

Why twelve? Perhaps because the twelve tribes were named for the sons of Jacob and they made up the Old Israel. The apostles were to be the fathers of the New Israel. This point is stressed by Luke in 22:30.

Why were there no women among the twelve? This question has been raised often in recent years. One possible answer is that Jesus deliberately chose men to show that it should be men who should lead and govern the church. The Roman Catholic Church still holds to that position. I belong to another tradition. I believe that it would have been thought improper at that time for women to belong to such a close company of travelling disciples and then to assume leadership. It was a male-dominated society. But we live in a very different world, where women may become leaders in every walk of life. We also remember that there were women among the followers of Jesus and they played a major part in the gospel narrative. It was women who were the first witnesses of the resurrection. They became heralds of the gospel and so, in practice, apostles. But in this series of readings we concentrate on the twelve men who are named and who are honoured in Christian history as the apostles. They lead us to the calling of Christ for women and men to be apostles today, sharing the way, the truth and the life we find in him.

Enrolled in the school

It was after a night of prayer that Jesus called and named the Twelve. This emphasises the importance of the choice; there was nothing casual or hasty about it. For Jesus it was a vital matter to have a small group of committed friends who were to become his messengers. In verse 13 we have both words: 'disciples' and 'apostles', learners and speakers, pupils in the school of Christ and missionaries who will carry the message. These twelve men were to be both.

There is a little uncertainty about the list of names. Here we have two named Judas. In Mark and Matthew we find a Thaddaeus in the list but no second Judas. It may be that after the betrayal by Judas Iscariot that very name carried a stigma, so the second Judas was called by another name from his family and so Thaddaeus comes onto the roll.

The most significant aspect for us is that Jesus chose and called people to be with him. We still use that language of call. We say that a person is called to the work of priest or pastor and that ministry is a calling. Yet the voice that is heard is usually a human voice, perhaps a committee of the church, and it may be mistaken. Our judgements about people are not infallible. Does God call? Surely yes. We are all called to a life of faith and service. But we do not always hear or interpret what God calls us to do. Ministry is a calling every day; the voice comes through scripture, a mourning family, a prayer in a hospital ward, the eagerness of young believers and all the adventure of Christian fellowship.

✴ *May we listen, Lord Jesus, for your call;*
   and when we hear, may we be ready to obey.

Apostles and deacons

We jump forward today to a passage which helps us to understand the special tasks of the apostles. There were many people who followed Jesus. We know by name the Twelve and some of the women, but most are unknown to us. Here in Acts, after Jesus had ended his earthly life and after Pentecost, the distinctive work of the Twelve had become clear.

They took as their great calling by God the ministry of prayer and preaching. So an apostle had to be focused on the dynamic relation of God and humanity. He prayed, and this includes both public leadership and private meditation, so that God's will might be done in this unruly world. He preached because the events and the words of Jesus had to be shared as widely as possible so that the revelation of God might be known to all.

Other people, equally spiritual, equally blessed, had to concentrate on the practical tasks, and those listed here were called deacons. 'Deacon' and 'minister' both mean 'servant'. Jesus sets the model. As he washed the disciples' feet, taking on him the form of a servant, so those called by the Spirit are servants too.

✳ *Whatever our special calling*
may we respond with joy
and give all we are for the kingdom of God.

Tuesday August 26   *John 1:35–42*

Take a friend

How significant John the Baptist was for all the story that followed! We often forget him as we read of the apostles and their preaching, but he was the key preparer of the way. It was his gift and vision to see that God was speaking to the world through Jesus, and his humility enabled him to step aside and point others to the Lamb of God. If the preacher can do that, and if the whole church can do that, we shall be witnesses, directing attention away from ourselves and saying, 'There is the light of the world who has brought truth and healing and freedom for you.'

Verses 40–42 tell us of the Andrew spirit, the reason why Andrew is often regarded as the patron of missionaries. The first thing he did was to run off to find his brother so that they could both meet Jesus together. Have a thought for the brother or sister, the close relative who can make a pilgrimage with you, rather than going alone. Take a friend. One of our frequent false assumptions is that we have no influence. 'I'm not a preacher. I can't do anything to build the church.' But in the family or the workplace or the leisure club there may be someone who does listen to you and may respond to an invitation.

In verse 42 Jesus gave a new name to Simon. It is Cephas in the Aramaic language, Petros in Greek and 'rock' in English. It was some years before Peter showed a rock-solid character but Jesus was hopeful. When we know the confidence that God places in us, we become stronger too.

✳ *We think of our own family. Is there someone who needs to*
meet the Christ-friend today?

Sons of Thunder

Although Luke does not mention this name, it comes from Mark's list of the Twelve (3:17) and may have originated in this incident on the road to Jerusalem. Here is the human nature which says, 'Let us punish those ungenerous people', and here is the grace which replies, 'No, we just move on.'

That human voice is loud in our ears. 'Let's lock them up and throw away the key.' 'Put them on the next plane back to where they came from.' 'That lot took our land a century ago and now we'll get our own back.' We hear and read it, this spirit of revenge, alive in our world – perhaps in our town. It is an animal instinct and it occurs in all racial groups.

The way, the truth and the life are very different. 'Father, forgive them for they don't know what they are doing.' As James and John followed Christ and heard that dying prayer, they entered into God's way of forgiveness, the only hope of peace and real human fellowship. We are called to live that way in the church so that the human family may not be poisoned by the passions of pay-back. We pray for all who now seek revenge in useless feuds in many parts of the world.

✳ *Father, forgive us our sins*
as we forgive those who sin against us.

The loved disciple

What an amazing title – 'the disciple whom Jesus loved'. Who was he? In the gospel of John we never find the name John mentioned. But we find this phrase four times: 13:23, 19:26, 20:2 and here. Those are all very significant moments in the story of Jesus: the last supper, the cross and the empty tomb on Easter morning. This disciple was so trusted by Jesus that he committed his own mother to his care. Now in today's passage we find that he is the disciple whose witness to Christ is given in this gospel. He was John, son of Zebedee, brother of James, who lived to old age at Ephesus. That is the testimony of the early church.

In verses 20–22 we find Peter asking a foolish question in his usual impetuous way. 'What will happen to John? Will his future be like mine?' Jesus did not answer directly but told Peter not to worry about the fate of others; he must simply follow Jesus and take what comes. What is going to happen to those non-

believers? We may ask but it is not for us to know. We are called
to have faith and follow all the way.

✳ *I cannot see what lies ahead for me,*
but you are there, and that is peace, dear Lord.

Friday August 29   *Acts 8:26–40*
Philip the interpreter
This high official from Ethiopia was already a seeker for truth. He
had come a long, hard journey to Jerusalem as a pilgrim and was
reading the Jewish scripture as he returned south. So he was
prepared for the new light of the gospel.

Philip was one of the first to be called (John 1:44) and was close
to Jesus throughout the ministry. Here in Acts we find him as the
evangelist in Samaria (8:5), then sent by God to meet the Ethiopian.
He knew his purpose was to interpret the ancient scripture as
pointing to Jesus. The passage in Isaiah 53 may be seen as
referring to Israel as a whole, this suffering, wounded people, and
most Jews have understood it that way. Philip saw it as pointing
directly to Christ who was wounded for us all, the Lamb of God.

So the preacher is still the interpreter. 'What does this verse
mean, pastor?' In response we seek to relate the ancient text both
to ourselves and to Christ, so that we may know God's word for
today. Philip certainly fulfilled that task. The result – a changed
official who was baptised and returned to his country and (so
tradition says) founded the church in Ethiopia which still lives today.

✳ *Guide us in our reading, Lord.*
May your Spirit be like Philip for us,
showing us your light in old words.

Saturday August 30   *John 1:43–51*
Suspicion and conviction
Apart from this passage, the only other reference to Nathanael is
John 21:2, so we know nothing of his background or trade, or of his
future life. But we do know he came from Cana in Galilee. When he
spoke so slightingly about Nazareth it was local pride speaking.
What good can come from that dull and dusty place over the hills?
How could the local carpenter's son be the Messiah?

When Nathanael met Jesus he was soon convinced. The
conversation in verses 47–51 hinges on the name Israel. 'Here is
an Israelite indeed' and 'King of Israel', followed by the vision of

angels ascending and descending, all point to the story of Jacob/Israel in Genesis 28. Jesus was telling Nathanael and the others that they would be like Jacob and see the glory of God, and, through faith, would lead the way for a whole people.

Here suspicion was changed to conviction. We live in a sceptical generation and it is when people actually meet Jesus – in the Bible, through preaching and worship, in acts of love and healing – that they can respond in faith. Come and see. Can your congregation say that with confidence?

✷ *Son of God and King of Israel,*
be our ladder between earth and heaven,
so we may glimpse your glory.

FOR REFLECTION – alone or with a group

● Think of what we mean by a calling. Do we sense that God calls a few people to be part of his kingdom, or all people? Is it just ministers who are called by God, or is every Christian called to a ministry? Think of people you know who have a conviction about their task in life. Pray for them. Think again about what God calls you to do.

2. Chosen

Sunday August 31   *Matthew 9:9–13*
The tax collector

There can have been few people in Palestine more disliked than Matthew, son of Levi. We are not generally very fond of tax collectors, although they are good citizens. But in those days they were hated for working on behalf of Rome, the occupying power, and also lining their own pockets at the expense of the common people. We meet another, Zacchaeus, in Luke 19, and he was 'very rich' from his corrupt dealings. So Matthew was a man most Israelites would have shunned and many would have feared.

Jesus called him and joined him in a meal, then numbered him among the Twelve. No wonder the Pharisees were highly critical. Would a genuine holy man lunch with such an outcast? Jesus replied unambiguously. He came to heal those who knew their need and unworthiness, not those who considered themselves to be righteous.

An African proverb says that no one is so hard to wake up as the one who is pretending to be asleep. There are people so persuaded of their own rights, decisions, gifts and authority that they cannot be woken up to grasp the hand of God. Yet still among the religious leaders of the day were Nicodemus, Gamaliel and Joseph of Arimathea who saw something wonderful in Jesus; we cannot write off any group as beyond the call of God.

✳ *Help us to respect all people,*
to see possibility in everyone
and to know that we all may be changed by grace.

Monday September 1   John 20:24–29
The honest doubter
The mentions of Thomas in the gospel of John suggest a remarkably honest man. In the story of Lazarus (chapter 11) he declared that all the Twelve should go with Jesus to Bethany 'that we may die with him'. He saw trouble ahead. At the last supper he was prepared to question Jesus. 'Lord, we don't know where you are going, so how can we know the way?' (14:5). Here he was unwilling to accept the amazing news of resurrection unless he could see Jesus as the others had. His need was met by Jesus, the man with scars.

Jesus comes to us, doubters that we mostly are, with scarred hands. How can God be good and just and loving when such terrible things happen in our world and in our lives? If God is responsible for all this then he should suffer too! Jesus stands with scarred hands and says, 'Shalom'. Christ is the suffering of God, the tears of God.

He is the healer too. His presence made Thomas cry out with confident faith. Tradition tells us that he went on to become the first witness to Christ in India where the Mar Toma Church still remembers him with thanksgiving.

✳ *Lord, I often wonder, can the world be saved?*
Can we live together as one family?
Can your kingdom come?
'Look! The tomb is empty!'

Tuesday September 2   Matthew 27:3–10
One who was lost
Although we are familiar with the story of Judas Iscariot, it is not clear what motivated him. Some think it was politics. Judas may have had links with one of the nationalist movements, urging

rebellion, and when Jesus refused to go that way he had to be removed. Many think it was about money and greed. In John 13:29 we read that Judas was the treasurer of the group and he may have been corrupt in his dealing with the money, desperate for more silver pieces. Or perhaps he was bitter about not being in the inner circle with Peter, James and John. We cannot be sure. The gospel writers only tell us that 'Satan entered into him' (Luke 22:3).

We cannot read of Judas without facing our own betrayals of our Lord. They may not be dramatic, just words or actions which bring sorrow and shame to Jesus – the cruel insult, the careless rejection, the narrow-minded church, the trivial judgement of others. We know that it happens. So we are thankful that we do not end in despair and horror. Judas saw no way out; we know there is a way. When we face honestly what we are then we meet a forgiving God who always stands ready at the door to welcome us home. That is good news.

✳ *As we live our compromised lives*
in this complex and tempting world,
save us from betraying our Lord.

Wednesday September 3   *Acts 1:21–26*
An unknown disciple
The empty seat at the table was a constant reminder of Judas. It seemed right to the eleven to fill that place and this short passage tells us how they set about it.

First came the qualification. He must be a personal witness to the ministry of Jesus from the time of John the Baptist through to the resurrection. Then came the short list, just the two names. We know nothing of Joseph or Matthias; they disappear from this moment onwards. The vote by lots was like taking the names out of a hat and we may think that unsuitable for such a serious matter.

There must have been many people who followed Jesus whose names we do not know and who get no mention in the New Testament. In Luke 10 we read of seventy-two messengers sent out to announce the kingdom, and we don't know any of them. We rejoice in all who have followed Christ who never get honours awarded, never hit the headlines, decline leadership positions and yet who are there at Jesus' side. I think of pastors in the Pacific islands faithfully serving their people, steadfast over the years in isolated places. Unknown to the wider church, perhaps, but honoured in the Lamb's book of life.

* You know all the faithful witnesses, Lord;
  they are pillars in your house.
  May the Spirit keep them strong.

Thursday September 4   *Luke 9:1–6*

Sent out

There are surprising things in this passage. Here are twelve men
with only a little experience of being with Jesus, no long training,
sent to be the heralds of the kingdom. They are sent into a
dangerous world with no equipment, to throw themselves on the
hospitality of the villages. It was surely a very risky business. But
they were sent with the authority of Jesus, so that just as he had
power to heal, so did they; as he proclaimed the kingdom in his
own person, so they can tell about him.

I do not think we can deduce our missionary methods today
from this passage. Our world and situation are very different.
What we can learn is that being called to live close to Jesus also
means being sent out into an unbelieving world. There is no holy
huddle, no cosy security for the disciples of Christ. In every age
they have to live among the temptations and ridicule,
misunderstandings and cruelty of secular society, proclaiming
God's reign in the way they live and serve. That does not change.

In verse 6 'they told the good news' is just one word in Greek:
'they gospelled'. Do we?

* We pray that the way we treat others,
  the way we listen and share,
  may be a gospelling to heal a broken heart.

Friday September 5   *Matthew 10:5–15*

Critical days

This Matthew passage is a more elaborate version of what we
read in Luke yesterday, providing more detail of the commission
of the Twelve.

First, the mission is limited. Jesus was not rejecting Gentile
and Samaritan towns but concentrating on the first priority, the
people prepared for the coming of Messiah.

Second, there is a strong emphasis on the way of life. They
are to be dependent on the hospitality of the people and so will
not need their own camping equipment. They are volunteers, not
paid employees. It is a venture of faith.

Third, they are to bring peace, Shalom, to those who receive them. There is a blessing of God when the messengers are welcomed. Those who reject them fail to find God's peace.

Fourth, this mission becomes a time of judgement. By rejecting the messengers some people will be saying 'No' to the greatest opportunity of their lives. That will be their sorrow for ever. In Genesis 19 Sodom was destroyed through its failure in hospitality to strangers. How critical is the way we listen for the good news of God's self-giving love.

✳ *May we have open hearts and open minds*
for all messengers of your grace.
May our churches be open too
for all who seek mercy and truth.

Saturday September 6   *Matthew 10:16–31*
What to expect

There are always some people who enrol in a movement because they expect grand days, good profits, long life or fame – the blessings that the world proclaims. Even among the Twelve there were times when they argued about who would have the best seats in the kingdom of God. It can infect the church in any age. We may begin to think about the rewards we deserve rather than the service we can offer.

Here Jesus is direct in his challenge. The outlook for an apostle is grim. Arrest, imprisonment, family anger and rejection, exile – all are possible. It is like the Churchill speech in 1940, offering nothing but blood, toil, tears and sweat. Such realism is a tonic, for it engages us in a critical struggle; we know that we are not playing with something trivial. So here we realise that following Jesus is to engage in the life and death issues of our human family. Even in our ordinary, peaceful life of daily duty when nothing exciting happens, we are enlisted in the eternal purpose to reclaim life for life's Creator.

Assurance comes at the end. God's care is universal and for ever. We can never slip out of God's hands. Crisis or calm, gloomy outlook or bright dawn, death of deaths and hell's destruction – have no fear.

✳ *For those in danger, in prison, in loneliness*
because they love the Lord
we pray: may faith and fellowship be theirs.

FOR REFLECTION AND ACTION –
alone or with a group

- Modern apostles – make a list of people you would put under this heading.
- Share your list with a small group: what do you learn about the nature of apostleship today?
- Write a song or prayer of thanksgiving for those who have given a good witness.

BIBLICAL STORIES
1. Who is on the Lord's side?

Notes based on the New International Version by
Bao Jia Yuan

Bao Jia Yuan graduated from Nanjing Union Theological Seminary in 1966. Unable to work as a minister during the Cultural Revolution, he worked in the countryside for many years. It was not until 1986 that the Reverend Bao began full-time church ministry. He was ordained in 1987. Bao is currently Associate General Secretary of the China Christian Council and Director of their Nanjing Office, where he is responsible for overseas relationships. He has been much involved in Bible publication, church development and ministries among minority nationalities for many years.

The explosive growth in church membership in China in recent years is a cause for rejoicing but also a cause for concern as the Chinese church struggles to minister to and care for its new members. It is not an easy task for the church to reflect faithfully God's image in Chinese society during this huge transition period in China's history, a period when China has opened itself in substantially new ways to the wider world. Nevertheless, despite the enormity of the task, we believe that God is using ordinary Christians like you and me – as well as others – to do his work and to fulfil his mission. 'God chose the foolish things of the world to shame the wise; God chose the weak things of the world to shame the strong. He chose the lowly things of this world and the despised things – and the things that are not – to nullify the things that are' (1 Corinthians 1:27–28).

Sunday September 7   *Judges 7:1–22*
A faithful witness

It is obvious that before God's call came upon Gideon, he lacked confidence and had limited vision. God's mercy transformed his limitations and his failures. It was his humility and his faithfulness to God's guidance that eventually made it possible for his name to be listed among the great heroes of faith (Hebrews 11:32). Gideon's conquest of the Midianites was not because he had a powerful name (his name means 'mighty warrior'). It was not because he commanded a strong army, nor was it because he was skilled in military strategy. It was simply because God expanded and used the abilities which he had already built into Gideon. God showed his power through Gideon's weakness and his faithfulness. The term 'the day of Midian's defeat' is well known as a testimony to the power of God's salvation (Isaiah 9:4).

One day a Chinese scholar boarded a ferryboat carrying seven heavy suitcases. The suitcases were packed with health, wealth, power, wisdom, faithful and true witness, knowledge and merits. Soon a terrible storm arose, and the ferryboat was at risk of overturning due to its excessive load. Upon the request to throw overboard some suitcases in order to reduce the weight in the boat, the scholar finally picked up the box of faithful and true witness. He thought this box was less important to him than the others, and consequently threw it into the river. He did not realise that he had thrown overboard his life's foundation. We too need to realise that a faithful and true witness is the gateway to releasing God's power in our lives and in our world. It is thus vital in our Christian formation, and not to be easily or lightly abandoned.

✳ *Almighty God, help us to trust in you,*
to obey your will, and allow you to be the ruler of our lives.
Grant us strength to live out a holy life,
and give us the courage to witness faithfully and truthfully
to you.

Monday September 8   *1 Samuel 17:41–58*

A person of reliance on the Lord

The story of David the giant-killer has been narrated from age to age and is a favourite amongst many Jews and Christians. David's bravery and his willingness to 'put his head into the lion's mouth', so to speak, have inspired and encouraged many adults and children down the centuries to imitate his courage and daring. There is a Chinese saying, 'Little strokes make great oaks'. This means that real strength lies in softness. The Bible also says, '[God's] power is made perfect in weakness' (2 Corinthians 12:9). God chose the young boy to defeat the giant enemy.

Have you ever thought about what the real secret is behind this scripture? How is it that the young boy could so act without fear to overcome such an assailant? The clue lies in Psalm 27:1, where David asserts, 'The Lord is my light and my salvation – whom shall I fear?' David puts his trust in the Lord. His words to the giant Goliath testify to this when he says, 'I come against you in the name of the Lord Almighty, the God of the armies of Israel, whom you have defied' (verse 45). David's complete trust in the Lord wins the heart of God and his trust is not betrayed.

A big round of applause is given to the acrobat when he finishes the breathtaking performance of walking on the tightrope. Then the actor challenges his audience by inviting one of them to sit on his shoulders as he walks for a second time on the tightrope. The whole hall is suddenly dead silent. Nobody dares to try. Suddenly a little boy comes up, saying, 'I will do it'. Who is this child? He is the acrobat's only son. Why will the little boy do it? He completely trusts his father and knows that his father loves him. This is such a trust as the young David displayed. How does it compare with our own?

✳ *Lord, help us to be your faithful people,*
those who demonstrate our trust and obedience in you,
living fearless lives because we know that we can trust in
you absolutely.

Tuesday September 9   *Matthew 4:1–11*
Rooted in the ground of love
We do not live in a protected laboratory or a spiritual vacuum, but in a world that is full of danger and many kinds of temptation. Our physical, emotional and psychological needs and desires make it easy to fail in all sorts of testing situations. Of course, temptation itself is not a sin; it is only the giving in to the temptation that results in sin. Temptation is often the combination of a real need and a possible doubt that creates an inappropriate desire.

The question is how to overcome the test of temptation. Every day we pray, 'Do not lead us into temptation', but we need also to be alert and ready for the test when it comes. How can we learn to deal with the trials and temptations of life? In the first place, we can look to Jesus and see how he combated the temptations with which he was faced. Jesus demonstrates both the importance and the effectiveness of knowing the scriptures and applying them as a protection against temptation.

There are numerous icebergs and pieces of floating ice in the sea around Greenland. These icebergs and floating pieces of ice are, surprisingly, moving in completely different directions, due to the dual impact of the winds on the surface of the sea and the underwater currents which pull and push in different directions. Temptations and misfortunes in our lives are like sea winds that can easily cause us to lose our way, pulling and pushing us in contradictory directions. However, the words of God and his eternal love are like the deep currents beneath the sea that keep us rooted and stable in the ground of God's love, no matter what is happening on the surface.

✳ *Dear Jesus Christ, keep us rooted and grounded in your love so that our lives are not thrown off centre by the trials and temptations that beset us.*

Wednesday September 10   *Esther 7:1–10*

Guard your heart above all else

Many Bible scholars have criticised the secular nature of the book of Esther, but, although God is not mentioned in this text, from the story of Esther we can sense God's sovereign rule and plan over history. Esther was an ordinary woman whose beauty and character won the king's love. In a death and life conflict between Mordecai and Haman, Esther used her favoured position and risked her own life to speak out on behalf of her people to the king. Her immediate action made God's deliverance possible, even though she risked her own security. She seems to have known that security in this life carries no guarantees: possessions can be destroyed, beauty can quickly fade, relationships can be broken, and death is inevitable. The ultimate security lies in serving the Lord on behalf of one's people, as Esther shows us – even if such action could lead to the loss of all worldly goods.

Even in today's civilised societies, women's issues continue to be hotly debated. An expression often heard in China is, 'Women hold up half the sky'. This means that women's work and contribution to family and public life help to create the world in which we live. It is obvious that women's status and importance in society have improved in many places. Nevertheless, there needs to be a greater recognition of the gifts and abilities of women, not least within the church, as well as a continuing struggle to achieve women's liberation in places where women are still denied the right to use their God-given gifts. Christian women should be leading the way in this, claiming and using all their gifts for the good of others and the glory of God, as Esther did.

✳ *Heavenly Father, help us to recognise and value the gifts you give us and to be willing to use them, as Esther did, for the good of others and for the liberation of all.*

Hear my prayer, O Lord

Elijah was the most famous and dramatic of Israel's prophets. Through him God accomplished many amazing miracles. He was also an earnest man of prayer. He prayed not merely with words but with his whole self, with his body bent to the ground and his face between his knees. In this passage we see Elijah going alone to face 850 false prophets of Baal on Mount Carmel. Alone? No, for he knew that the Lord was with him and that he was on the Lord's side. He prayed to God, 'I am your servant and have done all these things at your command.' Through his faithfulness, he manifested the power of the true God – just as Esther did and as Gideon and David did.

Prayer is our daily communication with God. We must pray with hearts full of trust in God's will, earnestly and sincerely. We do not have to use pretty phrases or speak in a particular way. We may pour out the language of our hearts which are burdened with a sense of need. For we know that our heavenly Father loves us and that he will not despise a broken and contrite heart (Psalm 51:17).

✴ ***God, grant me the serenity to accept the things I cannot change, courage to change the things I can, and wisdom to know the difference.***

The fear of the Lord is the beginning of wisdom

The passage today mentions several women: Shiphrah and Puah, two midwives; Amram, Moses' mother, and Miriam, Moses' sister. These women all worked together, unbeknown to them, to save the life of baby Moses. Together they performed a wonderful miracle. Yet they had little in common beyond the fact that their hearts feared God.

The Bible says in Proverbs 9:10, 'The fear of the Lord is the beginning of wisdom'. If one fears the Lord, one will follow the Lord. Whoever fears the Lord will dare to obey God, even if that means defying the words and authority of human leaders and thus risking condemnation or even death. Shiphrah and Puah feared God and therefore defied the injunction of the Egyptian king to slay the Israelite boys. We do not know whether Pharaoh's daughter feared God but we do know that she risked punishment by taking the Hebrew baby into her home. The faith of these women gave them the courage to take a stand for what they knew was right. Faith can embolden us, too, to take a stand for the right.

* **O God of mercy,**
  help us to take the risk of defying the forces of evil
  so that your new life can be born again and again
  in a world that badly needs it.

Saturday September 13   Genesis 34:1–29

Healing the broken world

This story is indeed a page of tragedy in the book of Genesis. The name of God is completely absent from this sordid chapter. A romantic tale of 'love at first sight' turns into a narrative of suffering and lifelong regret. Things went wrong from the very beginning: sexual abuse led to deception and revenge and finally to the terrible slaughter of innocent people. The whole chapter is a mirror of the dark side of human nature, and is full of every kind of wickedness and sin: greed and hate, lust, envy, murder, fighting, lying, bitterness and gossip (see Romans 1:29). And the tragedy continues in our own time. This story reflects our current world: a world of brokenness in which there is no peace among nations but violent abuse and cruelty, a world in which many families and individuals suffer terrible abuse and cruelty at each other's hands.

What can Christians do? A father wanted to read the paper, but was being bothered by his little daughter, Vanessa. Finally, he tore a sheet out of his magazine, on which was printed the map of the world. Tearing it into little pieces, he gave it to Vanessa and said, 'Go into the other room and see if you can put the map back together again. That should keep you quiet for a while!' After only a few minutes, however, the daughter returned and handed her father the world map correctly pieced together. The father was amazed and asked how she had done it so quickly. 'Oh', she said, 'It was easy. On the other side of the paper is a picture of Jesus and when I put the picture of Jesus together the world came together as it should.'

Only Jesus has the power to transform the whole world into his kingdom of justice and love. When we focus on the face of Christ in our world rather than the problems and our own inadequate resources, we will discover solutions to problems we did not think possible and resources will be given us which we could not have found for ourselves. Let us then join hands with love and compassion to reach out into the world which he longs to heal.

* **Jesus, we pray for this broken world.**
  May your Spirit inspire us to work for healing
  so that all humankind may know your goodness, grace,
  forgiveness, and reconciliation.

FOR REFLECTION – alone or with a group

● How have you reacted to the different stories of this week's readings? What thoughts and feelings have they generated?

● How is it possible to know we are on 'God's side'? What are some of the distinguishing marks of God's way?

● What risks may it be necessary for you to take in order to obey God's call in your life at present?

FOR ACTION

Choose one of the biblical characters in this week's readings to think about at greater depth. Explore the details of their life and character, including their strengths and weaknesses. Share with one or two others what you have learned from this biblical personality.

BIBLICAL STORIES
2. Sons and daughters

Notes based on the Lutheran Bible by
Margarete Pauschert

Margarete Pauschert is a retired Lutheran minister who has served in two parishes of Berlin-Kreuzberg and Berlin-Moabit, Germany. She was responsible for the religious welfare of women and for the teaching of women ministers. She has been a regular broadcaster on radio. At present, she runs a centre for adult education with a friend in a village by the Elbe river.

The stories of sons and daughters are at the same time the stories of their families. Names, property, possessions and values are all passed on to sons and daughters by their parents and forebears. In addition to such material inheritance, there is also a powerful emotional inheritance that links the generations: powerful feelings, such as love, tenderness, indifference or even hatred bind parents and children, as well as sisters and brothers, together. Sons and daughters live within this chain or line of family inheritance. They don't exist on their own. They are involved in the history of their families and sometimes we have to look as far back as the third or fourth generation to understand the feelings and the behaviour of sons and daughters in the present. The biblical stories set for this week take us into the world of family relations.

Sunday September 14   *2 Samuel 18:19–33*
Lord, don't call my children before you call me

In the life of parents there is no greater misery than suffering the death of a child. This is what fathers and mothers always told me when we were preparing for the funeral of a deceased child. Life ceased to make sense when there were no sons and daughters to succeed them. But the situation is even worse if death comes at a moment when parents are on bad terms with their child. In such cases, parents not only feel depressed and stricken with grief; they reproach themselves and feel terribly alone in their misery because they feel guilty for their unresolved relations with their child.

David could not comfort himself because his son Absalom was dead. Nobody understood David's grief for Absalom because he had been the enemy of the state and died in the war that he himself had plotted to overthrow his father, King David. However, the root cause of this violent death lay not in the relation between father and son but in the hatred between the two brothers Absalom and Amnon. Amnon was the first-born son of David and he raped Tamar, Absalom's beloved sister. After that, Amnon did even worse and kicked her out of his house, unable to bear the sight of what he had done to her. Now David weeps and laments the loss of Absalom; he is utterly distraught in his sorrow. He is as distraught as Tamar was after her brother had dishonoured her and her father did not call Amnon to account. David is as distraught now as his son Absalom had been when he, David, had not punished his brother for his terrible crime.

Sometimes our children live out our dreams and often they do what we have not dared to do in our time. Being our reflections, they may reveal things to us that we would rather hide. They are like mirrors of us. And on the day that a child of ours is dying, a part of ourselves dies also.

✳ *Heavenly Father, let there be peace between fathers and sons, and let them respect each other and learn from each other. Do not let our children die before calling us. Show us how to come to you as your beloved daughters and sons, and how to live with you in peace and justice.*

Monday September 15   *Genesis 27:1–29*
Reconciliation of brothers and sisters – a lifelong process
Here are two sons: one is the mother's darling while the other is the father's beloved child. Such a dynamic between brothers and sisters is common enough. A daughter may make great efforts to win the love of their mother who, sadly, only has eyes for her brother. Sons, likewise, may struggle to be recognised by their father and may be disappointed again and again when they do not receive such recognition. Every family has its own stories about jealousy between brothers and sisters in the struggle for the love and appreciation of their parents. Throughout our whole lives, we are shaped by the patterns learned in childhood from our families. And the desire of parents to treat their children alike often turns out to be a vain hope.

Jacob and Esau were twins. They differed greatly from each other and they became lifelong enemies after Jacob betrayed his brother Esau. However, the betrayal was only successful because the whole family was involved in its perpetration. Every family member played their part in the deception and crime. The two brothers were only reconciled long after both parents had died and they themselves were approaching the end of their own lives, having suffered many torments. Such wounds can fester over many years.

✳ *Healing God, you alone can heal our hearts, you alone can reconcile us when we have caused or received fatal wounds. We pray to you, reconcile all hurting brothers and sisters and heal their wounded hearts; and especially we pray for our brothers Israel and Palestine whose wounds run deep.*

Tuesday September 16   *1 Kings 3:16–28*

Two mothers claim the same child

Sometimes it is reported that a desperate woman kidnaps a child because her own child has died. The child's room at home has been carefully prepared and the mother cannot stand the emptiness of the house after the sudden death of her child. It also happens that a surrogate mother is not able to give a child away after having given birth to it, although she fully intended to do so all the way through the pregnancy. And we know, too, about adopted children whose natural mothers are overwhelmed by feelings of guilt years after the child has been given away for adoption and start to search for the child they had given away.

A mother's feelings of devotion and connection to her child are some of the most powerful within human experience. If her child is unhappy the woman suffers greater unhappiness. If her child loses its way in life, she may be accused of failing in the child's upbringing, adding to the acute pain she already feels for her child. If something goes wrong in the life of a child we often blame the mother. But there is no such thing as a perfect mother. Every mother will, at some point, fail her child; yet this does not mean her love is not effective and real. Whatever mistakes she makes, a mother who truly loves her child cares passionately and above all else for the wellbeing of her offspring.

Solomon does not waste time wondering why two mothers are claiming the same baby. Instead, he proposes drastic action: to cut the child in two. At that moment, the real mother reveals herself, since she longs above all else for her child to stay alive, even if she herself must lose it. Her love shows itself in its true colours.

✳ *God, help us to love our children truly, even if we may not love them perfectly. And, loving them, help us to have the courage to let them go their own way, to have their own thoughts and their own faith. And let us never stop praying for them.*

The father's vow to the Lord causes the death of his daughter

How can a father sacrifice his own daughter for the sake of a vow he made to the Lord? And how can it be that the daughter even encourages him to fulfil this vow? We are shocked by such a fatal agreement and find no relief in the fact that this death was subsequently commemorated by an annual Memorial Day in Israel.

Today, still, there are daughters who are kept as the property of fathers or brothers, and later of husbands. They have no power over their own lives but have the will of their menfolk imposed upon them. A missing dowry or the loss of a girl's maiden honour may still be reasons for girls or women being killed in India and in some Islamic societies. Nor is Christian Europe immune, where child abuse is a common crime that causes invisible but untold suffering to many of our sons and daughters.

Children are committed to our care, but, however much we love them, they cannot provide meaning for our lives or meet our deepest needs and desires. We have to have the courage of facing our own deepest desires and finding a meaning for our lives that does not depend upon our children.

✳ *Living God, open my ears so that I do not ignore the crying of a child. Let me not turn my eyes away from wrongs done to children. Comfort and forgive me when I do harm to my child, and show us how to regain confidence in each other again.*

Who will be provided for a sacrifice?

The father and his son are on their terrible way to Moriah hill. They do not talk, since the son's questions cannot be answered by the father. Who or what is being sacrificed in this story? Who is paying the heaviest price? The son who is going to be sacrificed or the father who is to provide his only son for a sacrifice? The mother whose longing has not been accounted for and who is left out of the story? The son who has to suppress his fears or the father believing in a God who demands this killing of his son? Only God knows the answers to such questions. It is a story that defies explanation.

After the sacrifice, the son disappears from the story and Sarah dies immediately after the incident. The family no longer exists as a family after this event, and the son starts his own new family.

At each Jewish New Year celebration, this story, named 'the binding of Isaac', is read as a reminder that God's will may not admit of simple explanation. It tells us, too, that after dreadful horror a new start must be made. This passage is also read by Jews as a memorial to the Shoah, the Holocaust of Jews during the Second World War. Faith in God provides no answer to the question why God did not rescue his people from the Holocaust, but it is up to us to encourage each other to give an answer with our own lives now.

✻ *O God, we tremble and quake at the cruelties perpetuated in our world, and at our own collusion with terrible things when we allow evildoing to continue without challenging it. Show us how to respect other religions, trust the new generation and protect those who are most vulnerable. Give us determination through your love and the grace to desist from easy answers when there are none.*

Friday September 19   Mark 5:21–43

Give her something to eat

As youngsters, we sometimes felt that we were not dearly loved by our parents and that no one understood us. We may have thought we should be better dead since at least then our parents would remember what we meant to them! Such thoughts are not uncommon to needy children. Parents, on their side, must provide food, clothes, education and the right friends for their children. They have so many cares that they may have no time to listen to their children, take their fears seriously and help them when they have to make serious decisions. Then, one day, they may realise that they do not recognise their children any more. They wonder why their children take drugs or do not eat or are withdrawn. The children have been suffering and we, the parents, have missed it. In such situations, we need help from others to recover right relations with our children.

The presence of a person of wisdom and compassion may restore both child and parent, where medicine cannot help. Jesus is such a person. He believes in and is concerned for the life of the girl, when others have given up on her. At the same time, he has compassion on the suffering of the parents. His compassionate touch restores the girl to life and movement again, and restores the lost daughter to the grieving parents.

✻ *God of healing, we need your help to guard and protect our relationships with our children. As you do not treat us according to our sins, so let us be generous and loving in the way we respond to our children.*

A father who had two sons

When entering upon an inheritance, sisters and brothers often end up in conflicts which have their roots in childhood jealousies and rivalries. One of the sons in this story has been working many years on the father's farm, helping his parents to run the estate, while the other son was off squandering his share of property in a distant country. Who knows what took place in the older son's mind and heart during all those years when the younger son was away? And when the younger son returned home, seedy and desolate – what then?

Jesus tells this story to encourage us to keep hope for change alive in our hearts. The needy younger son may not be lost for ever and the faithful older son may not be right in everything, even though he has lived a decent life. Both sons are offered the opportunity of change, of forgiveness and of reconciliation. The story suggests that the younger son accepted that offer, but we do not know what the final response of the older son was.

✳ *Lord, rescue us from family patterns that are destructive. Help us on the way towards reconciliation and keep alive in us the hope that your love offers.*

FOR REFLECTION – alone or with a group

● As you reflect on the inheritance you have received from your family, what are you most grateful for?

● What do you find most painful and difficult in the family inheritance you have received?

● Which of the biblical stories considered this week do you most relate to? Why?

● What new insights into family patterns have you discerned this week?

● What needs to change in your family relationships for God's love to be released?

FOR ACTION

To be able to tell the story of one's life is the first step out of depression, anger or hate. Look for a group to share your own story with. Become involved in an organisation like Unicef which cares for children who are suffering from war.

BIBLICAL STORIES
3. On the run

Notes based on the Anglicised Edition of the New Revised
Standard Version of the Bible by
Sandra Pollerman

*Sandra Pollerman is a storyteller, author and workshop leader
now living in a Suffolk village near Bury St Edmunds. Sandra
focuses her attention on the spiritual journey, particularly on how
God's story and individual and group stories fit together.*

Each time I move house and community, I long for it to be the
last. Being rooted in one place has been for me a lifelong dream,
albeit unrealised. The readings this week invite us to journey with
seven biblical figures who have also, by choice and by
circumstance, abandoned their fixed abode and gone 'on the run'.
It proves true for each of them, and true in my experience also,
that no matter how long the journey nor how distant the land, God
remains always at hand, whether the individual acknowledges
God's presence at a given time or not.

Sunday September 21   *Jonah 1:1–17*
Running away from God

Poor Jonah! Running away from God didn't turn out to be quite so
simple. When Jonah chose to turn away, God in all creation
continued to invite his servant to service – with the wind, in the
waves, through events.

The twist in the tale is that Jonah's companions were more
responsive to God's calling than Jonah himself. The companions
approached this unknown God with prayer and sacrifice, willing to
respond even when the way ahead lay against their principles.
Jonah, prophet and servant of God, was the one who clung blindly to
personal convictions rather than abandoning himself to God's calling.

What a chastening image this servant of God offers. How do
we compare? In the face of an invitation to service which seems
daunting and contradictory to personal convictions, how do we
respond? Are we able to discern and embrace a mission to
express the love and reconciliation which the God of Creation
wishes to extend to all?

Monday September 22   *John 18:15–27*

Running from the truth

Denial is one way to cope. Faced with a proclamation that might have brought him into personal confrontation, Peter chose flight from the truth instead. Even after all these centuries, there remains a great deal of sympathy for Peter.

While his repeated denial kept Peter safe on the outside, it was no defence against a meeting with God on the inside. Hidden with the truth, deep within himself, Peter was made sharply aware of his flawed behaviour. From such an encounter no flight was possible.

How often in our own lives are we faced with such an acute awareness of our imperfections? Can we allow ourselves to acknowledge our own flights from the truth when faced with moments of illumination? Are we able to extend to each other a place of compassion, acknowledging that all fall short of the highest model of living?

* *Merciful God, thank you for caring for us in the midst of our shortcomings. We pray for healing and forgiveness. May all who receive your grace respond to others with compassion and truthfulness.*

Tuesday September 23   *Genesis 4:1–16*

Out of harmony with the earth

Angry and hurt by being given a place of lesser regard, Cain acted without restraint against his brother. Murder and destruction were the methods he chose to redress his grievance. Nonetheless, God did not expel Cain from his care; it was with the earth itself that relationship was broken.

Cain was to live in the land of Nod. *Nod* in Hebrew means 'wandering'. Cain would be marked among men and forever out of harmony with the earth. No longer would the earth yield its strength to him.

This story speaks deeply to our human condition. We continue to choose violence and destruction to defend our territories and redress grievances. We deny responsibility for the situations of our fellow human beings. As the earth is made barren by conflict and bloodshed, both shelter and nourishment are withdrawn. Yet God continues to call us. Through Christ we are marked with the love of God in such an enduring way that we are never beyond God's invitation of compassion and reconciliation.

✳ *God of compassion, we pray for the grace to continue to turn and return to you. Your love goes beyond our understanding. We give you thanks for your care of the earth and of our human family.*

Wednesday 24 September   *Exodus 2:11–16a*

Running away from the law

Moses, like Cain, chose murder as a vehicle for retribution. Although he escaped immediate punishment for his action, there was a costly reaction. He was exposed by his kinsfolk and decried by his adoptive people.

Moses became an alien looking for resettlement in a foreign land. From a space of favour and privilege he found himself alone and in a desert waste. Running away from the law took Moses far from the rules of the Pharaoh's court. It also set him apart from the faith tradition of his childhood. The land of Midian presented an unknown and lonely prospect.

Can you identify an action or event in your own journey that took you into an unexpected and unknown space? Do you have a memory of being so alone that you sensed even God was left behind? What encouraged you to move through such a time?

✳ *Creator God, we acknowledge you as keeper of the familiar and of the desert spaces. Bless and guide all those who feel they travel alone. Continue to call us all into new understandings of your presence and your action among us.*

Thursday 25 September   *Matthew 2:13–23*

Fleeing for safety

At a critical point God came so close to Joseph that he was inspired to take decisive action. Joseph was willing to risk a great deal for the safety of the special child, Jesus. The journey into Egypt would not be an easy one. Being on the run in the desert would mean shortages of food and water and risk from the natural elements.

The rigours of the journey would put them as a family at risk, yet the journey would also afford protection from the dangers of murderous human power. The earth did not offer shelter and neither did human community. The defensive action Joseph took offered them protection without violent conflict.

Under what conditions have you faced the choice of fight or flight? Were you aware of a process or presence that confirmed your choice? How are we able to discern the difference between personal strength and cowardice?

✳ *O God our strength, we pray that you will continue to be both inspiration and guide. Draw near to those who are in danger and at risk. We pray that you will make the way to safety clear.*

Friday September 26   *Numbers 11:1–15*
Weary of the road
Meeting the needs of a group of people is not a simple task. When the group is moving from one place to another as itinerants or refugees, it becomes especially challenging. Both individuals and those who accept leadership must listen and work co-operatively.

For people on the run, whether by choice or by circumstance, the uncertainty of it all is perhaps the greatest challenge. Even when daily needs are met, the lack of a fixed abode and an established order makes even the strongest weary and life seem very tough.

This story of life on the run reminds us that individuals and leaders alike experience discomfort, disharmony, and distress. Their experience was that God responded to human need. Yet the God of Israel offered neither fixed solutions nor easy options. God responded to Moses and to the people of Israel with a listening ear and the firm promise of companionship throughout the entire journey.

As with the people of Israel in Moses' day, so with us.

✳ *Faithful and eternal God, we trust that you will continue to journey with us. We pray that we may never lose the courage to turn to you nor the confidence to trust your word.*

Saturday September 27   *I Kings 19:1–18*
Retreat … on the run into silence
'There is only one God' (El) 'and that is the God of Israel' (Jah).

Elijah the prophet had been very successful in proclaiming the truth contained in his name. So successful in fact that he had exhausted his personal resources, enraged those who believed otherwise and put his own life at risk. He was weary and worn out. Turning from further encounters, Elijah fled deep into the desert, saying to God: 'This is the end. I've done enough!' Is this experience familiar to you? Do you remember a time when you gave God a clear ultimatum?

Elijah was redeemed from his despair by a messenger. Elijah was given 'just enough' nourishment and encouragement to enable him to move into a space where he could become very attentive to God. Forty days of deep listening proved to be a powerful restorative. In your own times of listening, how has God responded to you?

If you are at a turning point in your own journey, would a long retreat help you to become more aware of God's plan for your life?

✳ *God of all, we give you thanks and praise for your presence with us. Continue to refresh our awareness of you – in our daily round and in our times of silence.*

FOR REFLECTION – alone or with a group

● Individually, what have been your own experiences of being on the run? Have you moved or travelled on by choice or because in some sense you have felt 'driven out'? Have you been able to discern when it was God's invitation and when it was your own longing for escape from something tough?

● As a group, how have we responded to the 'newcomers' or 'outsiders' who have presented themselves? Has it made a difference if people have come one at a time, or in pairs or small groups?

● Is the group also aware of those who have left? Has it been 'chance or circumstance' which caused former members to move along or has there been something that happened within the group itself to spark the move?

FOR ACTION

Prepare a 'traveller's map' of the recent past of your life journey. Set aside at least an hour for this. Begin with a quiet time of turning to God. Ask God to help you identify the challenges you have met. Recall whether or not you were aware of God's presence. Chart these reflections in words or images. Notice your thoughts and feelings. End with a quiet time, aware of God with you in the moment.

BIBLICAL STORIES
4. Count your blessings

Notes based on the Revised English Bible by
Mary Cotes

A Baptist minister, Mary Cotes is tutor in biblical studies at Northern College, Manchester. She broadcasts regularly on radio.

Some years ago I was visited by a German Christian. Just before her departure we prayed together and I was very moved by her passionate repetition of the word *danke* as she humbly listed the many things she simply wanted to thank God for. It struck me then that I had a lot to learn about counting my blessings! I hope that the scripture readings for this week will challenge us not only to reassess and rediscover the blessings we take for granted, but also to find new blessings in places we never thought of looking before.

Sunday September 28   *Luke 19:1–10*
Not a mite would I withhold…?
What topics feature in your church's discipleship classes? Thinking back to my own preparation for believer's baptism, I recall that after I'd been taught something of God's love for me in Christ, I was instructed in the basics of Christian living. I was to read my Bible every day (with my Bible notes of course!), say my prayers and attend worship regularly, especially communion. I was to participate in the fellowship's activities and donate a tenth of my income to the church.

This passage dramatically challenges my limited vision of Christian lifestyle. For Jesus, salvation comes not when Zacchaeus promises to do his daily scripture reading or tithe his fat earnings to the Temple treasury – but when he decides to give half his belongings to the poor. If only we were to understand that counting our blessings includes counting our money and reassessing our finances in the light of God's justice, I suspect that the salvation we proclaim might seem more relevant to a world sucked dry by greed.

✳ *Righteous God,*
   help us never to condemn the world's injustices
   without first confessing our own.

O'er the world's tempestuous sea

How does your church respond to change? Of course we all readily sing hymns about the power of the transforming God to awaken new life and new hope in us, but deep down we're often depressed and frightened by the prospect of renewal, especially if it means allowing old ways to die. When a church activity that's been running for thirty years ceases to attract people we feel as if the whole place is about to disintegrate. We hanker nostalgically after past times, past ministers, and wail that nothing's like it was in *those* days.

Just because we worship the eternal God it doesn't mean that ways of being church have to be eternal too. The story of Noah reminds us that God can be as much in the collapse of the old as in the creation of the new. The destruction of the familiar is not necessarily a bad thing: it can be a blessing, leading us to a rainbow of new beginnings.

✴ *God of the flood,*
when the old ways fail,
and the structures of the past no longer hold us up,
grant us the faith to know we are upheld by you.

Every child of every race

I've always found this passage immensely moving, and have seen different blessings in it at different stages of my life. When as a child I was mourning a beloved grandfather, the story reassured me that God never abandons the lonely. At the time I discovered the feminist movement, it spoke to me of the support two fragile women offered to one another in the midst of an oppressive world.

But now I would say that the blessing here is Ruth herself. Here she is, a young foreign woman with no riches or security, an economic migrant seeking asylum in Judah. She comes from a different culture, practises a different religion and longs for a better life in the company of an older woman who is not even a blood relation. Yet she proves such a blessing both to Naomi and to the nation that receives her that she ends up as King David's grandmother. This story invites us to think of foreigners not as threats but as blessings, not as drains on our economies, but as treasures who can make a creative impact on our history.

✴ *Lord Jesus,*
give me the hope that welcomes the stranger,
the love that drives out fear,
and the faith that trusts that the best is yet to come.

Beginning with blessing
If you had to give an account of the gospel message, where would you start? As a child I was brought up on a gospel story which began with humanity's sinful nature. If the sermon didn't spell it out, the order of service brought it home. Worship began with a long prayer of confession, and by the time we'd wallowed before the Almighty in the shopping list of our failures, we were all thoroughly depressed. Consequently, the God we just about glimpsed through the cloud of despond was at worst a growling headmaster, or at best a loving father tearing his hair out in despair at his uncontrollably wayward children.

This passage reminds us that the scriptures begin the story somewhere else: with a God who delights in creation and showers it with blessings too numerous to count. If only we were to begin our gospel messages with the joy rather than the despair of God and the potential rather than the abject failure of humanity, I suspect our Christian living would take on a dramatic new lease of life.

✳ *Creator of life,*
grant us laughter and delight in believing,
and the playful spirits of children who know themselves loved.

Whose God?
Who exactly is this 'God of Abraham, Isaac and Jacob'? A cursory glance over the biographies of these three characters proves unsettling! Corrupted by the thought of greatness, Abraham committed adultery, used if not abused his wife's slavewoman and then thought nothing of sending her and his own son to their probable deaths in the desert. Isaac, undoubtedly scarred by a father who loved one son more than the other, fell into the same mould and caused havoc in the family by favouring Esau over Jacob. And surprise, surprise! Jacob was no better. As a child he was already using threats against his own brother, and by the time he was an adult he was ready to deceive his dying father in cold blood.

The God who bursts in upon Moses is none other than the God of control freaks and frauds, inadequate parents and damaged children. Do I really want to worship this God? Yes I do. Only a God who copes with human beings at their very worst and still works out a divine purpose can ultimately bless a world like ours run by people like us.

✳ *God of the broken,*
help me to trust
that when I can see only the person I am
you in your kindness can see the person I might become.

The church is not a building

What sort of issues give rise to strong debate in your church? As I look back over my own experience, some of the most heated discussions have been over what colour the walls should be painted, or whether the toilets needed refurbishing. Any onlooker would have been forgiven for thinking that the most pressing issues for the church were not doctrine and mission policy but building maintenance and bank balances.

Today's passage reminds us that the most valuable asset to a community of faith is its people: those like Ezra whose faith has stood the test of time and who have given themselves to studying the scriptures. Of course we may count beautiful buildings as blessings if they inspire us to worship, but without devout people committed to praising God and living the gospel, even the most magnificent cathedral is at best an architectural wonder and at worst an empty shell.

✳ *Spirit of God,*
help me find you
in the glory of creation,
the splendour of cathedrals
and the beauty of those who trust in you.

The scandal

In a local church service I was attending recently, a sketch was performed entitled 'Wonderful sacrifice'. It depicted Jesus giving himself readily to death whilst onlookers gazed at him adoringly, then leaped joyfully to their feet to embrace one another. This is the picture of the atonement I grew up with, and I become increasingly uncomfortable with it. The glorification of self-sacrifice seems to me to be morally dubious if not thoroughly pernicious – especially when it is used by the powerful to persuade thousands of young men to go to war, or to keep women economically dependent and confined to the performance of menial tasks.

Today's passage offers a healthy balance. Here the risen Christ who has endured the horror of crucifixion tells Peter honestly that martyrdom is not something he'll welcome. By all means let's give thanks for those many prisoners of conscience the world over who endure torture rather than bow to terror. Their courage glorifies God. But let's not say there's anything wonderful about suffering itself. Persecution is an abhorrence and instead of singing hymns about what a blessing Jesus' agony is, let's commit ourselves to eradicating all such human rights violations from our world.

✳ *Lord Jesus,*
grant that I may never hear your words from the cross
without hearing also the cries of those who suffer today.

FOR REFLECTION – alone or with a group

● What blessings have most affected your life?
● Is there such a thing as a 'blessing in disguise'? If so, how do we recognise God's blessings?
● How would the members of your church react to the suggestion that Christian discipleship includes the reassessment of personal finances in the light of the gospel?
● Is there a way in which Zacchaeus' example could inspire you to reassess your own giving?

FOR ACTION

Befriend a lonely person in your community, or join a volunteer scheme that will bring you into contact with people whom the community often marginalises.

THE LOVER AND THE BELOVED: SONG OF SONGS

Notes based on the New Revised Standard Version by
Kathy Galloway

Kathy Galloway is a practical theologian, writer and campaigner. She lives in Glasgow, Scotland, and works for Church Action on Poverty. She is the leader of the Iona Community.

The Song of Songs, 'the choicest song', is a series of lyric poems in which a woman and a man unfold the story of their mutual love, of its passionate eroticism and of their profound delight in the very being of the other. It is a celebration above all of the power of love to endure and grow, to give and receive pleasure, and to bring a sheer joy and intensity of life that is surely its own reward.

---

1. My beloved is mine and I am his

Sunday October 5   *Song of Songs 1:1–8*
The wisdom of love

Many have found it surprising that this beautiful collection of love songs, this 'Song of Songs' should have been included in the canon of the Hebrew Bible. It makes no mention of God, it contains the only unmediated female voice in scripture and it is an unashamed and jubilant celebration of human sexual love. These factors have not always commended themselves to commentators!

Some have seen the book, traditionally attributed to King Solomon, as a collection of wedding songs, perhaps drawing on ancient fertility rites uniting deity and nation in a sacred marriage. Others have read it, in a somewhat fanciful reconstruction, as the drama of a lass and her lad, for whom the course of true love fails to run smoothly when she is taken off to the royal harem, only later to be reunited with her faithful lover.

And both Jews and Christians have interpreted it allegorically, describing in the lover and the beloved the relationship between God and Israel, or Christ and the church, or God and the soul, or even Christ and Mary. But the Song does not read like a conscious allegory, and the language is too directly sensuous for a Hebrew to have used in describing Jahweh.

Perhaps we should simply be glad that the Wisdom literature of which it is part, based as it is on experience and reflection rather than exhortation, is a religious tradition which sees passionate, erotic love both as divine gift and as a reflection of God's self.

✳ *Blessed are you, beloved God, giver of love, who has made us to love in return.*

Monday October 6   *Song of Songs 1:9–17*
A language for love
It is a sad reflection on the church's history that it has come to be perceived as ambivalent at best and more often condemnatory and fearful with regard to human sexuality. Too often, Christianity has been associated with the repudiation of the body and of sexuality. For untold numbers, it has been experienced as an instrument of sexual repression, and sexuality has well been described as 'the church's noisiest problem.' Yet for all that, the church has seemed unable to find an honest, direct and positive language to speak of what is one of the most profound human experiences. I will never forget one middle-aged woman saying to me with such pain, 'My church taught me that sex was dirty and not to be talked about, and it has had a terrible effect on my marriage, and on my sense of myself and my own sexuality.'

A greater attention to the frank and free sexual imagery and descriptiveness of the Song of Songs, and its uninhibited celebration of the delights of sexual love, might have resulted in a more balanced approach to sexuality, to the benefit of both people and church. While it is always valuable to seek the spiritual learning present in human relationships, it seems positively perverse to do that while ignoring or devaluing the embodied sexual reality that leaps out of every chapter of the Song of Songs.

✳ *God our Maker, forgive us if we have forgotten that it was you who created us with the ability to give and receive bodily pleasure, and condemned others to shame and fear.*

Tuesday October 7   *Song of Songs 2:1–7*
'This one, and no other'
In a western culture which strives ever more ardently for the perfect lifestyle, the perfect home, the perfect body, it is curious how, on

the contrary, our sexual expectations seem to be getting lower by the day. You don't have to be a sexual repressive to feel that so much of what is represented as erotic is not a great incentive to passion but rather a depressing catalogue of depersonalised exchanges. The effect of this kind of deeply unappealing transaction, far from increasing sexual fulfilment, is actually to drain from it everything that is in the least bit erotic. Though there is plenty of appetite around, much of it artificially stimulated to sell us more things we don't need and didn't know we wanted, real heart-stopping desire seems somehow to be on the wane.

Today's passage from the Song of Songs, often read at weddings and included in anthologies of love poems, is one of the great erotic statements of literature and faith. Its universality lies at least in part in its intensely personal quality. It is this man, and no other, who awakens such trust and delight. It is a tremendous affirmation of the God-given uniqueness of persons.

✳ **Blessed are you, God who is Other, who has given us to delight in the other.**

Wednesday October 8   *Song of Songs 2:8–17*

'Now is the time for singing'

Desire, that truly potent alchemy of tenderness and longing, is awakened by and directed towards someone or something beyond the self, which attracts by its very being and otherness. So it is not the same as appetite. It is incompatible with the self-referential transaction, requiring as it does the capacity to go beyond oneself. And being at its intensest a slow-burner, it needs time to develop.

Today's passage catches the sweet constraint of anticipation, the discipline of waiting for something eagerly hoped for. It is perhaps one of the most difficult and yet most deepening aspects of our humanity. It is the last weeks of pregnancy, the last days of the school year before the holidays, the last long miles of the weary traveller's journey home. It is the waiting of Advent before incarnation, and the longest Saturday before the resurrection. It is the ending of winter and the coming of the spring. *Now* is the time for singing! And who could disagree that, in truth, the singing is not more joyous, the source not more deeply carved into our being, because of the anticipation. The longing of desire gives fulfilment its greatest resonance.

✳ **Blessed are you, God of the seasons of life, who makes spring to follow winter.**

The disciplines of love

Our fears concerning those we love – fears of loss, abandonment or obstacle – sometimes make their way into our dreaming when we cannot admit them in the bright light of day. We would be less than human if we did not have such fears; they are a measure of our love and our need. But they are also an important part of the growth and deepening of relationship, for no relationship will survive if it does not address its underlying fears and difficulties. Only in fantasy and fairy-tale does 'happily ever after' mean no problems.

The disciplines of eroticism require an understanding of the value of restraint to fully appreciate release. Self-limitation and letting go are only the two sides of the one coin. Struggling together with the difficult challenges that love and life bring, naming the fears, these are also the disciplines of the erotic.

And contrary to conventional wisdom, desire, not morality or law, is the driving force of religion – whether experienced as the attraction of the ultimate Other, or, more perversely, as the fear of abandonment by that Other which can so easily turn into moralising or legalism. There is a contemplative eroticism that will never be understood by those who measure sexuality by performance.

✳ *Self-giving God, help us to make gracefully the sacrifices love requires of us.*

Wholeheartedness

Today's passage describes the great procession of King Solomon coming into Jerusalem from the desert, crowned with splendour, surrounded by the trappings of military might and political power. The alternative title of the book, The Song of Solomon, has meant that sometimes the poems have been attributed to him, and certainly he was famed as a lyricist and also as a great lover. It seems much more likely, however, that his name came to be a focus for much of the Wisdom literature, and no doubt having his name attached to the Song assisted its inclusion in the canon of scripture. But his amorous reputation and his harem of women are far removed from the direct and unsophisticated passion of the lovers here, in their youthfulness and wholeheartedness. They are in that wonderful stage of courtship where nothing else really matters.

In the book *Schindler's Ark*, there is a moving description of how, in a labour camp in the shadow of Auschwitz, the older prisoners went to great lengths in the midst of appalling privation and brutality, to preserve the dignity and beauty and privacy of a young couple's courtship. In a context of the most absolute cynicism, they affirmed the joy and possibility of love.

✴ ***Merciful God, preserve us from cynicism and help us to celebrate the love of our young people.***

Saturday October 11   *Song of Songs 4:1–16*
Without prejudice

In the Song, the beloved and her lover dwell at length on the beauty of each other's physical appearance and characteristics. Lovers do this, but perhaps there is another reason for their insistence. The woman seems to be responding to a perception that her dark skin is considered less than beautiful. In the face of such a view, she asserts her own beauty and sense of self, and requests that she should not be looked down on because of her dark beauty.

Perhaps there is an issue of class here – women of a lower class did not have the luxury of remaining indoors and preserving a light complexion in the heat of the sun, but had to work outdoors; dark skin was therefore seen as less 'refined', less desirable. Or perhaps it is an issue of ethnicity. But for sure, the plea, 'do not look down on me because of my colour' has a resonance still, rooted in the perversity of racism. Her lover's insistence on her irresistible beauty to him must surely have reinforced her trust in his love. But there is also a hint here that their love went against prevailing norms, that it had to confront prejudice.

✴ ***Reconciling God, help us to break down the barriers that inhibit love.***

FOR REFLECTION – alone or with a group
● What do you think are the disciplines of love?
● How can we find a language to speak of sexuality more helpfully?

2. Love is strong as death

Sunday October 12 (Week of prayer for world peace)
Song of Songs 5:1–8

The overshadowing

In today's passage, we hear for the first time directly from the women of Jerusalem (or the Chorus), with whom the woman narrator seems to be having some internal debate – as if she had to make a case to them for the truth and integrity of her love, so that they will not interrupt or impede it. Well, women all over the world are familiar with this constraint of feeling they have to account to the prevailing culture for who they are and how they love! This tension is exacerbated by the fact that the women's viewpoint is not a consistent one – sometimes they are supportive, sometimes sceptical, sometimes celebrative. This too rings true to experience!

And it adds to the sense that this is a love which must overcome obstacles. That this is a real fear is vividly demonstrated in the dream of the lover already gone from the door, and the brutality offered to the woman when she goes searching for her beloved. Here, for the first time, is a discordant and violent note, even if it is only a reflection of her fears. It is a universal tragedy that this fear of violence should overshadow even the most innocent and harmless of pursuits. It threatens the security of childhood, the stability of maturity, the tranquillity of age and makes the destructive linkage between love and pain and fear.

✳ ***God of peace, help us to overcome fear and pain by the power of love rather than the power of violence.***

Monday October 13   *Song of Songs 5:9–16*

A woman's desire

Female sexuality has generally been regarded in both church and culture as problematic, and as requiring careful governing and serious restraint – on the supposed basis that unrestricted female sexuality would be so wanton, lewd and irresponsible that human society itself would break down! A cynic might observe that this is in fact a much more accurate description of much male behaviour and that by and large it tends to be the women who are both left holding the baby and then blamed and punished for it. Such projection suggests motives more to do with power and control than a genuine desire for truth. The forces at work here seem to be paternity and ownership and male fears of sexual inadequacy.

Fortunately, there have also always been men who could respect and enjoy the kind of frank expression of female appreciation and desire found in today's passage, and could recognise that equality, mutuality and reciprocity in love are the truest guarantors of lasting, stable and life-giving relationships. Sacramentality and covenant love do not flourish on double standards and implied threat.

Unfortunately, not enough of these men have had an authoritative voice in the church!

✳ *Loving God, help us to face the wounds in our own sexuality, so that we do not inflict them on others.*

Tuesday October 14   *Song of Songs 6:1–10*
With the eyes of love
There is an unashamed partiality in today's passage which is quite delightful. Here is a man proclaiming his beloved's loveliness against all the competing claims of the famous beauties of the day. Truly the eyes of love see in a special way. How often have we heard, 'I don't know what she/he sees in him/her.' And our own new-born is unquestionably the most beautiful baby in the world. But this partiality is one of the great gifts of our creation as human! To be seen with the eyes of love is to be set free from market valuations, fantasies of glamour, the need to conform to stereotypes of beauty. It is to be relieved of the burden of simply being the ego-enhancing prize possession of another. It is to see in the other the glorious image of God, and to see that image in the other regardless of beauty, rarity, utility.

In the security of that way of seeing, the attraction of numerous conquests pales into insignificance. Fidelity is a delight, not a duty, and no one can make us envious, because we have discovered, and must constantly revisit, gratitude for what we have.

✳ *God in whose image we are made, help us to look at those we love afresh with the eyes of love.*

Wednesday October 15   *Song of Songs 6:11–13*
The landscape of love
One of the most striking features of the Song of Songs is that in its evocation of a love between two people, it also communicates

239

the love of a place. So much of its imagery and its use of metaphor relates to geographical features and locations, and they too are powerful in their loveliness. This is a fruitful, fertile landscape of blossoming vines and ripening figs, of walled gardens filled with flowers and small fresh springs of water, of rich valleys and majestic mountains. That they are juxtaposed with images of the cloudy, dusty desert only makes the pastoral scene all the more enticing. The cities too are beautiful, breathtaking and splendid. It is as if all of nature and culture rises to its greatest heights in solidarity with the lovers.

Was it really like that? Of course, these are descriptions of one of the earth's most beautiful and fertile regions. For those of us more accustomed to harsher landscapes – those relentlessly barren because of drought, land degradation, searing heat, pollution, or those which are bleak, cold, raw and dark for half of the year – the delight of these descriptions may be even more intense. And for those whose experience of cities is of urban squalor, overcrowding, danger and disease, the contrast may be particularly poignant. After all, this text is from a time long before environmental disaster, poisoned rivers, climate change and global warming. The landscape speaks as well as the lovers.

✳ *Creator God, help us to love and cherish your good creation in all its parts.*

Thursday October 16   *Song of Songs 7:1–9*
A life of gift
The language of the Song is a celebration of the sensuous, a joyous capitulation to the senses, in which the lovers delight in each other's taste, touch, smell and the sound of the beloved's voice, as well as in what they see. Everything in their daily experience, the animals they tend, the vines they dress, the features of the landscape, is drawn into play in the effort to communicate what is ultimately a mystery beyond words: the delight of love and the attraction of the other.

It is a transformative power that love has, to warm all around with its own glow, so that not only the other but all around is seen more acutely in its own character and uniqueness. Notwithstanding the fact that nowhere in its eight chapters is God mentioned, nor are there any references to divine law, sacred history or prayer and liturgy, I find that this is indeed a holy book. St Irenaeus said, 'The glory of God is a human being fully alive' and the Song of Songs stirs body, senses, imagination, intellect, heart and spirit so much into attentiveness that the only appropriate response is to worship, to give thanks to God for a life which contains so much gift.

✳ *For the grace of life and love, great God, we give thanks.*

Friday October 17   *Song of Songs 7:10 – 8:4*
Many kinds of love

For these lovers, with their hasty departures and endless seeking out of the other, with their pleas not to be interrupted, there is a sense of urgency and even of secrecy. Is their safety or their reputation in jeopardy? The only way their love might be public and win the approval of society would be if they were related, when their relationship would cause no eyebrows to be raised. Again we are left with the question: did their society seek to keep them apart because of differences in class, ethnicity or colour? Whatever the answer, there is an appeal here through the universality of the poetry of love, to the possibility of reciprocal love and the fulfilment of intimacy.

That appeal is valid in many contexts. Our culture does not always understand or value the equal validity of many kinds of love, besotted as it is with a somewhat infantile Hollywood fantasy of romance and glamour. And, for many, the passion of the lovers is simply not a possibility. But the patient attentiveness of the carer, the mutual affection of friends, the deep bonds of brotherly and sisterly love, the companionship of many kinds of community and family life and the chosen solitude of the religious or artistic life also offer the fulfilment of love and intimacy. It is well that we should cherish them all, without feeling threatened by their difference from our choices.

✳ *Gracious God, we thank you that you offer many kinds of love for many kinds of people.*

Saturday October 18   *Song of Songs 8:5–14*
Being holy

The Song of Songs speaks not only to history and culture but to scripture itself. Some have seen it as a commentary on other portions of scripture which undermine human sexuality in general and female sexuality in particular. Without it, the prevailing stories would be those where women are penalised and shamed for their sexuality, confined to procreation without pleasure and rendered invisible by repressive gender roles. But this last passage describes a woman who, as much as her lover, is strong, passionate and faithful, and gives her love freely and sacrificially. She is not for sale; she asserts her love without shame, and in it finds contentment and peace. The rich and powerful can offer her nothing that compares.

Medieval commentators found in the Song a joyful allegory of the love between Christ and the human soul, in its respect for the otherness of the other, its longing, and its strength of desire and fulfilment. Whether we read starting from that perspective or from sheer pleasure in the delight of human love, we can all affirm the importance of attentiveness to the relationship, of allowing it to grow and be nurtured, and of making the necessary sacrifices for the wellbeing of the other. Spirituality and sexuality cannot be separated if we are to be whole and holy.

✳ *Beloved God, we give thanks for love more powerful than death.*

FOR REFLECTION – alone or with a group
● Where do you find positive affirmations of human love in the Bible?
● How do we nurture loving relationships of all kinds in our church communities?

FOR ACTION
Spend some time trying to look afresh at the people you love and often take for granted.

WATERS OF LIFE

Notes on the Revised Standard Version by
Alan and Clare Amos

Alan Amos is Trust Chaplain at the Medway Maritime Hospital, Gillingham, in Kent, England. He is involved in inter-faith partnership in the hospital and in Kent, and has previously worked as Chaplain in Beirut and in training ordinands in Cambridge and Canterbury. Clare Amos is Theological Resource Officer of the Anglican mission agency USPG. She has taught biblical studies in Jerusalem, Beirut, Cambridge and Kent and is particularly interested in studying the Bible in the context of the modern Middle East.

The image of water runs through the scriptures from the book of Genesis to the book of Revelation. It is fascinating to trace its metamorphoses: from womb of life to agent of destruction, from medium of new birth to symbol of chaos which will be excluded from the New Jerusalem. Water is all these things and more, lending the fluidity of its nature to the ever-changing metaphors of poet and prophet. Over the next three weeks we explore this rich symbolism, aware that water needs to be touched by grace to fulfil the aim of the Creator. In this transformation, water represents our plain humanity, which can also be touched by grace to become the bearer of God's Spirit.

1. Waters of creation

Sunday October 19 (One World Week)   Genesis 1:9–10, 20–23
In the beginning
As the story of creation unfolds in Genesis 1, we are made aware that *division* or *separation* is a necessary part of the creative process. God divides between light and darkness, between heaven and earth and the regions under the earth, and between the waters and dry land. This theme of separation anticipates the distinction between good and evil which is explored at such depth in the Old Testament. It also anticipates God's choice of a people who will be called to be holy, marked out from the nations around them whose hostility is sometimes compared to the roaring of the waves of the sea. (The sea often represents the forces of threat and chaos, in both Old and New Testaments, and the image of the sea may convey the fear of being drawn back and absorbed into the primeval and formless void.)

And yet the waters are also marked out by God to be life-bearing, to 'bring forth swarms of living creatures'. Included in the water creatures are the great sea monsters. It is notable that they are included in God's blessing, and are given his approval as creatures that are good in his sight. These days, one of the frontiers of exploration is the charting of the creatures of the deep, including the giant squid. Some of these creatures may seem strange and alarming, but they are known to God better than they are known to us! 'All things bright and beautiful, all creatures great and small, all things wise and wonderful, the Lord God made them all.'

✴ *Lord, help us in our choosing. May we be receptive to your will in the paths we follow this day. May we look beyond appearances, to discover the beauty which lurks in hidden depths. May we become celebrants of your creation. And may we learn to live together in harmony in the one world which you have made.*

Monday October 20   *Job 38:8–11, 16–18*

Humanity put to the test

Arrogance is a very human trait. We like to measure everything, and with the process of measurement we feel we can solve many widespread human problems. We live in an age when statistics are collected and almost made an object of worship. It is tempting to think that an improved bureaucracy empowered by knowledge of statistics will solve problems of health provision, educational achievement, and the efficiency of all public services.

Against this human 'wisdom' God sets some very radical questions. For all the extent of our knowledge, the extent of our ignorance is still greater – and the fear of the Lord is the beginning of wisdom. When we reflect upon the dynamic forces of nature, their creative power and ability to destroy and renew, then we begin to recover our humility.

And, surely, our processes of measurement are not in themselves sufficient to redeem us from the pitfalls of our broken humanity. The renewal of the human spirit is essential for true liberty and progress, and if we leave all that we mean by 'grace' out of our equations and solutions, we may wonder why little is achieved.

God sets Job a demanding questionnaire! Sometimes human beings who design questionnaires seem to think they are gods. Yet Job desires a face-to-face encounter with God, a living dialogue. Ultimately, it is through the stubbornness with which Job pursues his converse with

God that he attains wisdom. Let us not shrink from converse with our fellow human beings, and hide behind sheets of paper!

✳ *Help us, dear Lord, to cast aside the sins of pride and arrogance. Open our hearts so that we may greet your presence where it may be found in the lives of others. And where your divine image is defaced and marred, give us courage and perseverance to hope with your hope, and care with your love.*

Tuesday October 21   *Psalm 93:1–5*

The Lord reigns

This psalm contains an inner contrast between surety, firmness and foundation, on the one hand, and the threat of chaos on the other, represented by the raging of the floods. It celebrates the victory of the Lord over the forces of disruption, and very probably was used in dramatic acts of corporate worship which represented the triumph of God over raging chaos. Used in this way, it was a proclamation that ultimately God is in charge of the affairs of nature and of humanity.

By proclaiming the reign of God, we challenge and subdue in his name the forces which refuse to recognise his dominion. We do this daily when we pray 'thy kingdom come', when we look to the fulfilment of God's reign.

And yet, the raging of the floods is a part of life as we know it. Time and tide belong not only to outer nature but also to inner nature, to the fluctuations of our human spirit. We probably all know those for whom these fluctuations are unbearable, and who may have to be cared for from time to time in a mental health setting. Often someone suffering in this way will come down to my hospital chapel to offer a prayer, quite frequently to write a prayer to put in our intercessions box. Some of these prayers are very moving, and show that God is at work within, in the deep places of their hearts. They sometimes display a wisdom which others lack. We should remember, too, that many of our great creative artists and thinkers have suffered acutely for their life-giving art.

In ministering to those in mental distress, we try to bring them the assurance that indeed 'the Lord is mightier' than all the troubles that beset them, whether we feel we can use words of faith, or whether we are called to wait alongside them in a spirit of hope. Words do not always convey the compassion of God.

✳ *Lord, we thank you for the kingdom which you have proclaimed among us. May your kingdom come. We thank you*

*for your victory over the forces of death and hell. We pray
today for all those who are deeply troubled in mind and spirit.
May they know you as a light that shines in the darkness, and
which endures to lead them to the fullness of the day.*

Wednesday October 22   *Psalm 65:5–13*

Hope and joy

Key words of this passage are 'deliverance', 'salvation', 'hope'
and 'joy'. These words of assurance are rooted in the action of
God as Creator: the God who established the mountains and
controlled the seas and governed light and darkness. God
showed in the tasks of creation that strength which is further
displayed in his acts of deliverance for humanity. He is a God who
saves. The Hebrew word for 'salvation' is *Yeshua*, which is also
the name we know as 'Jesus', given to the Messiah at his birth. At
times, Jesus displayed the power of God in creation, not least by
stilling the roaring of the waves, when the disciples began to
tremble at who he might be.

The psalm moves on to culminate in a wonderful rejoicing at the
blessings of God which may be experienced in nature. This psalm may
have been used in the worship of Israel as a prayer of supplication and
expectation, calling upon God to sustain life through the blessings of a
good harvest and the gift of plenty. But the whole meaning of the psalm
cannot be understood without returning to the opening verses, where
God's forgiveness is portrayed as the supreme gift, and the presence
of the Lord is revealed as the supreme joy.

✳ *Lord, we thank you for your good gifts in creation. We
remember also those who experience not harvest but
famine, not abundance but poverty. Help us to struggle for a
world in which abundance is shared, so that there may be
enough for every mouth.*

Thursday October 23   *Isaiah 35*

God's promise

These words of encouragement to Israel speak of God's power
and promise to transform both the landscape and the prospect for
God's people. The poetry of verses 1 and 2 presents a vision of
the desert being crowned with gifts of beauty which seem foreign
to its nature. These verses introduce a vision of the
transformation of humanity, at least of those human beings who
are receptive to the divine word. As God by the exercise of his will

may bestow beauty and fruitfulness upon a land that has been waste and arid, so he may restore courage and hope to those who are weak and full of fear.

At the centre of this chapter we find the life-giving power of water (verses 6 and 7). Upon those who believe and trust, God's grace comes with an equally dramatic effect and impact, as sorrow and sighing are banished, and redemption is accomplished. These words point us forward to the 'living water' of John's gospel (John 4:1–31; 7:37–39). The words may also suggest to us that the 'foot washing' of John 13 was not just an act of cleansing, but an act of commissioning. The feet of the apostles are cleansed, rested and prepared for the journey ahead, which is to be as arduous as it was for those who followed a highway through the desert. Feet are washed in preparation for fresh use, as is written elsewhere in Isaiah: 'How beautiful upon the mountains are the feet of [the messenger] who brings good tidings, who publishes peace, who brings good tidings of good, who publishes salvation, who says to Zion, "Your God reigns"' (Isaiah 52:7).

The chapter concludes with the picture of the way to Zion stretching forth through the desert. It is the joyful path for all the redeemed, a path which is protected by God and which requires holiness of those who would walk upon it. As the prophet well knew, most paths through the desert are traps for the unwary, and perilous for those without a guide.

✳ *Lord, guide us on the path that leads to your kingdom, and grant us the courage and trust that we need for the journey.*

Friday October 24 (United Nations Day)   Isaiah 55
Free grace
I well remember the cry of those selling water melons on the streets of Beirut. All of a sudden, doors and garden gates are flung open, and people hurry out to stop the cart as it goes by. How surprised they would be if the vendor were to call out, 'All free today! No charge!' Isaiah 55 begins with such an unlikely invitation. And yet it becomes clear very quickly that it is the words of God through the prophet which are real meat and drink, which alone have the power to satisfy. For it is those who listen to the word who will be brought to life, life that belongs to a covenant which is everlasting. Truly God's ways are very different from the ways of humankind (verses 8 onwards) for God's greatest gifts are bestowed freely. Being priceless, they are bestowed without price. Verses 10 and 11 carry forward the description of the divine word as active and effective.

God's word produces results, just as the rain and the snow, gifts from God, produce fruitfulness upon the earth.

Many are the New Testament passages which can be said to draw upon this chapter of Isaiah, from the temptation of Christ in the wilderness to turn a stone into bread (Matthew 4:3–4) to the living water given to the woman of Samaria (John 4:5–30), and the parable of the sower (Mark 4:3–20). The book of Isaiah has itself become a spring from which living waters issue forth.

The chapter ends in song and a kind of calypso performance by 'the trees of the field'. It is an overwhelming expression of joy. I shall never forget the funeral of a friend, where we sang the words of verse 12 as we left the church. This was just as he had suggested and asked of us. The words of Isaiah are still alive, summoning us to the life that does not know an end.

✳ *Lord, you have set Jerusalem as a sign in the midst of the nations, and yet we still long for your promise of peace to be fulfilled. We long for the time when war and bloodshed shall be no more. Help us to play our part in the struggle for a just and peaceful order in this world. May your Holy Spirit refine what is good in humankind, and purge away hatred and malice.*

Saturday October 25   *John 3:1–10*

A new beginning

Nicodemus is a leader who needs to begin over again in his spiritual life. He senses this. He comes to Jesus 'by night', by which the evangelist probably indicates Nicodemus' ignorance. And yet he 'knows'. He 'knows' that Jesus is a teacher who has come from God. Perhaps he thinks that this confession is enough. (Sometimes Christian people have imagined that knowing and saying the Creed is enough.) But the heart of the message of Jesus is not about knowing at this superficial level. The message of Jesus is only fulfilled in an *encounter* with God which transforms. This is what Nicodemus has not been able, so far, to imagine.

It is ironic that the gospel tells us 'Jesus answered him...' (verse 3) because what follows is very far from an answer to anything that Nicodemus has said! If we pursue the words of the chapter through to verse 21, it becomes plain that, in a sense, Jesus himself is the answer to Nicodemus' question, if it can be said to be a question at all. In fact, Nicodemus was close to the truth without seeing it: for John is telling us that truly Jesus is for us 'the presence of God', if we really know him rather than just the facts about him.

But before we reach that destination, we have to pass through water and know the activity of the Spirit (verse 5). Nicodemus is being called to 'let go' – let go of most of the things in which he has trusted for his security. Like most of us, he likes to see where he is going and make it one step at a time. But grace remakes us. And at what cost! For such a birth, there is also a death (see Romans 6:3 ff.).

✳ *Lord, grant us the grace to begin anew in our lives, in*
confidence that you have remade us and will remake us
according to your promises.

FOR REFLECTION AND ACTION – alone or with a group

Choose one day in which to become very conscious of your use of water. Think about how much water you use. Enjoy sipping slowly a glass of pure water, perhaps instead of another drink during the day. In the early morning, walk on grass without shoes and socks, feel the dew and the blades of grass with your feet. If it rains, stop to trace like a child the journey of a raindrop down the window pane. If it is wet, spy out a spider's web and its glistening beauty. Wash your feet and your face slowly in cold water, taking time to feel the refreshment which water gives. Think of those who live in the desert, who sometimes use sand for the cleansing of their bodies. In the evening, look back and remember your encounter with water during the past day.

2. Waters of destruction

Sunday October 26   *Genesis 6:11–22*
God's cataclysm

Creation had begun with earth being heaved dry of the waters; now creation is apparently to come to an end with earth being totally covered by those waters once again. It is indeed a return to chaos, to a sort of pre-creation state. That is what the biblical writer is seeking to convey.

Yet in reality what was to happen was simply God giving expression to the chaos that had already taken place, for the 'earth was filled with violence' (verse 11). One of the remarkable features of the story of the great flood is that the earth itself is not treated merely as an object, but almost as an active participant in the drama. The earth was 'corrupt' – and it was going to suffer for this.

Of course this strikes us as unfair – but it is also realistic. Whether we like it or not, our actions as human beings affect the earth and its wellbeing. We have begun to realise more clearly how fragile is our environment – and how its long-term balance and health depend on our care. The saga of the ozone layer is a notable example. But this is something that happens imperceptibly and over a period of time. It is no accident when people reflect on the dangers of nuclear holocaust that they have often turned to the biblical story of the flood. Both are sudden cataclysms which could make our earth utterly uninhabitable.

Yet even in this darkest moment of prediction a tiny note of hope is sounded. There will be a few survivors – and God promises to continue in relationship with humanity. Will we be so fortunate if such a cataclysm were to happen again?

✳ *God of the deepest depths, we cannot sink so low that your love is unable to reach us. This is the ground of our hope.*

Monday October 27   *Genesis 7:11–24*

God's ark

There are two small and contrasting notes in this passage which remind us that it comes from a worldview quite different to our own. The first is the comment that this great flood was caused not simply by rains falling incessantly from the sky – but also by 'the fountains of the great deep' being burst open. The ancient Israelites believed that the dry earth rested on a vast subterranean ocean which had been sealed tight at creation, though of course the springs of water on which people depended for life were necessary 'drips' in the system. But if major leaks were to occur – as now apparently happens – then catastrophe would inevitably result, as with a dam bursting. So the reference to these fountains emphasises just how total was the disaster.

But this is countered by another observation. 'The Lord shut him (Noah) in' (verse 16). It is the personal name of God that is being used here, and he is doing something very personal for Noah. He is taking the tenderest care of him, by making sure that this ark is properly shut – perhaps almost as a parent would check the car door for a young child. So in spite of the awful deathliness of the final verses of this chapter we have been reminded that even now God is not – quite – finished with his creation. Tiny and tossed about on the seas though it is, this ark will keep Noah safe for a new future.

✳ *Keeper of the ark, with fatherly care you cherish us. Lead us into the future.*

God's voice
This psalm reminds us of the religious context in which Israel lived its life for hundreds of years. It was a world in which nature was fearful and unpredictable – and it was the task of gods to control such forces, and ensure that human beings were kept safe and in *shalom* (verse 11). The winter season in particular was a time when sudden storms could wreak havoc – with gales and flash floods trapping the unwary. The myths of Canaan tell of battles in which their gods subdued such destructive waters. Such conflicts with natural forces seem to be echoed in this psalm – though it is noticeable that the psalm also suggests that there is, in reality, no contest. The Lord is simply too powerful – he is God of the heavens (verse 1) as well as of all the powers of earth. So he does not have to fight the waters to control them (verses 3, 10), since he is already enthroned as their King with his voice thundering out for all to hear. Even the mighty cedars, the greatest trees known in the Mediterranean world, bow their heads in homage before his power.

What a vision of God and his power! Yet, as Elijah came to realise perhaps a couple of centuries after this psalm was written, God's strength can be shown in other ways too. For on Mount Horeb (1 Kings 19) it was not in the fire or the mighty wind that he heard the voice of the Lord, but in the gentle stillness of the deepest silence.

✳ *Lord of the cedars, your voice is both magnificent and awe-full. May we never be afraid to listen to the breeze of your Spirit.*

God's watchtower
Life was unpredictable in the cities of ancient Israel. Aside from such natural hazards as drought or plague, there was always the possibility of falling under attack from human enemies, whether local or international. So cities had walls – and strong gates – and watchtowers on the walls to try and ensure that plenty of warning could be given if an enemy decided to drop by. Then people would be able to come in from the field, the gates could be shut and defenders could take up their positions.

This quite complicated chapter is comparing the role of the prophet to such a watchtower. It is his task to give warning of what lies ahead – and possibly, just possibly, this warning may be enough to avert the danger. Otherwise terrible indeed will be the devastation which is graphically described by the prophet, to match the terrible deeds that the people have done. But in the midst of these doom-laden predictions comes the startling interruption, 'The earth will be filled with the knowledge of the glory of the Lord, as the waters cover the sea' (verse 14). We pause for a moment at a wonderful vision in which the dirt and filth of the people's current life will suddenly be swept away by the reality of God which will not allow anything to stand in its way. As the prophet himself had been consumed by the presence of God, so too would the world in which he lived.

✳ *Eye of vision, faithful tower, help us to know your will more clearly, and to focus on your glory alone.*

Thursday October 30   Exodus 15:1–22

God's terror

The miraculous crossing of the sea by Moses and his followers became the root experience of Israel – a sort of touchstone by which all later history was measured. It is, for example, recalled even in the Book of Revelation where in 15:3 those who have conquered the 'beast' sing the 'song of Moses' – a clear allusion to these very verses. We ourselves will be returning to this story and what it means for us, the spiritual heirs of the Exodus, in our section 'Waters of deliverance' next week.

But today's reflection presents the other side of the coin. Deliverance for some seems to mean inevitable destruction for others. The note of terror is clearly present throughout these verses. It is salutary to think what it would feel like for an Egyptian Christian to read them. They lie at the heart of the difficult particularity of the Bible, and with all that that has meant throughout history and even today. In truth there are no easy answers. Perhaps, though, it is important to say that those who sang so joyfully of God's terror being wreaked on others (verses 11–12) did eventually come to realise that God was no puppet to be manipulated for their own selfish ends. The God who is incomparable will eventually show his sovereign freedom by his refusal to be pinned down to human agendas – and that may one day prove to be painful for the descendants of those who sang this song – or, indeed, for us.

✳ *Fearsome God, show mercy on us when we fail to recognise the wideness of your terrible love.*

God's wisdom

These verses, half parable, half verbal illustration, come at the end of the great Sermon on the Mount. These 'words of mine' (7:24, 26) refer to the demanding teaching of Jesus that we have heard in the last three chapters of Matthew's gospel, beginning with the Beatitudes. So we are being presented with quite a challenge with the demand to both 'hear' and 'do' them.

For many people in the United Kingdom the image of floods which destroy housing has become all too real in recent years as winters have become suddenly so much wetter. Is it a result of global warning? We can guess, but at this point in time it is probably too early to be completely sure. What we can say is that the events of the recent past – whether due to natural forces or to human wickedness – have brought home to us in a new way the fact that we cannot 'opt out' and try and pretend that our own actions do not matter. The demands of the Sermon on the Mount may seem almost too challenging to bear – but unless the rich world is prepared to live in a way that also accommodates the needs of the poorer 'others', sooner or later we will find that a deluge will fall upon us. That would indeed show our foolishness!

✳ *Wise One, you have taught us that to fear you is the beginning of wisdom. Lead our steps on this path of life.*

God's coming

Like many passages in the 'apocalyptic' sections of the gospels these verses are difficult and perhaps even distasteful to modern readers. Their central message though is clear – that we need to be continually prepared for the God who will come to us when we least expect him. The language with which this advent is described sounds threatening – but is this the whole story?

God is certainly coming, but whether we view this as judgement or as salvation ultimately depends on ourselves. The allusion to the waters of the flood is telling.

Among my favourite pictures is a tapestry that shows the symbol of water flowing through the Bible. Creation, flood, exodus, wells which quench the thirsty and the river of the water of life are all depicted. Some of the scenes are shown in deeper blue, some in lighter. The dual sense of water is thus represented – the darker blue represents the fearsome, destructive side of water, the lighter blue its life-giving nature. Yet these two 'sides' of water are woven together in one and the same picture: they belong together and make up part of the same whole. So it is with the coming of God – will we perceive it as a cataclysmic flood, or as a delightful coolness which refreshes us as on a hot summer day?

✳ *Divine artist, in our lives you paint for us a many-hued canvas. Be with us in all the shades of our life.*

FOR REFLECTION AND ACTION – alone or with a group

Listen to a recording of a piece of music that portrays the fearsome majesty of the sea, for example, Wagner's *Flying Dutchman*, Benjamin Britten's *Peter Grimes*, Vaughan Williams' *Sea Symphony* or Debussy's *La Mer*. Allow yourself to be caught up with the exquisite terror and excitement of the sea. Afterwards, reflect alone or with others on your reactions in the light of the week's readings.

3. Waters of deliverance

Sunday November 2   *Exodus 14:15–18, 21–23*

God acts to save

The crossing of the Red Sea and the deliverance from Pharaoh's army became a touchstone for Israel's faith and life. The powerfully-told episode has been returned to again and again to renew and empower those of the Jewish faith. Its retelling in the annual Passover celebration reminds all those present that they have been 'brought out of Egypt'. They have been ransomed from slavery and bondage, and set on the road to freedom.

This narrative of deliverance is also recalled by Christians at Easter. In churches which hold a vigil service on the Saturday before Easter Sunday it is usually one of the scripture readings, reminding us that Easter can be understood as the Christian Passover, the celebration of the great act of deliverance from death to life in Jesus Christ. The waters of the Red Sea then speak to us not just of a past event recalled and made present, but of the life-giving waters of baptism. We can picture the adult candidates for baptism in the first three centuries of the church's life, gathered together on the Saturday evening, listening to the scripture which anticipates their baptism and birth to new life. But imagine what it must be like listening to and reflecting on this passage as an Egyptian Christian in the context of today's world. That really requires an ability to locate the inner voice of scripture, the heart of its message, to make the journey from the land of the temporal to the land of the eternal.

✳ *Heavenly Father, help us to overcome all obstacles and fearfulness through trust in your grace and power to save. Free us from all anxiety, as we wait in joyful hope for the coming of our Saviour, Jesus Christ.*

Monday November 3　　　　　　　　　　　　　*Psalm 107:23–32*

The hushing of the waves

The context of this passage is a psalm of thanksgiving for the redemptive works of the Lord. Here we have one specific example of God's redemption, set alongside other examples given in the psalm. We may be reminded of that classic hymn of the sea, 'Eternal Father, strong to save'. The words of the hymn, by W Whiting, blend with the chromatic musical setting of J B Dykes to conjure up the mighty power of the sea against which God's intervention is sought. (Dykes named his hymn tune 'Melita', the ancient name for Malta, the island where St Paul landed after shipwreck.)

But if we note the words of the psalm carefully, we find a difference from the assumptions of the hymn. In the hymn, God is invoked to restrain the fury of nature's power. In the psalm, in verse 25 we find it is the Lord who commanded the stormy waves to arise, before calming them in answer to the prayers of the desperate sailors. The psalm does not explain why God should choose to command a storm, but perhaps hints that sailors, like others, need to learn the limits of their own power and ability, and their dependence upon God.

In the Old Testament, God is often the causer of all manner of destruction as well as the bringer of salvation. This does not fit too well with our contemporary ways of looking at God and the world. The Christian perspective, based on New Testament insights into the life and teaching of Jesus, is that God allows us to suffer and that in some deep and mysterious sense suffering is necessary. But we could not live with a God who inflicted each act of suffering in a deliberate and purposive way. In the end, we are forced to say that suffering happens within God's providence, and that we are never outside his reach and his care.

✳ *God did not say 'you shall never be troubled'. God did not say 'you shall never be tempested'. But God did say 'you shall never be overcome'.*

Julian of Norwich

Prayer conquers despair

What can we do when we plumb the depths of despair? The answer we find in the scriptures is that the darkness recedes when we face it not in our own strength alone, but by calling upon God. Job offering a psalm in the belly of the whale is one example of such prayer *in extremis*; the song of the three young men in the fiery furnace is another (an addition to the book of Daniel which can be found in the Apocrypha). This psalm is another. According to tradition, David is its author, and it expresses the hope he put in God in the darkest moments of his life.

If we allow ourselves to be fully human, then there will be times when we feel as if we are drowning in sorrow, sometimes our own sorrow, sometimes that of others, sometimes the two combined. While this is a part of normal human experience, sometimes the agony becomes intensified and prolonged in clinical depression, which is one of the most painful states known to humanity. Those who have suffered in this way know what it is to feel completely incapable of helping themselves, or even to stretch out a hand towards God. It is then that often we find another person reaching out towards the sufferer, being the means by which God finds them. And gradually, as the darkness lifts, prayer becomes possible again and renewed communication becomes communion.

In the Eastern Orthodox icon of the Resurrection, the risen Christ descends to the underworld to tread down the gates of Hades and rescue Adam and Eve, representing our fallen humanity. He reaches out to us too, in the darkest places that we have known or may yet know.

✳ *Thou mastering me*
God! giver of breath and bread;
World's strand, sway of the sea;
Lord of living and dead;
Thou hast bound bones and veins in me, fastened me flesh,
And after it almost unmade, what with dread,
Thy doing: and dost thou touch me afresh?
Over again I feel thy finger and find thee.
　　　　　Gerard Manley Hopkins, 'The Wreck of the Deutschland'

Wednesday November 5   *Mark 4:35–41*
Who is this?

It is helpful to read this passage bearing in mind Psalm 107:23–32 (Monday's scripture portion). We can then see how Mark shapes the gospel story to pick up the wonder of Jesus speaking words to control the force of the wind and the waves. This is placing a human being in control of forces which are at divine disposal. No wonder the disciples are filled with awe. We notice how they express their amazement to one another. What Jesus had done was so shocking that they were not ready to question him about it but could only confer with one another. We are used to gospel passages where the scribes and Pharisees accuse Jesus of blasphemy; here we see that the disciples could not get their minds round what at first seemed a shockingly blasphemous idea: that Jesus was more than a human being like them. Who then could he be? Who alone in the Hebrew scriptures had authority to do such things?

But the gospel story is not just about the first disciples and Jesus, it is about Jesus and us. It is about the way we are overcome by anxiety and panic in the midst of the stress waves of life. The noise inside and outside us can become deafening. We need to be delivered by a divine word calling us to peace and recollection. We need God to stop us in our tracks (perhaps as Saul of Tarsus was stopped in his). Sometimes we hear the word of peace and renewal from others; sometimes we suffer before we can hear it from the depths of ourselves, for our resistance to hearing the word which calls us to be still can be very fierce.

✳ *Lord, help us to find your peace at the centre of our being. Deliver us from the temptation to set ourselves or others impossible targets. Give us this day our daily bread, and help us to be satisfied with the strength which it provides.*

Thursday November 6   *John 6:16–21*
Do not be afraid
St John tells the gospel story in a way designed to highlight its inner meaning. Firstly, we are told 'it was now dark, and Jesus had not yet come to them' (verse 17). Then we are told of the storm arising, and the effort of the disciples in rowing a considerable distance – three or four miles. The message for the reader is that we may not experience the presence of the Lord just when we feel we need it. We may have to endure a time of darkness and some experience of tempest, and we may have to make our own strenuous efforts to advance in our lives, before we experience the deliverance of the Lord. It is remarkable how when Jesus enters the boat, it completes its journey very quickly, arriving at the safety of land quite suddenly.

The main part of a church building is often known as 'the nave,' from the Latin *navis*, ship. It is a place where the body of disciples meets, in expectation of encountering Christ in one another and in word and sacrament. But the encounter cannot just be stage-managed by 'those in charge'. We are called to be the Body of Christ, but it is only when we respond whole-heartedly to our calling that we truly become what we have the potential to be. Sometimes fear holds us back; living out our faith is a risky business. But the presence of the Lord is perfect joy, and casts out our fear.

✳ *Let nothing disturb you,*
Nothing afright you;
All things are passing,
God never changes.
Patient endurance
Attains unto all things;
Who God possesses
In nothing is wanting;
Alone God suffices.

Teresa of Avila

Friday November 7   Romans 6:3–11

Emerging from the waters

The following poem or hymn by the contributor explores the theme of water in creation, baptism and new creation:

Living water, flowing free
From the rivers to the sea
Bringing life to plant and tree,
Growing, thriving in God's world.

When the earth is parched and dry
We seek a blessing from on high
Life that streams down from the sky
Bringing greenness to God's world.

Living waters, through us flow
Make the Spirit's gifts to grow
Tend our faith that we may know
How to flourish in God's world.

Sign of death and sign of life
Sign of hope where sin is rife
Sign of grace for Adam's strife
As we rise to face God's world.

Tears of anger, tears of grief
Tears of sorrow and relief
Tears of joy beyond belief
As we struggle in God's world.

258

Sister water, God we praise
For your sweet and subtle ways
Known to us in all our days
As we journey through God's world.

Suggested tune : 'There's a spirit in the air'

✳ **Lord, upon those who are baptised, may the blessing of
living waters be ever renewed;
And for all who seek your face, may your bread be sufficient
for their journey.**

Saturday November 8   *Isaiah 43:1–2*

Beyond fear

To God who creates us, glory;
To God who redeems us, glory;
To God who calls us by name, glory.

To the Lord who is with us through waters and floods, praise;
To the Lord who is with us as we pass through fire, praise;
To the Lord the Holy One, who is our Saviour, praise.

To God who has ransomed us, glory;
To God who values us above price, glory;
To God who calls us beyond fear, glory.

To the only wise God, Father, Son and Holy Spirit,
   be praise and glory,
Now and to the ages of ages, Amen.

FOR REFLECTION – alone or with a group

● We are told that water is likely to become a cause of wars later
in this century, as countries quarrel about the use of limited
resources. Discuss how Christians may contribute to the
struggle for a fairer sharing of the world's water. Do you know
of any projects which are relevant to this concern ?

● What does the statement ' I am baptised' mean to you? If you
are not baptised, do you think baptism is important? What
'happens' in baptism ?

FOR ACTION

Find out about one particular project in the developing world
where water is a key focus: for example, the building of a dam or
a well, or the supply of clean sanitation. CAFOD, Christian Aid
and other charities will have information. Hold an event to raise
funds for this project.

WORK AND WORKERS
1.God the worker

Notes on the New Revised Standard Version by
John Vincent

Since 1970, the Reverend Dr John J Vincent has worked in the Sheffield Inner City Ecumenical Mission, the Urban Theology Unit, and the Ashram Community, of which he is leader. Recent Ashram Community projects have included the development of an inner city shop and retreat centre, the Burngreave Ashram, and the writing and publishing of four volumes of a new introductory course to basic Christianity, called Journey, *a guide to contemporary 'Explorations in Discipleship'.*

There are in the Old and New Testaments over two hundred titles and images for God. Most of them, naturally, are pictures derivative from human activities or attributes. God is portrayed in 'anthropomorphic' language: God appears in the shapes of human beings.

'The works of God', and the 'works of God's hand', are familiar ideas in the Old Testament, as are ideas of God 'working' in history, or through Israel as a nation, or through individuals. The passages we study this week pick up singular, dramatic and picturesque images for God as worker. In them, God appears as Creator, Potter, Shepherd, Celebrator, Lover, Beloved and Investor.

Sunday November 9   *Job 38:1–11*
The creator

All religions and many worldviews have myths of how everything came into existence. The Old Testament has several of them, including the rather different stories of Genesis 1 and Genesis 2. In this passage, too, we have a kind of creation story. Here, God is the great designer, the global craftsman, the divine architect and engineer.

Science may have answered the 'How?' questions, and perhaps the 'From what?' questions – but not the 'Why?' questions, or the 'Where?' questions, or the 'With whom?' questions.

The passage raises questions of its own, too. The contest with the wretched Job was, after all, conceived by Jahweh who set Satan onto him to test his love of Jahweh. So Jahweh can have little moral reason for now turning on him with this over-the-top rhetoric. Of course, Job did not lay the foundations of the earth, or organise the planet, or shut up the sea, or form the clouds or the night. He never claimed to have done so.

Is this the unseen, dark, millennial, hidden side to the force behind existence, who does not appreciate human meddling?

✳ *May I not speak when I have nothing to say.*
Let my silence be as deep as the mystery.
In all my knowledge, keep me humble,
let me get on with my tiny vocation,
regardless.

Monday November 10   Jeremiah 18:1–12
The potter
God the potter does not get it right the first time – 'the vessel he was making… was spoiled in the potter's hand' (verse 4). So the potter has another go, as he chooses (verse 5). Right, says God the potter. It's up to me whether I pick you up, or pull you down, or destroy you (verse 7). If you change your ways, I might change my mind (verse 8), but if you go back on your goodness, I'll go back on mine, and punish you again (verse 10).

One would have to admit that there are more chances for a destroying God than a reconstructing God, in the world. The image of the potter here is one of breaking up. Only if we turn from evil and do good does God 'declare concerning a nation or a kingdom, that I will pluck up and break down and destroy it' (verse 9).

✳ *You seem to wait for us to make the first move, God.*
Things always seem to go wrong, and you do nothing.
The goodness, the initiative, has to come from us,
which you then take and mould into your kingdom.
So be it.
Let me be the clay for your moulding.

Tuesday November 11   Psalm 23:1–6
The shepherd
After God the remote architect and God the regenerating potter, it is good to have God the loving shepherd.

I have known this psalm – of course in the Authorised Version – most of my life. I have had it ready, on the tip of my tongue, many times when visiting distressed or sick or dying people. I have said it out loud, slowly, and seen the lips of others join me as we repeated together the familiar words.

261

It always seems to me to be a psalm that goes deeper and deeper as it goes on. The shepherd is the guide, finding the best places for me (verse 2), and the leader finding the way for me (verse 3). But there is more: the shepherd has rod and staff to ward off death (verse 4), and provides a banquet to combat my enemies (verse 5).

✷ *O Shepherd of Israel, and mine,*
cling to me as I seek to cling to you.
In the shadow of death be my rod and staff;
before my enemies let me eat and drink and grow.

Wednesday November 12   Luke 15:1–10

The celebrator

Jesus tells the stories of the shepherd going after the one lost sheep, leaving behind the ninety-nine (verses 4–6), and of the woman cleaning out the house to find the one lost coin, after leaving the nine safe (verses 8–9). Both stories are designed to justify Jesus' own actions of leaving behind the faithful in Israel, and going to find those lost to the faith, the tax-collectors and the sinners.

And, says Jesus, God (as identified with heaven in verse 7 and the angels in verse 10) is more pleased with the 'one sinner who repents' (verses 7 and 10) than with the ninety-nine or the nine who do not need repentance.

We might find this notion excessive, 'over the top', if it is God who is the implied shepherd or woman. The numbers, anyway, are reversed today! It's more like to be the solitary one righteous inside and the ninety-nine or nine outside.

I especially like the idea that the woman spends the coin she has just found on having her friends and neighbours in to rejoice with her at her lucky find (verse 9)!

✷ *Rejoice with me, Celebrator Divine:*
pieces of your world are coming together,
bits of people are getting sorted out,
one in a hundred has a vision,
one in ten is working with you.
Amen! So be it!

Thursday November 13   John 15:1–11

The lover

The key to this passage is not God as the husbandman who has to trim the vine to keep it good (verses 1–3, 6), but rather God as the divine lover, who has set up the vine, which is Jesus, and surrounded it with his love (verses 9–10). The divine love plants and nurtures the divine son, who in turn plants and nurtures the divine brothers and sisters (verse 10). This is imaged in the creator of the vine (God) setting up the vine, which lives the divine life on earth (Jesus), and has branches which are also part of the divine life (disciples).

The dominant emphasis is therefore on the disciples abiding in the son, and bringing forth fruit (verse 5) which glorifies the father also (verse 8), at the same time bringing the disciples into the same reality which the father lives, which is his son (verse10).

God becomes what we are, so that we might become what God is. Divine love takes human form, so that the human form may conform to divine love.

✷ *Within this vine, I am branch, twig, stem, leaf, fruit.*
Within this love, I am pulse, artery, ligament, cell.
Wow!

Friday November 14   *Isaiah 5:1–7*

The beloved

Isaiah sings of his 'beloved' (verse 1). The beloved is God, who creates his chosen 'loved one', the 'house of Israel and the people of Judah' (verse 7). God passes on to his beloved people everything they could need – a fruitful hill, a vineyard, a fence, choice vines, a tower, a winepress (verses 1–2), and the 'pleasant planting' (verse 7). But out of all this provision and care, all that comes is wild grapes (verse 2).

So, too, God has set up the means of judgement, which is the law, and righteousness, which is the way of the Lord. But out of it, all that comes is oppression, and the cries of distress. So verse 7.

One thing remains: Isaiah, the human being who, in the midst of it all, still speaks of the divine lover, whom he calls his 'beloved' – twice in verse 1!

✷ *Love has to be a two-way thing.*
God sets up everything so that we can be happy.
God's care is for justice and goodness.
God's love is visible in the enfolding arms of existence.
God's passion is for human and cosmic wholeness.
God my Beloved!

The investor

This parable is, in my view, part of Matthew's armoury to demonstrate that the Christians not only fulfil the Old Testament law, but also make it even more demanding. So the old opposition to usury disappears, and the five and two talent individuals are rewarded for doubling their 'Lord's' loan by investing it (verses 20 and 22). Meantime, the faithful servant who delivered back what he was given (verse 25) rather than putting it to the money market (verse 27) loses what little he has, and is thrown out (verse 30).

An additional problem is the whole notion that if God is thought of as the lord, then God is responsible for the gross inequalities of the gifts, or loans, or 'talents', given to the three servants. Whereas our experience is that 'success' comes to people for a variety of reasons apart from 'native talent' (!), such as heredity, class, place and opportunity.

Usually, in the parables, there is at least a level playing field – as with the ten women who all get the same amount of oil in their lamps (the parable preceding this one, in 25:1–13).

Either way, God is the Investor, and we are those in whom God invests parts of his riches.

✳ *All the riches within me,*
mind, knowledge, history, community, place,
activity, vocation, product, performance, love, relationship,
are riches reflecting the ultimate,
are bounties from a giving God,
which open in return to me
the mysteries of the Giver.

FOR REFLECTION – alone or with a group

● Which of the seven images of God with which we have lived this week are compelling and full-of-grace for you?

● What actions, attitudes or projects in which you are involved might be hints of divinity? What does God 'in your image' look like?

FOR ACTION

Is there any way that you or your group could incarnate, embody or manifest in action any of the images and stories of God which we have studied this week?

WORK AND WORKERS
2. Workers for God

Notes based on the Student Bible, New International Version by
Marjorie A Lewis-Cooper

Marjorie Lewis-Cooper is a minister of the United Church in Jamaica and the Cayman Islands. She is currently a postgraduate researcher at the University of Birmingham in Britain. She has served as a pastor to churches in rural Jamaica as well as in ecumenical institutions, as project officer for Oxfam, as a missionary to the United Reformed Church in Britain in the role of a racial justice worker, and as a prayer companion, using the tradition of Ignatian spirituality.

How can you know if God has called you? Does God only call those in officially recognised, ordained ministry? Is there a special personality type, a particular gender, a particular ethnic group that is called particularly or even exclusively by God? This week's readings introduce us to a variety of persons who are called by God. They are different in temperament, in talents, in their journey to becoming workers for God, and in their experience of ministry. God calls us all to the privilege of being God's workers, with all that we have and all that we are.

Sunday November 16   *Amos 7:10–17*
Called to give bad news
Amos the prophet did not at first glance have the right qualifications to be a prophet. He was an ordinary man, a farmer. He was not from the officially recognised group of prophets. Yet God called him and gave him a mission. He was sent to prophesy in Israel in the north, although he was from Tekoa in the south. What right did a foreign southerner have to claim that the places of worship and the royal house of Israel would be destroyed? Perhaps unsurprisingly, Amos' prophecy was rejected. He was expelled from the royal sanctuary at Bethel and accused of inciting a conspiracy against the royal household.

For Amos, being a worker for God was not a comfortable experience. He had to tell the unpalatable truth. And who was he, this herdsman, to be chosen by God for such an important role?

The story of Amos reminds us that God, in God's grace and wisdom, calls each of us to a specific task or series of tasks. We have been elected for this task. Often we – or others – may question whether we have the qualifications for the task or are worthy to be called. Nevertheless, God calls us and we are accountable to God for the responsibility with which we have been entrusted. We may experience discomfort or rejection, but we are called to obedience. In our obedience God's word is proclaimed and God's will is done for the benefit of the whole community.

✻ *Thank you, God, for loving me and calling me. Help me to discern your call to me. By the power of your Holy Spirit strengthen and support me in your service.*

Monday November 17   Luke 5:1–11

It is possible!

In this story of the call of Simon, James and John, Jesus used a sign to demonstrate that what the three fishermen thought was impossible was indeed possible. Simon, James and John had worked all night and caught nothing. Although they were sceptical, they obeyed Jesus and cast their nets one more time. The catch of fish that resulted was so large that the nets started to break and they had to call other friends to help them.

Simon agreed to try, just once more, because Jesus said so. Jesus invited the men to a vision beyond the disappointment of their previous experience. They were invited to embrace a vision of provision in the midst of lack and deficiency. This enlarged vision was, itself, a sign of the larger life to which they were being called. Jesus invited them to do something much more profound than perhaps they had ever thought themselves capable of. They were being called to become agents through whom others could be brought into the kingdom of God.

In the struggle for a just and peaceful world, we are encouraged to continue trying even in the face of disappointments and delays. We are encouraged to keep always in mind a vision of the world as God intends it to be. We are urged to remember that by God's grace and God's power, *it is possible*!

✻ *Gracious God, strengthen and encourage those who are in the leadership of movements for justice and peace in different parts of the world. May your will be done on earth as it is in heaven.*

Enabling leadership

The story of Dorcas (whose name can also be translated as 'Tabitha' or 'Gazelle') demonstrates in part ways in which workers for God can enable each other. Dorcas is identified as a 'disciple'. This seems to be important, as the feminine form of the word for 'disciple' is only found once in the Bible, in this story. In the book of Acts, other women are mentioned, but Dorcas is the only one who is specifically identified as a 'disciple'. For the early Christian community, therefore, Dorcas was a highly respected and acclaimed worker for God.

Dorcas' ministry seems to have been cut short because of her death. The Christian community mourns Dorcas' death as a loss to the entire community. Peter responds to the request for his presence and restores Dorcas to life. Peter acts and, in the context of prayer, enables Dorcas to continue her ministry. Peter and Dorcas are divided by gender – one is male, the other is female. Yet the story shows the respect and appreciation they have for each other's ministry, and the commitment they share to the raising up of the other, so that a ministry made dormant can be exercised for the benefit of the entire community.

Dorcas seems to be a 'widow', who demonstrates a creativity and enabling power in her ministry, including to other widows. She assists these other widows to obtain the basic necessities of life. She also, by serving others, demonstrates that being single does not necessarily make one a victim and object of others' generosity, but may open up new possibilities and opportunities for serving God.

✳ *We pray, O God, for those who are single, whether by choice, or through circumstances beyond their control. Grant them/us joy in your service and the experience of the abundant life.*

From sinner to disciple

The invitation of Christ to Levi required a response both from Levi and from the wider community. Levi's response was an act of repentance in which he left everything behind and followed Jesus. But what exactly did Levi leave behind? Was it a way of life that was changed? Was it his priorities that were different?

Was he, perhaps, one of the tax collectors who were dishonest and would overcharge the taxpayers for their own benefit?

One thing that is certain is that Levi did not have the high standards of observance of Jewish ritual laws that the Pharisees thought appropriate. What should be done with one who was perhaps something of an outcast, and whose life had not conformed to strict religious discipline, when such a one repents? Jesus' response provides an example for the church. The sick are to be healed, and repentant sinners are to be forgiven and restored to fellowship with the community. The whole community should celebrate this restoration and reconciliation, as happened with the banquet that Levi held.

Repentance such as Levi demonstrates has often been understood as applicable only to individual sinfulness. Some Christians have, however, explored ways in which groups and nations can engage in acts of repentance. One such act has been the campaign for the cancellation of the debt owed by poor countries, notably through the Jubilee 2000 campaign. For over five centuries some European countries and the United States of America benefited from slavery, colonialism and economic exploitation of marginalised groups and nations. Christians from Europe and the USA have participated in the Jubilee 2000 campaign through which the eight richest countries in the world have been challenged to write off the debt owed by the poorest countries. Some rich countries have written off debt owed to their governments. In many developing countries, however, governments still have to use funds, which should have been providing health care, education and basic amenities for their citizens, to pay debts, especially those owed to the International Monetary Fund (IMF) and the World Bank.

✴ *As we seek to follow you, O God, as individuals and as communities, reveal to us those things that we have to leave behind, in order to serve you. Grant that in your church all outcasts who desire to serve you may be met with welcome and celebration.*

Thursday November 20   *Acts 18:1–4*
Partners in God's service
Information about Priscilla and Aquila can be found not only in this passage, but also in Acts 18:24–28, Romans 16:3–5 and 1 Corinthians 16:19. In today's passage we are informed that the two have been forced to leave Italy, as the Emperor had ordered

all Jews to leave Rome. Like so many persons in the world today who are exiled, fleeing persecution, or who are refugees or migrants searching for a better life, Priscilla and Aquila had to uproot themselves, leave the familiar and make their way in uncertain circumstances. Yet the picture we have of this couple is not one of hopeless or dependent persons who become a liability in the community. They are skilled workers, tentmakers, and faithful in exercising their discipleship by hosting a church in their home and as teachers. They work as a team and in concert with other Christians, for example Paul. In changing circumstances, some of which were outside their control, they proved to be resourceful and faithful, an asset to their new community.

Priscilla and Aquila present an example of a leadership of co-operation and shared power among men and women, in God's service. As a married couple they contrast sharply with Ananias and Sapphira (Acts 5:1–11), who colluded to deceive and to disobey God.

Aquila and Priscilla also remind us that our homes can be places in which we bear witness to the good news, even in informal ways and through small acts of hospitality. They remind us that God has gifted men and women to share leadership and to exercise their gifts in the service of God's kingdom.

✳ *We pray for migrants, displaced persons, refugees and asylum seekers throughout the world, that they will find refuge and a chance to live in safety and have opportunities to develop and contribute to society. Grant wisdom and compassion to governments and agencies which make decisions about their welfare.*

Friday November 21   *Proverbs 31:10–31*
The perfect woman worker
This poem in praise of a wife of noble character is a carefully structured acrostic in the original Hebrew, each line starting with a successive letter of the alphabet. The careful structure of the poem and the details of the virtues of the woman described, suggest that the writer wanted to emphasise the authority and conviction underlying this idea of the 'perfect woman'. The woman described has many admirable qualities. She provides food and clothing for her household, she is a shrewd businesswoman, she increases the assets and wealth of her family, she is kind to others and she is God-fearing.

There are some troubling aspects to this picture, however. At the time when this poem was written, women's rights were restricted. All the assets that this woman acquired and increased in value would have been under the control of her husband. Her welfare to a large extent depended on her husband's favour. She also does not seem to get much rest! She gets up before daylight (verse 15), and hardly gets any sleep at night (verse 18). Sacrificing oneself for others is a virtue that has often been praised, but Jesus not only urged that we love our neighbours, but he implied that we should also love ourselves. Are there sacrifices that God does not want us to make? Do we as women (and men) who work for God devote enough time to rest and seeking the quiet places of solitude as Jesus himself did? Does God ask us to sacrifice for the benefit of others without protecting our own rights? Does God sometimes ask us to question accepted ideas about who is a 'perfect' woman worker, or a 'perfect' male worker?

✳ *God, who created the world and rested, who established cycles of night and day, activity and rest, bless those who work, especially those in stressful situations. May they find rest in you, and moments of joy and encouragement to strengthen them for their work.*

Saturday November 22   *Acts 8:26–38*

An African serving God

For centuries the contribution of Africa to the development of Judaism and Christianity was played down in the west. However, in the last century many scholarly works have been written exploring the ancient links of Africa and Africans to the Judeo-Christian tradition. Within the Bible itself, mention is made of many prominent Africans, for example the Queen of Sheba (1 Kings 10), Simon of Cyrene (Luke 23:26) and the Ethiopian eunuch. Some of these persons were powerful leaders, intellectually gifted, and God-fearing. The Ethiopian, for example, was reading from the prophets, indicating that he was a well-educated and reflective man. This image stands in stark contrast to the dominant image of Africans which the media in Europe and the United States have portrayed for many years, as people who have no education and no knowledge of God.

In the order of the book of Acts, the Ethiopian is the first Gentile convert to Christianity who is mentioned. His home was Napata-Meroe (modern Sudan), a place that at the time was considered to be the end of the known world. With the conversion of the Ethiopian and his return home, the gospel was seen to have spread beyond Jerusalem and reached everyone, both Jew and Gentile, even to the ends of the world. The inclusiveness of the gospel was further highlighted by mention of the Ethiopian being a eunuch. Traditionally, eunuchs were placed outside the community of Israel and not allowed into public worship (Deuteronomy 23:1). The conversion of such a person demonstrates the inclusive welcome of God in the new dispensation of the gospel.

Perhaps most significant of all was the fact that the conversion of the Ethiopian eunuch was God's initiative. God was already at work in the Ethiopian as he sought to know God by reading the prophet Isaiah. God was at work in Philip, telling him where to go and what to do every step of the way. It is God who calls us, provides for our nurture, and sends us on our way rejoicing in God's service.

✳ *May God's reign of justice, love and peace be experienced in nations and communities and overcome racism, inter-ethnic violence and prejudice, wherever they are found.*

FOR REFLECTION – alone or with a group

● What are some of the obstacles faced by people who are called to serve God? What steps can churches take to help all members exercise a variety of ministries in the church?

● What support should be available to clergy, teachers, social workers and others who lead and care for other people, especially those working in difficult circumstances?

● Who are the 'outsiders' in the church and other groups to which I/we belong? What could God be saying to me/us through the voice of those who are different from the majority?

FOR ACTION

Prayerfully consider what specific action you can take this week, either to respond more fully to God's call on your own life, or to enable someone else to respond to God's call.

WORK AND WORKERS
3. Guidelines for work

Notes on the New Revised Standard Version by
Victor Premasagar

Victor Premasagar, who has served as pastor in both rural and urban situations, was for many years Moderator of the Church of South India. He is well known internationally for his writing and as a teacher of theology. He is currently Professor of Biblical Studies at the Gurukul Lutheran Theological Institute in Madras.

'Work' is God's creation – gift to humans and not, as some argue, due to the Fall. God placed the first humans in the garden of Eden 'to till it and keep it' (Genesis 2:15). God also blessed them to multiply, cultivate the land and rule over the animals (Genesis1:28). In India there is a prejudice against work (*karma*), as it is believed to entangle one in bondage to endless rebirths (*samsara*) and hinders the individual self from realisation of oneness with the ultimate self (*Brahman*). Nevertheless, our readings this week help us to see that work and wages are basic human rights, which give dignity, security and a sense of fulfilment to all.

Sunday November 23   *Luke 19:1–10*
Work should bring blessing to others
Zacchaeus worked in the Revenue Department but used his position to amass wealth. Earlier, some tax collectors and soldiers had come to John the Baptist and asked him what they should do. John exhorted them to be content with their wages and collect only the prescribed amounts. When crowds asked him, John advised the ones who had two cloaks to give away one and similarly share food also.

Why did Zacchaeus, unasked, want to give to the poor and make restitution? Jericho is not far from the place where John baptised in the Jordan. Could it be that Zacchaeus was among the crowds and tax collectors who had come to John to be baptised? Perhaps John's message had challenged Zacchaeus but he found that he could not change his ways. Now meeting with Jesus moves him to respond to the demands of the kingdom.

Jesus declares that Zacchaeus is also a son of Abraham inasmuch as he has practised righteousness and justice through giving half to the poor and making restitution. The kingdom demands radical action on behalf of the poor and the oppressed.

✴ *Lord, we thank you for giving us work through which to serve and find fulfilment. Keep us from the temptation to misuse our position and privilege and give us the heart to share what little we have with those in need.*

Monday November 24   *1 Peter 2:18–25*

Work should be for doing the right, even if it means suffering

This is not an exhortation to accept oppression and injustice. The word used for 'slave' is not the usual one but indicates one serving in the family within a good relationship. When things seem to be oppressive, one is enjoined to do good and not wrong, even if it results in suffering. But the interpretation of this text depends on how one understands the suffering and death of Christ upon the cross. Was Jesus on the cross bowing down to evil or challenging and overcoming it?

Liberation from slavery is the ultimate goal, but meanwhile, whilst you work towards this goal, do good and do not be disgruntled and resort to evil. Oppression and evil should be protested against, following the example of Christ, so that justice and righteousness may prevail.

✴ *Lord, open our eyes to discern oppression and exploitation in the day-to-day patterns of life. Give us courage not to be co-opted into the dominant culture but to take the way of Christ, even if it means following him to the cross.*

Tuesday November 25   *Luke 3:12–14*

Work should be without corruption and misuse of power

John the Baptist was calling people to return (*shub*) to the Lord. John's call moved people to come to him asking what they could do for the kingdom.

The Pharisees and the Sadducees (religious leaders), tax collectors and soldiers were all professionals misusing their professional opportunities to oppress and exploit the common people. John exhorts them to repent, to stop exploitation, to bear fruit worthy of their calling (Matthew 3:7–8) and, as children of Abraham, to practise righteousness and justice (Genesis 18:19). The common people had become selfish in their struggles against oppression. John asks them to share what they have – an extra cloak or food – with their poorer neighbours.

In this age of globalisation and open market economy, the poor are becoming poorer and the rich richer. There is a culture of pursuing one's own progress at the expense of the other, especially the poor and the weak. However, in contrast to such an ethic, the kingdom demands wellbeing for all.

✳ *Lord, in this world of oppression, make us sensitive to the needs of others. Give us the heart to share with others, especially the poor, the weak and the unemployed in our midst.*

Wednesday November 26   *Leviticus 19:9–13*

Your work should benefit the poor and the weak among you

The different codes of law in the Old Testament express a special concern for the poor and the weak in the society. This passage from the Holiness Code (Leviticus 17–26) stipulates that one should not glean the harvest but leave it to the poor (verses 9–10). One should not deal falsely, nor lie to one another (verse 11), not defraud the neighbour, not hold back a labourer's wages until the next morning and not revile or hurt the physically impaired (verses 13–14). These are all neighbourly concerns related to work and wages. Leviticus gives these neighbourly concerns equal status with the Ten Commandments and the ritual laws of sacrifice. The general principle enunciated here is: share what you earn by hard work with those in need and also be honest and compassionate in your dealings with your neighbours.

This chapter also has the second part of the summary of the Law and the prophets: 'love your neighbour as yourself' (verse 18). Jesus combines this with the *Shema*, with its command to 'love the Lord God, with all your heart, and with all your soul, and with all your might' (Deuteronomy 6:4–5), and indicates that love of the neighbour is equally important as love of God (Matthew 19:19; 22:39; Mark 12:31).

✳ *Lord, you ate with the outcasts and the publicans, healed the sick and fed the hungry crowds. Grant that we too may be compassionate towards our neighbours and work together with them for their liberation and wellbeing.*

Work and wages in the service of the Lord

St Paul is here using a pun on the Hebrew word *pe'ullah* which means both work and wages. Work naturally results in reward and so the worker is worthy of his or her wages. It is a human right. Paul cites examples of different workers who are supported by their work. Even the oxen that thresh the harvest have the right to eat the grain! But Paul says that he and Barnabas had never made use of this right. They did not take advantage of their ministry as preachers of the gospel. They worked to support themselves and others.

Roland Allen, an Anglican missionary in China, wrote his epoch-making book, *Missionary Methods – St Paul's and Ours?* in 1912. In this book he advocated a tent-making ministry like that of St Paul and his associates, in which ministers supported themselves by their own labour. The pastoral ministry has in many places, however, become a full-time ministry which is supported by congregations. Nevertheless, the principle still holds that pastors and church leaders should not take undue advantage of their privileged position and make undue demands upon their congregations.

✳ *Lord, we thank and praise you for calling men and women into the full-time ministry of the church. Grant that they will be mindful of their call and not take undue advantage of their privileged position in the church. May they dedicate themselves to serve you, the servant Lord, and your people.*

Work without change or purpose is against God

The author of Ecclesiastes (*Qohelet*), a Wisdom writer, surveys the entire world of human work and sees nothing new. God also works. He created the world and humans and assigned work to them. But what gain do workers derive from their toil? Their work does not endure as God's does. Nevertheless, whatever God has done endures for ever and evokes in humans a sense of God's action in the past and also in the future. It is God's creation gift to humans that all should eat, drink and be happy. But they should also be concerned about the poor and the oppressed, who are denied these creation gifts of God.

In verse 15, *Qohelet* introduces a somewhat strange notion of God who 'seeks out what has gone by'. The early translations into Greek (*Septuagint*), Syriac (*Peshitta*) and Aramaic (*Targum*) assert that God seeks out the poor and the oppressed. Here the writer emphasises the prophetic teaching about justice to the poor in the community.

✳ *Lord, liberate us from the monotony of the work you have given us to do. Help us to see our work as contributing to your kingdom. Grant that we may struggle against all injustice and oppression and work for equity and justice, sharing what you have given to us with those in need.*

Saturday November 29   *2 Thessalonians 3:6–13*

Do not be idle while waiting for the Lord's return

St Paul's letter about the Lord's coming impressed the believers in Thessalonica so much that they stopped work and were simply waiting for the Lord! Paul was appalled at this and exhorted them not to be idle but to work and support the weak.

Work today is more complex than in Paul's day. In this competitive, open market and technological age, many are unemployed. Globalisation, the open market, the multinationals and the state all play their part in controlling the nature of work and employment in our time. Many are without work, which goes against God's desire for human beings.

This passage reminds us of other New Testament passages about work. The parable of the labourers in the vineyard, with its emphasis on the master's generosity, expresses God's concern for the unemployed. The steward found awake and working when the master returned is commended for his alertness and readiness to act. The Lord wants his disciples to be active in work when he comes again in glory.

✳ *Lord, we thank you for the promise of your coming again to establish your reign of justice and peace. Grant that when you come we may be found faithful and active in the service of others.*

FOR REFLECTION – alone or in a group

● How can routine work be made interesting and challenging?
● As a Christian, what types of work do you consider to be a witness to the Lord?
● Worship should challenge the faithful to engage in acts of liberation. How can the local congregation become a witness to Christ by its service and action in the world?

FOR ACTION

As a church, undertake a study of the patterns of employment and unemployment in your area. Consider what contribution the church could make to fairer work practices in the community.

ADVENT – LUKAN THEMES
1. Redemption drawing near

Notes based on the New Revised Standard Version by
Maureen Edwards

Maureen Edwards, now retired, has compiled and edited many books for IBRA, and is still the editor of the Methodist Prayer Handbook. Having previously worked in mission education for the Methodist Church, she now enjoys being involved in the mission and ministry of her local church and in particular helps with a club for people with mental health problems.

We live in troubled times: ethnic conflict and continuing violence in the Middle East and many other parts of the world. Make your own list. Jesus too lived in a violent society: acts of terrorism by fierce nationalists known as Zealots, brutal massacres by Roman armies, the elimination of hundreds of infants by King Herod, racial hatred and xenophobia. Advent 2003 is little different.

Yet the Advent message is one of hope. We are encouraged to look forward to God's redemptive activity. God enters this rescue mission through the Son of Man, one who comes down and is human like us. The good news is that this mission has begun in Jesus Christ himself – that in him, and through the activity of the Spirit, we have hope that God's kingdom of righteousness and peace will transform the earth.

Sunday November 30   *Luke 21:25–36**
Transforming people
Jesus talks of 'the Son of Man' coming on clouds, the human one, flesh of our flesh, whose glory is not in victory but in his silent, immovable resistance to human violence and power. Such a life as his cannot be swallowed up: God can remake the world through life that ends in apparent failure and intense suffering. In neither history nor Jesus do we see God with manipulative control trumping the actions of nations and terrorists.

Yet a new order is possible and its signs are as obvious as leaves on the trees in summer: women are given respect and justice, the marginalised are brought into the centre, the words of children matter, and there is the potential for a jubilee for debtors. These signs of the kingdom are indestructible; they are all around us if we have eyes to see. There is every reason to hold on to our faith and pray that the nations will share this vision of a new earth, so that people, no longer oppressed, do not have to resort to terrorism, and so that through prayer we may find strength and courage to live through difficult and testing times.

✳ *Come, O Emmanuel, your love never fails.*
Set us free from all that destroys, that we may share with you in your mission to reconcile all people.

Monday December 1   *Romans 8:18–23*
Transforming the earth
As I write this (almost two years before you read it), a massive volcano has just erupted in Goma, Congo. Think of other recent natural disasters. Add to those our growing concern about the effects of pollution and the depleted ozone layer. Hold in your mind countries in the South Pacific that will disappear if global warming cannot be halted.

Paul reminds us how fragile the world is; how subject it is to decay; how prone to accident. Scarred landscapes, polluted rivers, dying forests cry out in agony to be set free to share 'the freedom of the glory of the children of God' (verse 21). He also reminds us that we human beings are inseparable from the earth: we share its pain. Together we pray for redemption. A similar insight comes from the native American tradition: 'This we know: the earth does not belong to man; man belongs to the earth. All things are connected like the blood which unites one family' (Chief Seattle).

✳ *In trepidation and terror*
we watch our shores
lest the high waters drown our beaches.
Lord, hasten the day when all creation is renewed,
with us, in faith, hope and love.

           Sione Amanaki Havea, Tonga
           From Oceans of Prayer (NCEC)

Tuesday December 2   *Luke 2:22–35*
Light of the world
Jesus' parents, faithfully carrying out their Jewish religious rites, brought him to the Temple in Jerusalem – the city to which he was to make many pilgrimages, the city for whose future he would weep (because it did not recognise the time of its redemption – Luke 19:41–44), the city outside which he would be

crucified, deserted and lonely. Little did Mary and Joseph realise that the words of this strange eccentric would come true. Simeon saw beyond their limited expectations to a better future, not only for his own community, but for all peoples. In this tiny fragile babe he saw God's light shining in the world's dark struggle for power.

We need inconspicuous people like Simeon, who do not fit into our category of the 'normal': people with learning difficulties, disabled people, psychotic depressives, lonely people. For God speaks through them. 'God chose what is weak in the world' to surprise and challenge 'the strong' with fresh insights (1 Corinthians 1:27b). Simeon's message is that this child's way to save the world turns its power structures upside down. He will be very vulnerable, and Mary herself must be prepared for this.

✳ *Praise be to you, O God,*
  for in Christ you have stretched our vision.
  We see your light, the salvation 'you have prepared
  in the presence of all peoples'.

Wednesday December 3   *Luke 2:36–38*

Lifting up the lowly

I have thought of Anna, on more than one occasion, when I have been introduced to others as 'a minister's widow', as though I am not a person in my own right.

Anna was a loner. She had been a widow for most of her life, dropped out and excluded from 'normal' activities; she had no status; she was marginalised even by the community of faith. In his gospel, Luke focuses on people who are 'different': shepherds, a childless ageing couple, Simeon and Anna, the 'poor'. In his first two chapters, he is saying that King Herod, the Emperor Augustus and Quirinius the governor of Syria (2:1–2) actually inhabited a smaller world than the poor. The poor are lifted up by God whose redemptive plan turns the world's values upside down. Recall the words of Mary: 'He has brought down the powerful from their thrones, and lifted up the lowly' (Luke 1:52).

It was Anna, out of her experience of isolation, who encouraged the congregation in the Temple to look beneath the glitter of the world's elite to what is small and hidden to discover the way that God would save them.

✳ *Isolated God, challenge our limited vision;*
  open our eyes to see you in the lonely
  and our minds to receive and learn from their insights.

A new community

This letter, written to a congregation of masters and slaves, rich people and poor, speaks of them as a community of love (verse 4) and hope (verse 5), whose influence is felt in 'the whole world' (verse 6). The writer gives thanks for their faith and prays that they may have strength to endure difficult times.

Read again verses 13 and 14, for here he points to the heart of the gospel: a new quality of life is possible because their past is forgiven. Redemption is a present reality.

Knowing that, through the grace of God, we are forgiven and can make a new start each day also transforms our relationships in the family, the community and eventually the world. We may not even move from the community where we were born, but our children and grandchildren, who go to work in other places, carry with them the values they have learned from us. We will probably never know the chain of renewed relationships which have flowed from our homes into 'the whole world', but a difference will have been made where people are in pain, isolated, divided by race and culture, searching for truth.

✸ ***Come, O Emmanuel, forgive and renew us
and use us as channels of your redeeming grace.***

God's long-term plan

Redemption, says the writer of this letter, is not a new strategy; it has been part of God's plan from 'before the foundation of the world' (verse 4). God 'chose us in Christ', but we need to remember that God's choice is never exclusive as ours tends to be, for God's plan, in 'the fullness of time', is to bring 'all things', the whole history of the universe, into completion in Christ. God's love extends to all people and the earth, despite our wars and factions and the pollution, flaws and catastrophes of our environment. Notice here the emphasis that we are redeemed not merely as individuals but in community, as 'God's people' with 'all things'. As we saw in Sunday's reading, the natural world and humankind are one: they cannot be separated.

And finally, in this whole process God's extraordinary loving, sacrificial way will be vindicated. The glory of God (verse 14) is seen supremely in the cross, in the blood of the innocent Christ. The climax of history from God's perspective is not the kind of victory the world expects, but bitterness and hatred will have been redeemed by perfect love, by the blood of Christ and the blood of martyrs, and by the witness of all who have lived in a Christlike way. In God's kingdom the thrones and victories of the powerful have no reality. Instead the victims and servants are truly blessed, to God's eternal glory.

✳ *'Blessed are the meek, for they will inherit the earth' (Matthew 5:5). Forgive the pride and stubbornness that separate us from one another and from you, that we may share in your eternal, upside-down kingdom.*

Saturday December 6   *Hebrews 9:11–14*
With his own blood

Christ offered himself for our salvation: his perfect life, his own blood. He did not offer a substitute. The writer speaks from his Jewish experience of the Day of Atonement, when the High Priest entered the Holy Place and sprinkled the blood of animals to atone for the sins of the people. Christ, on the other hand, poured out his blood on a hill where criminals were executed, and yet God was powerfully present, for God is always with the poor, the outcast, the victims. There Christ entered 'the greater and perfect tent (not made with hands...)' and offered himself, a sacrifice so perfect that it affects our conscience, changes us and sets us free to worship God for ever.

The writer points back to the tent of the wilderness experience (verse 11). Read chapter 13:12–15 where he reminds us that Christ died 'outside the camp'. True worship which takes us straight to the heart of the eternal, ever-loving God makes us one with God's poor who mostly live 'outside the camp'.

✳ *We are your temple not made with hands.*
We are your body.
If every wall should crumble, and every church decay,
we are your habitation.
Ours are the eyes with which you, in the mystery,
look out in compassion on the world...
Take us 'outside the camp', Lord.
Outside holiness.
Out to where soldiers gamble,
and thieves curse,
and nations clash
at the cross-roads of the world...
                                    George F MacLeod (1895–1991) ˙
                                    (Wild Goose Publications; permission sought)

FOR REFLECTION – alone or with a group

● Reflect on recent international events and try to identify those areas where you see God's kingdom present.

● Where do you see Christians bridging the gap between church and society?

● Which of your own activities are 'outside the camp'?

FOR ACTION

Listen to and reflect on the insights of children and people whose words and actions usually go unnoticed.

LIVING PRAYERS series

● Compiled by Maureen Edwards, a former IBRA editor

● User-friendly for individuals, groups & churches

Living Prayers For Today:

● Prayers for private devotions & public worship

● Modern and well-known older prayers from different parts of the world

More Living Prayers for Today:

● Focuses on the Christian festivals

● Includes some prayers for everyday use

UK price £15.50 each
(includes postage and packing)

**International
Bible Reading
Association**

Order through your IBRA representative, or from the appropriate address on page 303

ADVENT – LUKAN THEMES
2. The voice in the wilderness

Notes based on the King James Version and interlinear Greek by
David Hart

David Hart has worked as an Anglican university chaplain, a theatre critic and an arts administrator, and is now again a freelance writer, working as a poet. He grew up in mid-Wales and has lived for many years in Birmingham, UK.

In approaching these texts I have not felt I had anything to say. I couldn't do better than Luke and Matthew in saying what seemed necessary but I have, as it were, asked what was there that might show itself to me here and now in poetry. I am using poetry as a kind of research, as a way of wondering aloud. Poems will always be partial and fragmentary, suggestive and not definitive. The gospels offer themselves as if we were there, only we are not, we are here.

Poems work by a variety of means, by, for instance, taking short cuts, holding images up for closer inspection or offering an emphasis by way of repetition. They may hesitate, may leave a line unfinished so as to suggest the pause may be significant. Perhaps most of all they try to keep language out of its routines, out of its assumptions and worn ways. Success, of course, is not assured.

Perhaps responding to the gospels with poems suggests the infinite possibilities there are in language and in the discovery of images. We are speaking and image-making animals. Not least does this mean that empathy is made possible for us, taking on other people's voices and feelings, allowing, to a degree at least, what is there wanting to show itself.

Prayers too, being poems, are, one might say, experiments in translation, in trying to find ways in which to speak, to connect, to offer, to bring towards, to allow.

Sunday December 7   *Luke 3:1–6**
Here comes God
    Every ravine of us filled in,
    every mountain of us flattened,
    every twist straightened,
    every roughness smoothed,
    here comes God

and then the ups and downs again
differently.
Tiberias is sunbathing,
Pilate is sunbathing,
Herod is sunbathing,
Philip is sunbathing,
Lysanias is sunbathing,
John is having a crazy turn.

* *Holy Spirit,*
do what needs doing
to our imagination
to make us even if momentarily
as if knowledgeable.

Monday December 8   Luke 1:5–25

It's too late
It's too late,
it's too late,
it's too late,
it's all but over,
it's too late,
nothing else of interest now,
it's too late.
Then the messenger.

* *Holy Spirit,*
into the womb of my possibility
come.

Tuesday December 9   Luke 1:57–66

And, and, and
And, and, and, the *ands* pile up,
time carries the stories and us on *ands*,
until the *but* in the form of
an *and* and a *No*.
Not so fast with the assumptions, she says,
we are in the first chapter
of a book of surprises.

* *Holy Spirit, let me know*
when and *must become* but*,*
when OK *must become* No*.*

Shown the way

We were shown the way before
and we were shown the way again
and we were shown the way again,
his holy-since-time-began prophets
showed us the way
as they were themselves shown
and now we are being shown again.
Through I AM's bowels of compassion
this baby
will prepare the way.

✳ ***Holy Spirit,***
***here* again**
in the* afterwards *of the stories
and in the* always before *of what will come,
hold us
towards.

Trust the evidence

'I'm in prison,
are you the coming one,
the *other*?'
'Trust the evidence'.

✳ ***Holy Spirit,***
my breath,
my language,
my seeing,
my hearing,
my questions,
without certainty
ask me.

You missed him

So you missed him.
No one out of the human gene-pool
has been more to be taken notice of
(but still the gene-pool in heaven
is something else)
and you missed him.
He hasn't come off the catwalk

and the bank manager would have
smiled and
shown him the door.
He's Elijah,
he's the messenger,
poor bloke.

* *Holy Spirit,*
I'm going to get this wrong every time
but for all that
don't abandon me.

Saturday December 13   *Matthew 14:1–12*
Another man's head
To save face he had delivered
another man's head
and now it seemed that head
and the rest of who it had been
had come back
and was out there again
playing havoc
with the air waves.
There was a lot to fear
out there,
in here.

* *Holy Spirit,*
my head
out there
in here
still on my shoulders,
so.
Amen

FOR REFLECTION – alone or with a group
● How has the poetry of this week's notes helped you find new
  ways of reading the Bible?
● What has surprised you, shocked you, puzzled you or
  provoked you in the poems?
● In what ways do you see the gospels themselves as poetry?

FOR ACTION
Try writing your own poem response(s) to one or two of the
week's readings. Share your poem with another person.

ADVENT: LUKAN THEMES
3. Repent and change

Notes based on the Revised English Bible by
Joy Mead

Joy Mead is a poet and a writer who broadcasts occasionally on BBC radio, leads creative writing groups and is involved in development education and justice and peace work. She is also a new member of the Iona community.

All this week's readings are variations of a call to look long and hard at the way we live. There is much talk of the coming dawn and seeing the light – pointing to the way repentance as a *process* of healing (not a cure) leads out of the dark and has the creative potential to bring hope. This is not about personal evil alone – there is no such thing as totally private repentance – nor is it an abstract concept. It's firmly grounded in how we live and relate and connect. Repenting is implicitly about changing: personally, socially, and politically.

Sunday December 14   *Luke 3:7–18**
Something's coming...

The story of John's appearance out of the desert is full of wonderful elemental imagery: fire, water, stones, roots, fruit, chaff. There is something basic and earthy about this big, surprising character in his camel hair coat. He is unkempt and unbending. His cries are loud and insistent: 'Wake up! See the light! Repent!' His simple message – many would say he is naïve, or simply doesn't understand the complexities of the situation – puts the fear of God into the oppressors, the powerful, the men in suits! He isn't asking for restructuring or adjustments in programmes. He's calling for a complete change of heart so that all may share in the earth's good gifts. Share, deal honestly, don't bully or oppress, 'prove' your repentance – a message that is the basis of the gospel and holds good today. Big changes need to be made but there is hope and John has a strong sense of expectation. Something good is coming. John's world-ending wrath and call to repentance are an essential prelude to the coming joy, the new wholeness, the better world waiting to be born.

✳ *Spirit of love and anger, stir us up so that we may be angry at greed and seek passionately the use of our skills and resources to sustain and cherish all life.*

Forgiveness

'Speak the truth,' Paul says. This isn't a little homily about not lying; it's a big message about the truths at the heart of life: how to be, how to relate to others. The instructions are clear enough: be 'generous ... tender-hearted ... and ... forgiving...' The weight of the gospel lies behind the word 'forgiveness'. It's inseparable from repentance. Forgiveness deals with the past and makes the future possible.

In his book *No Future Without Forgiveness* (published by Rider in 1999), Desmond Tutu writes about *ubuntu*, an African concept which is difficult to put into a Western language. It is about the essence of being human – not 'I think therefore I am' but 'I am a human being because I belong'. If someone has *ubuntu*, she recognises our inter-relatedness – she participates and shares, is open and available to others and knows herself part of a greater whole. Harmony in community relies upon generosity, tender-heartedness and forgiveness so that people may survive, repent and emerge still human in spite of all that tries to make them less than human. There is a future for all.

✳ ***Vulnerable God, make us generous, tender-hearted and forgiving when faced with our own and other people's frailty.***

Peace with justice

Jeremiah, one of the Exile prophets, learned his trade from Amos and Micah, the great social justice poets. He is a hands-on prophet. With eyes wide open, he seeks to save what he can out of a national calamity – and isn't put off by ridicule or persecution. He wants his people to grow and mature, to amend their ways, beginning with a hard look at the words they use repeatedly. To make a place the 'temple of the Lord' needs more than saying that's what it is. Jeremiah distrusts slogans and flag-waving. He knows that repentance is about letting go old thought-patterns and images, re-structuring the way we come to know, making words and lifestyle agree, making the needs of others our own. No amount of shouting 'Peace, peace' where there is no peace, no amassing of weapons, or dependence on your past, no missile system will protect you. Jeremiah's message is that we should live lightly and let others be, cease to oppress, care for the weak, trust difference and welcome the strangers. The only true security is justice.

✳ *God of holy process, move us to change our ways as well as our language so that our weapons may become ploughshares in practice as well as in poetry.*

Wednesday December 17   *Isaiah 58:1–9*

Letting go and letting be

What is expected of a nation returning from exile in Babylon and rebuilding after a disaster? People are full of hope, excitement – and temptation. What are the proper religious practices? The answer isn't so much about laws and ritual fasting as about with whom you share your bread; not so much about doing as not doing – relinquishing control. We go to great lengths to protect our right to control with whom we share bread. George MacLeod, the founder of the Iona Community, said: 'The greatest community problem of our modern world is how to share bread.' No issue raises questions of justice more than food. Each time we gather for a meal we link ourselves with those whose plates are empty.

Isaiah's prophetic words, like all good poetry, are grounded in being, not abstraction. He sees repentance as practical healing. What is hurting the people is greed and national pride. Fasting as sharing is more costly than ritual fasting but is the way through to resurrection hope. Act justly: house, clothe, feed, share, and let go. Loose, untie, set free; then your religious practices and symbolism will reflect your life and 'your light will break forth like the dawn'.

✳ *Naked God, unclothe us of pride, unweave our thoughts, uncomplicate our hearts.*

Thursday December 18   *Ezekiel 11:17–20*

A heart of flesh

Ezekiel, another Exile prophet, is an astute observer of political events. He lives during a time of tragedy and transformation when God's promise to Israel comes to be understood as being about community rather than land. Ezekiel looks for changes in feelings: in relationships and, especially, attitudes to foreigners.

The people must recognise their responsibility and not try to shift the blame for their own fear and guilt onto the foreigners they cannot love. If they repent and change, they will be transformed into a fully human and loving people. 'A heart of flesh' is an evocative way of talking about compassion. For it is compassion which gives a community its 'singleness of heart' and transforms relationships between people. Compassion is elusive and hard to define. It isn't a virtue. It isn't altruism. It isn't religion. It isn't a fruit of the Spirit. It's a connected way of life: not individual but communal consciousness and feeling. Compassion enlivens and enfleshes the hearts, making people imaginative, questioning, vulnerable and open to the needs of others. Compassion leads to acts of mercy and love, makes transformation possible.

✳ *Spirit of gentleness, we have need of hearts that feel the hurts of others as if they are our own. Make such hearts in us.*

Friday December 19   *Ezekiel 33:10–16*
Live in this day
If you read the earlier verses you will see that Ezekiel is the 'watchman' at the gate, sounding the alarm, warning and encouraging. In this chapter he, like Isaiah, has taken a wonderfully daring step away from logic into the realms of love beyond reason. Ezekiel's life-giving, life-enhancing message stresses the freedom to choose to give up wrongdoing without the coercion or fear of punishment. Implicit in what he says is the need to be aware of the way that what we do impinges on the lives of others. He has that sense of interdependence and immediacy typical and necessary for the 'watchman'. Perhaps today he is waiting at the gate for the rich countries to acknowledge connections between power and powerlessness, between overfilled supermarket shelves and hunger, between poverty and terrorism. We still have choice but there is much we choose not to understand. Ezekiel's message is clear and hopeful: the good or bad of your past will not help or hinder you. Confess and be humbled. Your sorrow will transform this day and move the people towards a better future.

✳ *May we bear no grudges, carry no reserves. May we live this moment fully and wholly.*

Saturday December 20   *Romans 13:11–14*
Day is near
Paul goes through dark times but never loses his sense that the light, of love not law, is with him.

New life begins in the dark – in the earth, in the womb – but needs the light. Sometimes it seems we would rather stay in the dark, half alive. The coming day is feared. Its light will show all our blemishes and faults: 'debauchery ... vice ... quarrels ... jealousies' (verse 13). There is much that the dark keeps hidden.

But unless we choose to greet the dawn, see what is wrong and meet it in the full light of day, there will be no new beginning. Repentance and change don't happen in the dark. In the light, we're all human, with our faults and our differences, and we are all loved. As we reject the darkness and meet the light, we feel the forgiving, healing, renewing warmth of the sun. We can greet the dawn and delight in all the beauty around us. We rejoice, walking freely and without fear on the good earth.

✴ *May we wonder at the beauty of the dawn without trying to make sense of all the light.*

FOR REFLECTION – alone or with a group

● Think about repentance as owning your responsibility for what happens in the world. Where does that lead you personally?

● Do this week's readings lead you to any change of heart, personally, socially, politically? Does this change make you look at your thought-patterns and lead you to seek different images of God?

FOR ACTION

● Listen and look with open hearts.

● Make the anguish of others your own.

● Challenge injustice wherever you meet it.

ADVENT – LUKAN THEMES
4. Mary

Notes based on the Revised English Bible by
Ruth Shelton

Ruth Shelton is a poet and illustrator who has worked within a wide range of Christian contexts, including working for the Church of England as a Social Responsibility Officer for seven years. She has recently moved from London where she was Director of Pastoral Training at Campion House, Osterley. She is now freelancing, including working as Poet-in-Residence at the Shepherd Special School in Nottingham.

The mysterious beauty of these readings, captured in many great paintings in the Western tradition, feeds our spirituality and sense of wonder. However, the conventions with which they have been surrounded can also be a barrier to understanding and feeling what these stories might mean for our own context.

'What do you see?' the Lord asked Jeremiah at the time of the prophet's first call and visions. In answer to John the Baptist's poignant question, 'Are you the one who is to come?', Jesus replied, 'Go and tell John what you have seen and heard: the blind regain their sight, the lame walk…' (Luke 7:20–23). Shortly afterwards he asked the crowds: 'What did you go out to see'? (Luke 7:24–28). Shepherds, angels, stars… what are we being asked to see in our own streets and towns?

Sunday December 21   *Luke 1:26–38*
A woman is deeply troubled

A 16-year-old woman in a project for homeless people in Nottingham was white with shock, and crying. She was pregnant. She said to me, 'Christ knows what I'm going to do, but it feels like … like a present.' The gift was not only hers but ours too – if only we had acknowledged and recognised her child. I never saw her again, but it is likely that she and her child not only remained invisible to us, but were also scapegoated by our failure: by abortion, lack of support, lack of housing or education.

Mary was pregnant, unmarried, poor, and deeply troubled. Systematic theology expresses a degree of perplexity that such an extraordinary event should happen in an ordinary place. The story is viewed from the perspective of this woman. A 'servant of the Lord' who confesses that the Lord has looked upon her in her lowliness (Luke1:48) tells us that it is in our own ordinary places and our own ordinary troubles that God makes himself known – if only we can recognise the gift of his presence.

✳ *Mary, mother of us, lead us to your son.*
Where will we find him?
We will find him in the tears of the homeless.
We will find him in the cries of a child.

Monday December 22   *Matthew 1:18–25*
A woman is vilified
In Botticelli's 'Mystic Nativity', the paths and rocky walls leading to the manger zigzag angrily and the rocks are scarred like lances of which the sharpest point touches Mary's brow. How can we re-imagine the immediate feelings of the historical Mary in her journey towards the birth?

In Matthew's version of the events it is Joseph's humiliation which is the most easily imagined. The woman's suffering is invisible. The mutterings against her that are hinted at in Joseph's first decision to 'have the marriage contract quietly put aside' would not only have caused pain in her soul, but were directed against her very flesh. Then, as now, the sexual behaviour of men and women is judged by different standards. In order to bear the one who would 'save his people from their sins' Mary had to defy the notions of sin in the community in which she lived. The one whom she was suffering to bring into the world did not recoil from fleshliness like Mary's detractors but chose it as his dwelling-place. Mary turned the shame of what her body was saying to the world into a triumph.

✳ *Mary, mother of us, lead us to your son.*
Where will he be?
He will be with the women of the night,
watching with mothers who are alone.

Tuesday December 23   *Luke 1:39–45**
A woman responds
For a pregnant woman and those close to her, the heartbeat and kicks of the unborn child provide some of the most moving and exciting moments of the experience. Although the child as a personality is unknown, the deep sense of recognition amounts to a kind of knowledge.

The person whom Elizabeth honours in this account was a young pregnant woman in worn clothing, whose hands were calloused with work and whose ankles were thick from hours of standing. She had just struggled on foot to a town 'in the uplands' of Judea. We see such women, headscarved and old before their time, most nights in the background of some event on our television screens. They are the invisible and despised who carry out over two-thirds of the world's work for less than a third of the pay. Elizabeth recognises Mary's dignity and who it is that she carries within her – the very movements within her own womb are part of her response.

Elizabeth's question can be our question too – 'Who am I, that the mother of my Lord should visit me?' (verse 43) – as he continues to come to us within the abused flesh of the poor of the world.

✳ *Mary, mother of us, lead us to your son.*
What is he seeing?
He is seeing the beauty of the outcast.
He is greeting the dignity of women.

Wednesday December 24, Christmas Eve　　　　　*Luke 2:1–14**
A woman gives birth
In Botticelli's 'The Nativity', we can see an angel drawing back the hood of the shepherd's cloak as if to say, 'Look – open your eyes!' If we *close* our eyes and imagine the nativity, most of us would see a scene of calm beauty: mystical light emanating from the depths of the stable, the figures transfixed in an eternal transport of worship. Such images, often associated with childhood memories of Christmas, engender a sense of certainty and security – Christ has come into our world, and all will be well.

We need the aid of a seeing angel to draw back the cloak from our eyes. Symbol can neither replace history nor divorce itself from history and we need to return to the concrete history of Mary the village woman, undergoing one of the most painful and emotional events of her life – giving birth, far from her home and the neighbours and relatives who would customarily have helped her. It was terrifying for her and it should be terrifying for us – who is this child? Something we have waited and longed for is suddenly here – alive – to be loved, engaged with, responded to. But what will he ask of me?

✳ *Mary, mother of us, lead us to your son.*
What will he ask of me?
He will ask for your life and your love.
He will give them back a hundredfold.

A woman ponders

One day when I was holding my nephew, my sister looked at him intently and remarked how strange it felt to see him from another perspective – other than holding him tightly to her own breast. She said, 'I think I am surprised by him.'

Luke's narrative emphasises Mary's active meditation on the question of the meaning of her son's life. After the shepherds' visit he reports that 'Mary treasured up all these things and pondered over them' (verse 19). The prediction of Jesus' significance by Simeon is addressed specifically to Mary (Luke 2:34–35). Later, when Jesus replied to Mary's consternation when he got lost in the Temple (2:48–52) she 'treasured up all these things in her heart', the very place where she would be torn asunder, pierced by 'seven swords', the death by torture of her beloved son.

It is possible that throughout her life she would continue to be surprised by him, swinging between fear and love and doubt but always an active participant in his drama rather than a static worshipper at his shrine. If the coming of Christ does not disturb us and take us where we would rather not go then the incarnation remains a mere idea stuck on a dusty shelf. The real life of this real mother with her joyful suffering heart holds out the living Christ to us – to our continual surprise.

✳ *Mary, mother of us, lead us to your son.*
How will we know him?
We will know him when we least expect him.
We will know him when we feel afraid.

A woman challenges

Occasionally in the obituary columns one reads about a life which can be interpreted in terms of historical transformation – a philosopher, a revolutionary or a politician. They tend to be male, famous and dead.

In Mary's famous exclamation, a young, poor woman defines the historical realities of her time and commits her life to overturning them. She is also able, uniquely, to tell her people about the kind of God they are waiting for. Although he is holy – the *Tremendum* whose approach we can only await with reverential fear – his merciful heart hears the cry of women like Hannah, whose canticle of gratitude becomes the basis of Mary's Magnificat (1 Samuel 2:1–10).

The God who is coming is mighty, but he is not unknown – he has already intervened in the lives of ordinary poor people, as he transforms the life and the body of the woman who announces his reign.

The Magnificat is neither rhetoric nor optimism. Mary tells us that God's mercy takes historical forms and is made concrete in deeds. The ground on which she stands is that of a poor, occupied nation – and it is the ground on which we are standing today.

✳ *Mary, mother of us, lead us to your son.*
Where is his country?
His country is the place where you are,
his nation the deeds of the ordinary.

Saturday December 27   John 19:25b-27

A woman watches her son die

In my study is a still from Pasolini's film *The Gospel According to St Matthew*. A group of people are stumbling up a rocky hill. Among them is a stout matron dressed in black, her careworn face contorted in agony. This is Mary on Calvary. The doctrines and concepts in theology exalt Mary, but if that exaltation falls into mythology or 'succumbs to the numinous world of archetypes', as Leonardo Boff warns, we diminish both her and our own possibilities. For if Mary had such extraordinary powers, how can we ordinary humans stand at the foot of the cross?

In Palestine, Afghanistan, Africa and throughout the world women watch their sons die. They hold up photographs of their missing children, thus risking arrest. They take medicine and food behind enemy lines. The consequence of these actions – the suffering, the cross – will not lead to greater certainty, as can be seen in Jesus' own cry of despair on the cross. The more we love, the more we are endangered.

Why would we want to make such a journey? But Mary chose to, and her ordinariness shows us that we can.

✳ *Mary, mother of us, lead us to your son.*
Where will we follow him?
We will follow him to the foot of the cross,
where the mothers of the world are weeping.
We will find his hidden glory
in the lives of the ordinary
and the magnitude of small lives
will change all our lives for ever.

FOR REFLECTION – alone or with a group

- What are the problems and issues that young women are facing in your neighbourhood or locality?
- What visible evidence of poverty do you see in your town, village, or city?
- Who are the groups of people, individuals or agencies who are addressing these issues?

FOR ACTION

Take some positive action in response to these questions this Christmas.

ADVENT – LUKAN THEMES
5. Growing in wisdom and stature

Notes based on the New Revised Standard Version by
Joanna T Redhead

Joanna T Redhead is a primary mathematics officer and project co-ordinator at the department of education, the University of the Bahamas, Nassau. She is a Methodist local preacher.

The story of King Solomon's wisdom is well known. But Solomon proved not to be as wise as one would have expected, and did not always do right in the eyes of God. Let us then look at what is meant by 'wisdom'. Paradoxically, it is from the proverbs of Solomon that we may extract the meaning of 'wisdom'. In the Prologue to the Proverbs we read: 'For learning about wisdom and instruction, for understanding words of insight, for gaining instruction in wise dealing, righteousness, justice and equity; to teach shrewdness to the simple, knowledge and prudence to the young – let the wise also hear and gain in learning, and the discerning acquire skill, to understand a proverb and a figure, the words of the wise and their riddles. The fear of the Lord is the beginning of knowledge; fools despise wisdom and instruction.' (Proverbs 1:2–7). Solomon would have fared much better, both for himself and for his offspring, if he had heeded verse 7. However, he ceased to fear the Lord and paid for it.

'The Lord gives wisdom; from his mouth come knowledge and understanding' (Proverbs 2:6). Those who hear and heed the Lord's words gain wisdom through the knowledge and understanding so gained. All wisdom then, whatever its content or provenance, has to do with God and has its source in God. The insights gained from knowledge of the ways of God and applied to daily living are the focus of this week's readings.

Sunday December 28   *Luke 2:41–52**
Mild, obedient, good

Wisdom, it is said, is intelligent use of knowledge. During his visit to the Temple, Jesus is gaining knowledge, through 'listening to them (the teachers) and asking them questions' (verse 46). This is the only indication we have of Jesus' early preparations for his ministry, though we are told previously that 'the child (Jesus) grew and became strong, filled with wisdom; and the favour of God was upon him' (Luke 2:40). The words of a well-known children's hymn by Cecil Francis Alexander (1823–95) convey the wisdom of the child Jesus thus:

> And through all his wondrous childhood
> He would honour and obey,
> Love, and watch the lowly maiden
> In whose gentle arms He lay.
> Christian children all must be
> Mild, obedient, good as He.

But 'Jesus increased in wisdom and in years, and in divine and human favour' (verse 52). His wisdom grew as he did. He learned as he matured – learned to live and make intelligent use of his knowledge.

Jesus' knowledge was of God and of humanity. Jesus knew that his short ministry would be fraught with trials, including the ultimate test of death on the cross. Even though he prayed to have this final test removed, he was prepared to accept his father's will and proceed with it. He had prepared himself by developing the wisdom to face his suffering and death. For God's wisdom helps us to face all trials and tribulations, and sustains us through them with the hope of at last coming home to that place where we shall be known fully, and shall fully know:

> And our eyes at last shall see him,
> Through his own redeeming love;
> For that child so dear and gentle,
> Is our Lord in heaven above;
> And he leads his children on
> To the place where he is gone.

✳ *Lord, help us to grow in wisdom all the days of our lives, until at last we come to see you face to face.*

Monday December 29   *1 Samuel 2:18–20, 26**

Samuel the Nazirite

Samuel grew up in the presence of the Lord under the tutelage of Eli. His deportment, actions and attitudes were of particular note when compared to the behaviour and sins of Eli's sons. The sons of Eli showed no respect for, indeed no knowledge of, the Lord. Their deeds indicated a great lack of regard for their duties as priests of the people. Samuel, on the other hand, gained much knowledge of God and understood thoroughly the obligations of a 'Nazirite' to the people of God. He grew in stature – which denotes not only bodily but also spiritual development. His maturity of body and mind resulted in his actions being approved by the Lord and finding acceptance with the people.

The impression given in the second and third chapters of the first book of Samuel is that Samuel wanted to please. He was obedient to his parents, who had lent him to the Lord, to Eli his mentor, and above all to God who called him in the dark of night.

✳ *Lord, grant that our children today may be half as obedient and as willing to please as Samuel was. And grant that we may be worthy of such obedience.*

Tuesday December 30   *Colossians 3:12–17**

Wisdom from above

This passage chronicles the qualities to be found in persons who have grown, or are growing, in wisdom and stature. Such persons should exhibit humility, meekness, patience, tolerance, and forgiveness. But, most important of all, they should show love, while allowing the peace of Christ to rule their hearts. They should have knowledge, then, of Christ and his word as they 'teach and admonish one another in all wisdom' (verse 16).

James, the brother of Jesus, in his letter to the twelve tribes of the Dispersion, also lists the qualities of the wisdom from above – God's wisdom, in contrast to 'earthly, unspiritual, devilish' wisdom (James 3:15). According to James, 'the wisdom from above is first pure, then peaceable, gentle, willing to yield, full of mercy and good fruits, without a trace of partiality or hypocrisy' (James 3:17). These qualities are not unlike those cited by Paul in today's passage.

Paul had prayed unceasingly, he says, that the Colossians 'be filled with the knowledge of God's will in all spiritual wisdom and understanding' so that they 'lead lives worthy of the Lord, fully pleasing to him ... as (they) grow in the knowledge of God' (Colossians 1:9–10). As he did with the new converts in all of the places he visited, Paul gave advice and instructions about how the Colossians should live, and what they should do in order to grow in wisdom and stature. Ultimately they should 'do everything (in word or deed) in the name of the Lord Jesus, giving thanks to God the Father through him' (Colossians 3:17).

James exhorts the tribes to 'show by your good life that your works are done with gentleness born of wisdom' (James 3:13). This is good advice from both sources, which we would do well to follow even (perhaps especially) today as we near the end of this third year of our third millennium.

✳ *Lord, you are the only true source of wisdom. Grant that your wisdom may be bestowed on each of us that we may all act and live in accordance with your will. Help us to exhibit the qualities which indicate that we are growing in wisdom. Help us to lead lives worthy of our knowledge of you, now and for ever.*

Wednesday December 31 (New Year's Eve)　　　　　*Psalm 148**

God's universal glory

Throughout the Bible we are instructed in the ways of wisdom, both religious and practical. Colossians 3:17 directs us to 'do everything in the name of the Lord Jesus, giving thanks to God the Father through him'. The world and everything in it was made by God. We are to ensure that God approves the life we live by living responsibly and joyfully.

The book of Psalms includes songs of praise and thanksgiving, prayers and laments, all expressing the many varying aspects of life both then (for the Jews) and now (for us)! Psalm 148 is a song of praise, extolling God's universal glory, one of the many songs of joy. God's universal glory is displayed throughout the universe and beyond, from the divine life in the highest heaven to God's many creations in our world: sun, moon, stars, weather and its forms of precipitation, animals and plant life, land and sea, as well as peoples of the earth. So all the world is invited to praise the name of the Lord.

In an earlier psalm we are told, 'the fear of the Lord is the beginning of wisdom; and they who live by it grow in understanding. Praise will be his for ever' (Psalm 111:10, REB). This might form for us an apt thought for the end of the year and an excellent new year resolution for 2004 – to grow in wisdom and stature by living in humble trust in God and in obedience to his will so that we may be guarded and guided in the ways of life.

✳ *Heavenly Father, as we end this year in anticipation of a brand new one, we praise your name. We thank you for your guidance during the year past and joyfully look forward to the new experiences of the one to come. Help us, we pray, to go forward in faith, growing in wisdom and stature.*

FOR REFLECTION AND ACTION – alone or in a group

● God's wisdom helps us in many ways. List and discuss at least three ways in which you were helped during the year 2003.

● List three ways in which you are aware of needing to be guided and taught during 2004.

● Examine Colossians 3:12–17 and in particular study the qualities of the wisdom which comes from God. Where have you seen these qualities at work – in yourself and in others?

● Reflect prayerfully on your need to grow in wisdom during the next year. How will you help to enable this to happen?

INTERNATIONAL BIBLE READING ASSOCIATION

– a worldwide service of Christian Education
at work in five continents

HEADQUARTERS

1020 Bristol Road
Selly Oak
Birmingham
Great Britain
B29 6LB

www.christianeducation.org.uk

and the following agencies:

AUSTRALIA

Uniting Education (previously The Joint Board of Christian Education)
PO Box 1245 (65 Oxford Street)
Collingwood
Victoria 3066

GHANA

IBRA Secretary
PO Box 919
Accra

INDIA

All India Sunday School
   Association
PO Box 2099, Plot No 62
Railway Colony, Sikh Road
Secunderabad – 500 009

Fellowship of Professional Workers
SAMANVAY
Deepthi Chambers, Vijayapuri
Hyderabad – 500 017
Andhra Pradesh

NEW ZEALAND

Epworth Bookshop
PO Box 6133, Te Aro
75 Taranaki Street
Wellington 6035

NIGERIA

IBRA Representative
PMB 5298
Ibadan

SOUTH AND CENTRAL AFRICA

IBRA Representative
Box 1176
Sedgefield 6573

Scheme of readings for 2004

1. Special to Luke
Blessings and woes – Shared texts – Teaching – Lost and found – Faithfulness – On the way to Jerusalem

2. Prayer
Call to prayer – Cries of prayer – Confidence in prayer

3. Lent: Speaking about God
Husband – Father and mother – One and holy – Merciful and forgiving – Redeemer

4. Luke's Passion and Resurrection
Passion – Resurrection

5. Encounters with difference
The impact of difference on Jesus – The impact of difference on the early church – Biblical understandings of difference

6. 2 Corinthians and Ephesians
Trouble brewing – Trouble out in the open – Ephesians

7. Spirits
The Holy Spirit in the new covenant – Other spirits – What the Holy Spirit does

8. Jesus and the Law
The Law – Jesus under the Law – Jesus challenges the Law – The Law for followers of Jesus

9. Fair trade
Just deserts – Fair dealings – Extra-mile people

10. The Minor Prophets
Joel – Jonah and Nahum – Habakkuk

11. In town and country
Our beautiful world – Spoiled and restored – Urban culture – Jesus and some significant sites – Two cities

12. The Book of Ecclesiastes
Observations on life – Is anything new? – Towards meaning

13. Creating
Birthing: Bringing forth God's life – Crafting: Shaping God's life – Seeing: Envisioning God's life – Word-painting: Expressing God's life – Singing and dancing: Embodying God's life

14. Advent expectations
Whispers of redemption – Messianic yearnings – A new hope – Already and not yet – Towards fulfilment